Kellogg's
Six-Hour Day

IN THE SERIES

Labor and Social Change,
edited by Paula Rayman and Carmen Sirianni

Kellogg's Six-Hour Day

Benjamin Kline Hunnicutt

Temple University Press

Philadelphia

Temple University Press, Philadelphia 19122
Copyright © 1996 by Temple University
All rights reserved
Published 1996
Printed in the United States of America

♾ The paper used in this book meets the requirements of the American National Standard for Information Sciences—Permanence of Paper for Printed
Library Materials. ANSI Z39.48-1984

Text design by Betty Palmer McDaniel

Library of Congress Cataloging-in-Publication Data

Hunnicutt, Benjamin Kline.
    Kellogg's six-hour day / Benjamin Kline
Hunnicutt.
        p.   cm.—(Labor and social change)
        Includes bibliographical references and index.
        ISBN 1-56639-447-3 (cloth: alk. paper). —
        ISBN 1-56639-448-1 (pbk. : alk. paper)
        1. Work sharing—Michigan—Battle Creek—
History. 2. Shift systems—Michigan—Battle
Creek—History. 3. Hours of labor—Michigan—
Battle Creek—History. 4. Cereal products
industry—Michigan—Battle Creek—Employees—
History. 5. Unemployment—Michigan—Battle
Creek—History. 6. Depression—1929—
Michigan—Battle Creek. 7. Kellogg Company—
History. I. Title. II. Series.
HD5110.6.U62B384   1996
331.25'72—dc20   95-44326

Portions of and ideas from Benjamin Kline Hunnicutt, "Kellogg's Six-Hour Day: A Capitalist Vision
of Liberation Through Managed Work Reduction,"
Business History Review, Autumn 1992, copyright
© 1992 by the President and Fellows of Harvard
College, are reprinted by permission of Harvard
Business School

For the memory of my brother
ROBERT AYDEN HUNNICUTT, JR.

Contents

Acknowledgments

I owe much to the economist John Owen, who first asked why "Americans have had no net gain in their leisure . . . since the end of World War II." Not only did he start me in the direction that led to my first book, *Work Without End;* he encouraged me over the years, showing a gracious hospitality during my visits to Wayne State and a willingness to talk for hours about our topics.

At first the going was hard. In the early 1980s no one seemed to be interested in what happened to the century-long shorter-hours movement. Without a publisher for my early attempts, I was disheartened and ready to turn to more promising fields when David Montgomery encouraged me to keep trying. The result was a major breakthrough for me, the publication of "The End of Shorter Hours" by *Labor History* in 1984.

Since then, to my considerable relief, other scholars have joined the search for answers. With *The Overworked American,* Juliet Schor, more than any other writer, advanced the study of work and leisure. I am indebted to her for making our topics issues of considerable public and academic interest. I also thank her for the personal support she gave me when I was criticized for asking in the *Wall Street Journal* in 1990, "Are We All Working Too Hard?" and for her continuing advice and generous assistance.

I acknowledge my debt to Gary Cross and David Roediger, who have written excellent histories of working hours and leisure and who have allowed me to claim them as friends over the years. I also thank Nelson Lichtenstein, Stanley Aronowitz, and Carmen Sirianni for their help. I welcome Jeremy Rifkin's recent interest in *The End of Work,* a topic sure to enliven discussions of the economics and history of work and leisure.

Older voices still contribute to these topics. Long an admirer of his work, I was surprised by Ivan Illich's interest in *Work Without End* and delighted by the time we spent together at Penn State, and I remain grateful for the inspiration he gave me. Illich introduced me to André Gorz, Alexander King, and Clive Jenkins, each of whom has encouraged or assisted me in my writing. Indirectly, Illich was responsible for my meeting

Tom Bottomore. Bottomore's death cut short a collaborative effort he and I had begun.

Journalists and popular writers have helped to tell the story of overwork and the erosion of leisure. Suzanne Gordon, whose *Prisoners of Men's Dreams* is in my mind one of the best books around on work and leisure, gave me wonderful advice and support over the years. Amy Saltzman, Witold Rybczynski, and Vicki Robin have given superb accounts of "downshifting," empty front porches, disappearing weekends, and the choice of "your money or your life," and provided help anytime that I asked them. John DeGraff produced an excellent PBS special, *Running Out of Time,* and aided my research efforts in Battle Creek.

I also thank those people actively involved in promoting shorter work hours, especially Barbara Brandt in Boston for her friendship and encouragement and Bill McGaughey in Minneapolis for his research and writing.

Colleagues at the University of Iowa, Michael Teague, Richard MacNeil, and Ken Mobily, for twenty years have shared the bureaucratic burdens heaped on our little group by academic bean-counters. Together we have managed to flourish despite the cutbacks and busy-work that have replaced the easy atmosphere of support and encouragement that I found when I first came to this school. I am also grateful to Mary Anders for her support and invaluable help in preparing the book's manuscript.

Other colleagues in the field of leisure studies, Doug Sessoms, Jerry Dickason, John Hemingway, and Tom Goodale, have offered generous support and interest.

Hundreds of workers in Battle Creek answered my letters and patiently endured my visits and phone calls. Of all the interviews and visits, I will remember most fondly the hours sitting across the kitchen table from Joy and Charles Blanchard. I offer my deepest gratitude to William Brown, who preserved the papers of his father, Lewis Brown, and was willing to share them with me. I am also deeply grateful to Local No. 3 of the American Federation of Grain Millers for opening up the union's archives in Battle Creek to me.

Finally, I thank my wife, Francine, for her support, and for the relief from writing found in the pleasant company of my children and grandchildren: Benjamin, Chris, Emmalee, Hannah, and Henry. I am also glad once again to thank my mother, Cassie, for a lifetime of encouragement.

Introduction

On 1 December 1930, at the start of the Great Depression, W. K. Kellogg acted on the advice of company president Lewis J. Brown and replaced the traditional three daily eight-hour shifts in his cereal plant with four six-hour shifts. By adding one entire shift, he and his managers hoped to create jobs for laid-off employees and for some of the unemployed in Battle Creek.

The six-hour day was an instant success, attracting the attention of the national media and Herbert Hoover's administration. It was one of the biggest stories ever to come out of Battle Creek, already famous for its Sanitarium and cereals. The initiative won strong support from prominent businessmen and labor leaders all over the country and from community leaders and workers in Battle Creek. Observers throughout the world speculated that Kellogg's experiment offered a practical way out of the depression and, in light of the steady decline in hours of labor for over a century, a foretaste of things to come.

The first day of operations was relatively quiet. A heavy snowstorm delayed street cars, but time-clocks were reset to record everyone as on-time for the first six-hour shift. Personnel director N. D. Huff calmly reported that the new operations "are O.K.," and even though "many new people" had been hired to work the fourth shift, "it appears that if any readjustments are needed, they will be few and of a minor nature."[1] In the months that followed, local papers quoted George Bernard Shaw's and Julian Huxley's predictions of a two-hour work day, at most, by the end of the century, and cited education officials in Washington who were urging the local schools to "face facts" and concentrate on "education for the worthy use of leisure." Taking note of the widespread interest in shorter hours, H. G. Wells began to dramatize work's decline in *Things to Come* and *The Man Who Could Work Miracles,* which would become his most popular movies. Kellogg's, it seemed to many, was blazing a trail to a future where free time would replace work as life's central concern.

Through the depression years, the six-hour day functioned as Kellogg (known to all as "W. K.") and Brown hoped. Jobs were created as the company payroll grew, and plant employees seemed delighted to have more time of their own, especially since their weekly paychecks were only a little smaller—hourly wages were raised 12.5 percent that December and another 12.5 percent a year later. Moreover, when Kellogg's was organized in 1937 by the National Council of Grain Producers, one of the local union's first demands was that the six-hour day become "standard," and that the few eight-hour workers (such as night watchmen) be permitted to switch to six hours if they wanted to. This demand and the fact that two-thirds of the workers on the longer shifts then voted to switch are strong indications of worker support during the 1930s.

But the "standard" six-hour day and other union demands soured Kellogg management on the short shift. After W. K. turned over company management to a new team headed by the Chicago banker W. H. Vanderploeg, his and Brown's original vision faded, and the company began to discourage shorter hours. Complying with Franklin Roosevelt's executive order mandating a longer work week as a wartime measure, the Kellogg plant went to three eight-hour shifts in the early days of World War II. But, prompted by the union, management reluctantly promised to return to six-hour shifts as soon as the war ended.

After the war, management persistently tried to persuade workers to continue the eight-hour shift offering generous money incentives and using the issue as a bargaining chip in contract negotiations. The company's wartime promise notwithstanding, the local union had to struggle to regain the six-hour day, voting three to one in 1945 and again in 1946 to return to the short shift. Even after returning to six-hours, the company kept up the pressure, insisting that "those who want it" be allowed to vote to work longer. Workers were divided by this tactic, and, through the next four decades, department after department voted to return to eight-hours.

Through the 1950s and 1960s, Kellogg's six-hour workers were increasingly isolated in a town and a nation of eight-hour workers. As fellow employees deserted the cause, they were forced to defend their salient position in labor's historic fight for shorter hours, which became increasingly exposed. Still, they held on to six-hours for over forty years in the face of intense management, community, and even union pressure. As their numbers thinned, they retreated to six-hour enclaves in a handful of the plant's departments. Eventually even these hotbeds of shorter-hour sentiment were unable to hold out. The remaining 530 workers, over three-quarters of whom were women, surrendered in February 1985.

Unlike its birth, the passing of the six-hour day was obscure. Only the *Battle Creek Enquirer* carried the story. The assistant city editor wrote in the "Local Interest" section: "Kellogg Co.'s six-hour shifts were laid to rest at Stan's Place Friday with tears and laughter, Bloody Mary's and sloppy joes. A black cardboard coffin sat on the table in the Springfield tavern inscribed with the epitaph: 'Good Time 6 Hrs. Born April 1, 1931 [*sic*]. Died, Feb. 8, 1985. RIP."[2] The *Enquirer* also published a eulogy that one woman wrote for the occasion.

FAREWELL GOOD FRIEND—"OLD SIX HRS.":
We had become so attached to you.
'Tis sad but true!
You kept our families closer together.
But Mr. 8 hrs. said, "Go out and get 'em!"
He had the "win".
But we didn't "grin".
Now you're gone and we're all so blue . . .
Since you've taken some of our friends, too!
Loyal friends who'd rather "quit" than be without "you".
So off you'll go to lie beside our founder—"Mr. K".
Our bodies will never forget "you".
For you were good to them, too!
And now a moment of silence—let's shed those tears.
We'll try hard to banish our fears.
And now get out the *vitamins*—give your doctor a call
Cause old 8 hrs. has got us "all".
    Sorrowfully written by Ina Sides.[3]

This simple narrative continues to be retold in many ways in Battle Creek. In this book several voices tell the story or parts of it: this writer, trying to understand the history of working hours in the United States; various Kellogg managers interested in motivating employees and producing cereal efficiently; and the people who actually worked the six-hour shift over the years.

THE RISE AND FALL OF FREE TIME

A journalist might tell the story of Kellogg's six-hour day in the simple and direct terms used above. Seen from the historian's point of view, that story is part of a remarkable twentieth-century epic. Kellogg's experiment exemplifies major trends in the history of labor in the United States and illustrates several changes in workers' perceptions about, and public attitudes toward, work and leisure since the Great Depression.

In 1976 the economist John Owen sparked a lively scholarly debate with his observation that "employed Americans have had no net gain in their leisure . . . since the end of World War II." Historians and economists have struggled to explain why since then.[4] In my book *Work Without End,* I suggested that during the 1920s American business, reacting to the "threat of leisure"—the constant erosion of working hours that had cut working time in half over the "century of shorter hours"—discovered the "New Economic Gospel of Consumption." Instead of accepting work's continuing decline and imminent fall from its dominant social position, businessmen, economists, advertisers, and politicians preached that there would never be "enough" because the entrepreneur and industry could invent new things for advertising to sell and for people to want and work for indefinitely. Thereupon, in direct response to the spectre of work's fall to leisure, modern consumerism was born and a new kind of "necessity"—indeterminate and changing, but still somehow undiluted—came into being.

But the Gospel of Consumption soon faced a crisis, the Great Depression. On its own, without government support, infinite industrial and economic growth was a fantasy. Giving up on the absurd idea that people would keep working to buy anything and everything they could afford or borrow for, businessmen and conservative politicians tried to redistribute the work that was still left by the Machine to meet the crisis—a political course of action they called at the time "work sharing." Franklin Delano Roosevelt, however, in a stroke of political genius, came up with an alternative solution to unemployment: government-supported *work creation.* Enlisting the forces of the federal government, he used deficits, liberal Treasury policies, expanded government works projects, and enlarged government payrolls to "stimulate the economy," create more work for more people, and revive the Gospel of Consumption.

Business in the 1920s and Roosevelt in 1935 responded directly to the decline of work, inspired by a vision of perpetual growth in the economy permitting an indefinite expansion of work hours. In the New Deal plan, however, "full-time" work and economic growth would be guaranteed by government support and not left to the "free market." The most important political watershed of this century was crossed, and "JOBS, JOBS,

JOBS" became the domestic touchstone for subsequent politicians from both the Left and the Right. The goal of shorter hours was abandoned. "Work without end," based on consumerism, prevailed.

More recently, in her widely publicized book *The Overworked American: The Unexpected Decline of Leisure,* the economist Juliet Schor compounded the historical puzzle, arguing persuasively that leisure has actually declined since 1976. Bill Clinton adapted her argument to the 1992 presidential campaign with the slogan "Americans are working harder for less" than when Ronald Reagan was elected. Finding that the "average Joe" is working a full month more today, Schor concluded that the historical process of work reduction has not only halted; it has reversed. As I did in *Work Without End,* she attempts to explain this phenomenon through the rise of consumerism, the structure of capitalism, and labor's changing positions.

Subsequently, overwork has become a hot topic in television specials, popular books, and countless magazine and newspaper articles. The public and journalists in the popular media have joined academics in asking why people in the most technologically advanced nations in the world are starved for time. The general public seems to have recognized as obvious what scholars have struggled to disclose—that instead of the abundant leisure once promised by the Machine, time for life outside work is vanishing, and families, communities, and personal life have suffered as a direct result. Yet no one has seriously asked what workers themselves thought about leisure and work after winning the forty-hour week, or explored the reasons they give for abandoning shorter hours.[5]

Kellogg's six-hour day provides a rare opportunity to tell the story of the end of shorter hours from the workers' point of view. Kellogg workers advanced beyond the vast majority of workers on the shorter-hours front and, in the face of intense pressure, held their position and their extra two hours for fifty-five years. Why the majority initially supported six hours, why some held their ground for over half a century, and why they finally gave up are exactly the questions historians need to ask of workers in general.

Such a history might begin to discredit suggestions that workers have been helpless in the face of "economic necessity" by demonstrating that up until 1984 a group of workers, supported (in Herbert Gutman's words) by a strong "subculture . . . with deep roots in tradition," fought for shorter hours and questioned the primacy of work in their lives, just as generations of workers had done before them, continuing in the face of evolving "necessity" to find meaning and value in the time "outside" their industrial jobs.[6] Instead of helpless vessels carried along by the tides of the Economy or driven by a "natural" urge to work and consume, the Kellogg women and men better resemble the historical characters Gutman and E. P. Thompson described: "working people [who] were not simply overridden or manipulated . . . but, on the contrary . . . left their own clear marks on the nation's social and political evolution." Focusing on what Gutman called the "modes of thought and perception through which [the worker] confronted the industrialization process," the historian who pays close attention to what Kellogg workers did and said may discern the way they experienced the end of shorter hours.[7]

Following Lynn Hunt, William H. Sewell, and Gareth Stedman Jones, as well as Thompson and Gutman, I maintain that in Battle Creek the "necessity" to work "full-time" was a culturally produced outcome of class and gender struggles—the symbolic product of a forty-year-long discourse, echoes of which may be still heard in that city. In short, I argue that cultural change rather than "economic forces" or psychological "realities" best explains the end of shorter hours in Battle Creek.[8]

This analysis provides a cultural explanation for the end of shorter hours, going beyond the social and political explanations I offered in *Work Without End*. The Kellogg experiment demonstrates that changes in the language and the cultures of managers and workers in Battle Creek provide important clues to explain leisure's decline in recent years.

GENDER, CLASS, AND CULTURE: SUBVERSIVE LEISURE

Battle Creek and the community of Kellogg workers and managers there are ideal subjects for the historian. Superb records preserving workers' language and stories originate there. In 1932 agents from the Women's Bureau of the Department of Labor interviewed nearly all of the women who worked at Kellogg's about the six-hour day and other family and community matters related to their "extra time." All 434 reports are available in the National Archives. Hundreds of workers, managers, and union officials remember the six-hour day, and dozens have wonderful stories that they seem eager to tell. Many who worked six-hour days during the Great Depression can help reconstruct the old stories, phrases, and words that grew up around Kellogg's original experiment.

In the pages that follow, I analyze the themes and metaphors found in the accounts collected in 1932. I also pay close attention to popular family and community activities (such as canning, gardening, child-rearing practices, visiting, sports, family projects and outings) and community settings (such as softball fields, parks, front porches, and gardens), which gave symbolic structure to activities outside work.[9]

I use my own interviews and letters from living Kellogg workers and managers to show how the community discourse evolved from the 1932 baseline. Since 1988 I have received more than three hundred letters from Kellogg workers and managers who responded to my inquiries, and together with my students, and with some help from public television station KCTS in Seattle, Washington, I have conducted over a hundred interviews with Kellogg workers, managers, union officials, community leaders, librarians, newspaper reporters, and others. Comparing the "texts" of 1932 and 1988 reveals the dynamics of the debate about the six-hour day.[10]

It was no accident that women were the strongest and most persistent of the six-hour supporters, continuing to criticize the concept of work as the center of life and promoting alternative social structures, activities, and values outside the job in their "extra time." After most of the men had deserted the cause, the women continued labor's 150-year tradition, questioning the role of work discipline in their lives, looking more and more to the family, school, and community for meaning and satisfaction, and discovering new kinds of power and status in their time outside industrial capitalism and the marketplace.

As people worked less, work and the marketplace lost some of their importance. For many workers the two "extra hours" were enough to tip the balance between work and leisure. As work began to lose its place as the dominant social and cultural focus, the traditional patterns of status and control that had been established on the centrality of work were unsettled. Male dominance, for example, was assured in a culture dominated by work; it was much less secure outside the job. Males, threatened, retreated to the job and fortified its importance with new language and stories.

Class as well as gender helped determine the roles the historical actors played in the rhetorical drama. After World War II, Kellogg managers and senior male workers, with status and power at stake, propagandized work, trivialized leisure, and feminized shorter hours. A coalition was born as managers who recognized the "threat of leisure" and male employees united against the "other": the young, the sissies, the "misfits," and the "girls" who "didn't even know enough" to realize the importance of a "full-time job."

Typically, academic discussions of power, control, and conflict focus on money, ownership of property, job status, or political power. But historians and anthropologists have made the case that control in civil society also has to do with time: the daily, seasonal, and generational comings and goings, occasions, rituals, and celebrations in the community. Schedule appears to be a fundamental source of cultural authority. In fact, one might argue that time is to civil society what money is to the economic sphere and laws or votes are to the political realm—the medium of exchange, the symbol of value, and the way to get things done.[11]

Certainly, control of time was a point of contention during Kellogg's six-hour experiment, occasionally overshadowing political and economic struggles in the community. Who determined the daily schedule during the two extra hours, what activities were to be done and where, and the structure of the group doing the activity were critical and controversial issues. Men and women, workers and managers, waged a fifty-year struggle for control in Battle Creek on the most fundamental of social levels, forming alliances and contending for the extra time until the mid-1980s, when the issue was settled in favor of "full-time work." Within that narrow, two-hour opening, existing social forms became somewhat fluid; housework and child rearing, work and leisure, "recreation" and sports were rendered problematic. Kellogg workers were able to stand briefly outside the static social order and objectify established gender roles, customs, and duties. New possibilities were tried out, new structures of authority and control, role, identity, duty, and even mutuality and giving emerged from that interstice, only to fade with the disappearance of shorter hours.[12]

"AN INDEPENDENT DOMAIN OF CREATIVE ACTIVITY"

The promise or threat that the extra time would destabilize existing social structures and alter cultural roles was compounded by the possibility that perpetual disorder would be leisure's legacy. A spectre of unstructured time haunted Battle Creek for fifty years.

The resulting discourse about the meaning of the extra hours may be distinguished from the debates about what to do with the time. One of the most important parts of the discourse concerned the value of the two extra hours—whether they were worth keeping. The response ranged from complete rejection to enthusiastic support. Eventually, for many in the community, the two hours became a freedom "too far"—what Robert MacIver, writing about modern leisure, once called "the great emptiness." For such people the extra leisure seemed to lead to radical individualism and permanently unstructured behavior that by definition were bad—"idle hands" and the "devil's workshop" led vigorous metaphorical lives in the city. Abundant leisure seemed to be permanently outside meaning; on its face it was silly and aimless, leading to confusion and despair.[13]

For those who shared these fears, work was the obvious answer. In addition to preserving traditional class and gender roles, the job seemed to many to be the only social structure capable of providing the seriousness and purpose necessary to sustain individual sanity and family and community order. The threat of empty freedom and desolate time excited fundamental fears—fears that with gender struggles and job-status anxieties gave rise to a new rhetoric about "the necessity" of "full-time" work and the "silliness" of leisure. These idioms, becoming dominant, were finally responsible for the death of the six-hour day.

But for an important few mavericks, resembling Jacques Rancière's worker-poets, the extra time remained through the 1980s as a longed-for oasis, a time outside struggle and conflict, class, gender, and control, necessity and structure—beyond what Eugen Fink called the "architectonically . . . complex ordering of purposes" in which "all human work takes place." Beyond what Joseph Pieper called the modern "world of total work" and "universal utilitarianism that seeks to turn everything in the world to some useful purpose," the six-hour deviants found, in Victor Turner's words, "an independent domain of creative activity."[14]

One staunch six-hour worker, Joy Blanchard, saw new possibilities opening for her and for those around her in the two hours. Her job was important for economic reasons, to be sure—she and her husband were a "Kellogg couple," both working six-hours for years. But the extra leisure allowed them to experiment with "the way things were usually done." She was proud that her husband took an unusually active role in their children's upbringing and that he was the only male "grade parent" at their sons' grammar school.

Blanchard consistently talked about her own job as a means to other, better things, repeating that "work was never the center of my life" or "the most important thing." The two extra hours gave her a measure of time outside the job and housework, outside expectations and duty, conflict and control, for "other things" she claimed as her own. Certainly, housework took much of her time, as did "family business," discipline, and problem solving. But, as she phrased it, in the free time she managed to claim for herself she "was able to" read and do "fun, creative things" with her children. Such "free" activities were her reward, the goal of the day that gave meaning and purpose to her job and housework.

Blanchard eloquently described a respite at the end of household demands, jobs, established social roles, and financial concerns, a margin of time outside for walking, reading, gardening, learning, mothering, teaching, writing, appreciating, loving, thinking, playing, being a neighbor, caring for, talking, birding, for their "own sakes." Such "leisure" was not for resting in order to do more work; it was certainly not for passive "amusement" or mindless consumption. On the contrary, it was the most important part of the day, during which she believed she had found and crafted the best parts of her life, family, community, and citizenship.[15] Blanchard's experience was consistent with Victor Turner's conception of modern leisure as "potentially capable of releasing creative powers, individual and communal, either to criticize or prop up dominant social-structural values. It is . . . possible to conceive of leisure as betwixt-and-between, neither this nor that domain between two lodgments in the work domain, or between occupational and familial and civic [arenas]."[16] Those who embraced the new leisure as a "domain between two lodgments" continued to struggle toward meaning outside industrial work, consumption, and gender role, attempting to find something better to do beyond the "necessities" imposed by the job, housework, and the Economy. But they contended in a losing contest with those who, for a variety of reasons, denied such freedom, embraced "necessity" and stable social roles, and worked harder than ever.

THE COLLAPSE OF COMMUNITY

The six-hour mavericks tell their stories about the death of the six-hour day as part of another, larger story about the flow of time, energy, and attention from the home and community to work and consumption. Joy

Blanchard took a stand against television, for example, urging those around her to continue to use at least some of the extra time in active exchange with others, in traditional community-service and family projects. In her opinion, one reason the Kellogg workers went back to work "full-time" was that people in her city had emptied leisure of activity, failing to meet the challenge represented by the extra time. Most had even surrendered activities as fundamental as conversation to "Hollywood, TV, and radio types like Johnny Carson." Having "found nothing better to do" than watch television, shop, or gossip, "they might just as well go back to work."

For Blanchard and other six-hour mavericks, expanding leisure could have fortified the community, strengthened families, preserved tradition, and opened up new cultural opportunities. Overmatched and overpowered, they still aspired to lead their families and community to challenge the mass, popular culture that steadily eroded the local subculture and discourse. From the beginning of the six-hour experiment, outside cultural forces made deep inroads into the local discourse. An important part of the Battle Creek story is the increasing influence of commercial, media culture on leisure time. The expanding mass media competed powerfully with local forms of making, transmitting, and exchanging culture, such as the local production of language, story, entertainment, and interpretation of personal experience. Gradually, active culture-making and practice were transformed into commodities and hawked by "out-of-town" professionals and experts. Local culture-producing leisure activities, along with the extra two hours, were steadily devalued.[17]

Advertisers and professionals, ranging from sports figures to academicians, promised, for a price, to produce culture and leisure without the "bother." The six-hour women heard mass media and "professionals" asking their husbands and neighbors implicitly, Why take the time to go to see ("support") the women playing softball down at the plant when you can listen to the radio or watch the Detroit Tigers on TV? Why "bother" canning when you can buy anything you want at the supermarket? Why struggle to understand the world around you on your own and "make a fool of yourself" expressing opinions on local issues? Why make music, tell stories, paint, write, or observe nature when local "professionals" and experts at Ann Arbor and East Lansing are paid, and paid well, to understand and do such things, and do them so much better than you? After all, since you are not paid for it, why "go to all the trouble?"

Leisure as "the *freedom* to enter, even for some to help generate, the symbolic worlds" became a "bother" and "too much trouble," and was gradually replaced by passive amusement and empty free time. The value of time spent doing and making local culture and crafting homemade discourse, morals, and meaning was steadily discounted.[18] Instead of being the most active and important part of the day or "night of the proletarian" in which to escape capitalist controls, class, gender, and social role, an opportunity to speak, write, do, and make culture, leisure was identified with the lack of effort, commercialized, feminized, trivialized, and co-opted. Only a few continued to see the importance of active leisure in the local production of culture. Only a few recognized the threat that passive, commercial recreation represented to the essence of family and community. As one of the mavericks put it, "nobody was left to argue with."

The century-old view of work as a means to more important activities, the perennial dream of more time off work for "better things," gave way to new words and stories presenting "full-time work" as inevitable and abundant, increasing leisure as "unrealistic," "silly," only for "girls" or "sissies." Gradually, these ways of speaking ossified because of the lack of continuing discourse. Leisure as a realistic alternative to industrial work, an opening to social experimentation, and a challenge to mass amusement and passive cultural consumption waned as mass culture encroached on and then dominated the time spent outside the job. The traditional working-class remedy for the ills of industrialization, the "progressive reduction of the hours of labor," has been nearly lost to the language. Now the dominion of work stands virtually unchallenged and seemingly impregnable. The job resembles a secular religion, promising personal identity, salvation, purpose and direction, community, and a way for those who believe truly and simply in "hard work" to make sense out of the confusion of life. The few who still doubt that work is life's center are condemned as heretics, and time outside work and consumption, without "entertainment" and technology's toys, is a new wilderness.

Chapter One

Kellogg's Liberation Capitalism

In 1930 Kellogg's was the largest manufacturer of ready-to-eat cereals in the world, employing nearly 1,500 workers. On 24 November the company president, Lewis J. Brown, announced that the Battle Creek plant would institute a six-hour day on 1 December. According to Brown, the company would be able to hire an entirely new shift of workers, a fourth shift in the twenty-four-hour working day, thereby helping to relieve unemployment in Battle Creek. With this bold step, Kellogg's would take the lead among socially conscious businessmen and industrialists. The company would show Henry Ford and the other "welfare capitalists" how to combat the depression crisis and, at the same time, offer a new vision of progress to a nation sunk in despair—so Brown hoped.[1]

William Keith (W. K.) Kellogg, the company owner, told Battle Creek Mayor William Penty that "if we put in four six-hour shifts . . . instead of three eight-hour shifts, this will give work and paychecks to the heads of three hundred more families in Battle Creek." Lewis Brown told audiences in Canada and in the Midwest that the "market crash," "unsound credit," and "depression" had but one "remedy . . . shorter work periods."[2]

This remedy was much more than just a cure for unemployment, for it offered a new, capitalist version of liberation to the modern world, where machines were steadily replacing men and women at work and where individual liberties were threatened by the rise of authoritarian governments. Observers around the world agreed with Brown that Kellogg's was revealing the true miracle of welfare capitalism, the rebirth of freedom in the form of "mass leisure." Under the direction of scientific managers and enlightened industrialists like Brown and Kellogg, the free exchange of goods, services, and labor in the free market would not have to mean mindless consumerism or eternal exploitation of people and natural resources. Rather, capitalism's destiny was revealed as a new freedom from work for more and more people, achieved through the marketplace. Workers would be liberated by increasingly higher wages and shorter hours for the final freedom promised by the Declaration of Independence—the pursuit of happiness.

Unlike the authoritarian schemes of the Socialists, this liberation would be founded on freedom—on the free choice of the capitalist to reduce work time (a sound management decision) and the free choice of workers to accept shorter hours as a benefit, what economists called a "normal good," on a par with higher wages. Together, the worker, manager, and owner were making sound, free choices for their own benefit. The result would be a shift of the center of American life from necessity/work to freedom/leisure.[3]

"Welfare capitalism" was emerging from its chrysalis, revealing its true splendor as "Liberation Capitalism."[4]

PRACTICAL FOUNDATIONS

Brown argued that his vision was based on realistic considerations of the needs of both labor and management. First he explained that in order to "maintain the workers' purchasing power," the minimum daily wage for a male employee would be raised to $4.00. In other cases the loss of two hours of work per day would be partially offset by raising the basic hourly wage by 12.5 percent. He maintained that this would "give Kellogg employees . . . a purchasing power, in view of price declines, exceeding that enjoyed a year ago for eight hours of work." As a result, Kellogg's would be "paying the highest rate per hour of any of the larger firms in our city—and much greater than the average throughout the country."[5]

From the start, Kellogg management faced the issue of total weekly pay head-on, challenging those in organized labor who claimed that worksharers were putting the entire burden of unemployment relief on the workers. Kellogg's plan called for business and labor to share the costs of shorter hours equally: workers accepting a modest weekly pay cut and job-rules concessions, Kellogg's increasing hourly wages and expanding the total payroll and the number of employees. In late 1932, an influential group of New England businessmen gained national attention for offering exactly this "share the work, share the cost of shorter hours" scheme, calling it the New Hampshire Plan, much to the annoyance of Kellogg's management.[6]

There is no doubt that Kellogg workers were paid less weekly, at least until 1935, when Kellogg's raised wages a third time. But there is also no doubt that Kellogg hired more people and paid out more total wages, and that the issue of hourly wages, as distinct from total weekly pay, was still important for workers. Moreover, according to Brown the six-hour day was in keeping with Kellogg's tradition as a leader of industry and welfare capitalism. Brown reminded reporters in 1930 and 1931 that Kellogg's had been one of the first companies to institute the eight-hour day and try out the five-day week. As Brown saw it, Kellogg's was continuing to blaze the trail of industrial reform. The six-hour day represented the company's latest effort to "share the benefits of mechanization and increased productivity" with workers and fulfill its social obligation to the community.

Brown and "W. K." cited Henry Ford's leadership, noting that over the years Ford developed a strong case for shorter hours as a sound principle of industrial management. Ford had already "proven" that workers gave their best service over the long term if hours were shorter. He had shown that absenteeism, turnover, and accident rates improved and a "more stable workforce" resulted. He had also "demonstrated" that workers were happier, more cooperative, and less given to militancy and unrest. Brown and W. K. Kellogg agreed with Ford's claim that a shorter day was "one of the finest cost-cutting moves ever made" and was the way to higher productivity and therefore profits. This was quintessentially good capitalism, for it gave workers, managers, and owners what they wanted.[7]

As part of the deal, management presented the still-unorganized Kellogg workers with a package of benefits and concessions built on the six-hour initiative. In exchange for reducing hours and, in its view, maintaining weekly wages while expanding the total payroll, management insisted that workers accept the elimination of the night-shift bonus and the half-hour lunch break. Brown argued that each of the four shifts, even the 6 p.m.–12 a.m. and 12 a.m.–6 a.m. shifts, would appeal to enough workers that a free bidding procedure would make the shift bonus unnecessary— some people liked to work nights so they could have the "day-light hours free." He also maintained that most workers would prefer to work straight through lunch and leave the plant as soon as possible. Since the lunch break was expensive in terms of plant facilities and workers' time (according to the scientific managers, the least productive parts of the day were just before and just after lunch), the move would help pay for the larger payroll and higher hourly wages.[8]

Moreover, the overtime bonus would be phased out, replaced by a "production bonus" based on how much workers produced, not on how long they worked. Brown was particularly proud of this initiative, considering it a practical application of a basic but widely ignored principle of scientific management. Before the six-hour day, workers had a "psychological" incentive to stretch out their work to win premium pay. Now overtime was outmoded, for as the editor of *Forbes*, Chapin Hoskins, observed, the four-shift plan created "an incentive for getting all necessary work done within six-hours"—after six hours workers were paid at the lower pre–December 1930 hourly rate.[9]

Before six-hours, workers objected to such a scheme, calling it a management trick to speed up the line, and suffering the clear effects of fatigue. According to Brown, however, short-shift workers supported the "production bonus"; most said that they preferred to work faster and harder for the extra pay rather than put in tedious "overtime" hours. Moreover, the problem of fatigue had been reduced substantially— Brown used the analogy of a "relay-race" in which runners passed the baton well before they were out of breath.[10]

In contrast to Ford and other leaders of welfare capitalism, Brown further argued that shorter hours would provide "greater opportunity for recreation and enjoyment—outside of business hours" and that a shorter work day would "mean better living and working conditions generally." Unlike the eight-hour system with two undesirable shifts (those beginning at 3 p.m. and 11 p.m.) and one highly preferred shift (beginning at 7 a.m.), the six-hour day would offer "opportunity for an equal amount of outside recreation and pleasure" by providing four "equally desirable" work periods (beginning at 6 a.m., noon, 6 p.m., and midnight). Brown noted that "the six-hour shift will give them all time to rest up, to do the things they always wanted to do, if they hadn't been so pressed for time."

Through the 1920s, Henry Ford had stressed the economic importance of the additional leisure created by reducing the work week to five days. The extra free time would encourage people to buy and consume more industrial goods. As for the "humanitarian side of the shorter day and the shorter week," Ford cautioned that "dwelling on that subject is likely to get one in trouble, for then leisure may be put before work rather than after work—where it belongs."[11] For Ford, leisure was not an alternative to work but rather, within limits, the source of new "needs and necessities" and therefore the wellspring for new reasons to keep working "full-time."

Although Brown and W. K. followed Ford in most areas, they embraced the troublesome "humanitarian side" of shorter hours. In a "Personal Letter" to company employees, Brown wrote of "another income of which we do not often think, and yet it is the one by which much of our lives is governed. . . . Happiness has a bigger 'mental value' . . . than the gain in 'money income' . . . of the job. The mental income is satisfaction—the enjoyment of the surroundings of your home, the place you work, your neighbors, the other pleasures you have—[which are] harder to translate into dollars and cents" He claimed that the six-hour day would "revolutionize continuous industry operations" and laissez-faire capitalism because the balance of the workers' lives would shift from concerns about work and economic matters to the various kinds of "mental income" life offered. With six-hours, what Ford feared would come to pass—the "humanitarian side" of life would ascend.[12]

Such a watershed had been a long time coming, even though signaled by the eight-hour day and Ford's five-day week. With the advent of six-hours the focus of life would henceforth be on leisure—on freedom from necessity. Workers' attention would shift from economics and job issues to concerns about what to do with their lives, and a new day of liberty would dawn for the industrial worker, bringing "about higher standards in school and civic . . . life." But the company and industry would also benefit: "There is nothing more valuable to the industries of Battle Creek than to be able to draw its workers from a community where good homes predominate."[13]

Brown believed that the shorter day was industrial management's best hope for the future, and that it would save capitalism. When he announced the four-shift plan, Brown played openly to a larger, national audience, asserting: "We are going to start something that has been talked about for years, but nobody has had courage enough to do."[14]

BUSINESS REACTION

Brown was right; the business world was watching.[15] *Factory and Industrial Management* proclaimed on the front cover of its December 1930 issue that this was the "biggest piece of industrial news since Ford announced his five-dollar-a-day policy."

The editors reiterated Brown's claim that Kellogg's was on the cutting edge of industrial management:

Here lies our dilemma: On one side, millions of people wanting goods and unable to buy them . . . ; on the other side, industry . . . working at two-thirds capacity. . . . [Kellogg's] sends an arrow to the heart of the problem . . . to deny the ability of American industry to shorten hours for the present and for the future is to deny all the achievement of past generations. . . . We predict that this new policy of the Kellogg Company will do more to stimulate leaders to action and will make a far greater contribution to the solution of the unemployment problem than all the feverish temporary expedients being tried. American industry needs to apply . . . the best-known management methods. It is significant that [Kellogg's has] . . . the courage and the vision to undertake the experiment. Industry cannot turn back; it must go on developing new machinery and the new social values that arise from it. Therein lies profit; therein lies mass leisure, the next step.[16]

The magazine contacted leading political, industrial, and labor leaders throughout the country to elicit their views. Without exception, the comments were enthusiastic.

Arthur Woods, chairman of Hoover's Emergency Committee for Employment, telegraphed that "the Kellogg plan is a very significant move" and that such developments were evidence of "industrial ingenuity and determination in dealing with the unemployment emergency," a model of Hoover's voluntarist policies. T. R. Darrow of the Harvard Graduate School of Business Administration visited Battle Creek and used Kellogg's as a "case study" in his classes back in Massachusetts.[17]

Morris Leeds of Leeds and Northrop called the six-hour day an example of "constructive thinking and action which will help decrease unemployment now and may have permanent . . . value," serving as a "stimulating example" for other employers. Paul Litchfield, president of Goodyear Tire and Rubber Company, reminded readers that Goodyear had been on six-hour shifts for two months, an adjustment that "is justifiable in times of . . . unemployment." Edward A. Filene sent his "sincere congratulations," and the management of General Motors, including Alfred P. Sloan, Jr., indicated that they were "interested" in the experiment. Most impressive of all, John Edgerton, president of the

American Association of Manufacturers, called Kellogg's six-hour scheme "highly commendable."

William Green, president of the American Federation of Labor, used Edgerton's very words: "It is obviously impossible . . . to increase the number of employed workers unless working hours are decreased. . . . Kellogg's [six-hour day] is in line with this requirement . . . and is *highly commendable*. The increase in hourly [wages] . . . will enable workers to maintain a relatively high purchasing power." John B. Andrews, secretary of the American Association of Labor Legislation, thought Kellogg's move was "a wise step" and a model for industrial managers dealing with the problems of "this machine age." Don D. Lescohier, executive secretary of the Wisconsin Citizens Committee on Employment, thought the institution of a six-hour day would be necessary for "American industrialists generally as the basis for sound prosperity."[18]

National interest in Kellogg's experiment, and the broad political consensus favoring it, continued throughout 1931. Herbert Hoover asked W. K. Kellogg to come to Washington. (In 1955 Hoover recalled that he had been "very interested in the experiment" and had told Kellogg that it was "very worthwhile.") Senator David I. Walsh of Massachusetts, like Henry Ford an occasional "guest" at the Battle Creek Sanitarium, visited the plant and told company officials and the press that he "heartily approved" the plan and believed that it should be adopted by as many industries as possible. Hugo Black later used Kellogg's success to argue for passage of his thirty-hour work-sharing bill in the U.S. Congress. There are even some believable reports that FDR called W. K. during the first months of 1933 to congratulate him for what he was doing, at a time when Roosevelt supported legislated work sharing, and the Black–Connery Bill was known briefly as the Black–Perkins Bill.[19]

The *New York Times* followed the Kellogg story through the 1930s, reporting in 1931 that the six-hour day was "a complete success."[20] *Business Week* reported that employees were "completely sold on the plan," continuing: "Needless to say, Battle Creek has been a Mecca for far-sighted business executives, for students of management and all others sincerely interested in permanent stabilization of business. . . . Many [businessmen] are now seeing [the Kellogg experiment] in a more favorable light because not only does it please employees and appeal to the public but, on the basis of five months experience, it is profitable."[21]

Forbes's managing editor, Chapin Hoskins, visited Battle Creek the same year. Commenting that the experiment was "*the* topic of discussion" in the business world, Hoskins told how W. K. had begun two years earlier to build an executive force of "younger men" to carry the company through the next stage of its "existence and growth," hiring Lewis J. Brown as the new president. And it was Brown who had initiated this "striking formula of business administration." The fruit of the new "energetic and progressive business administration" was simply "good management," the best example of which was the six-hour day; and "good management . . . will probably, in time, bring the six-hour day elsewhere." Obliquely referring to then-current attempts to legislate shorter hours, Hoskins concluded that "nothing else" but enlightened management, working closely with employees, could make work sharing work.[22]

In the tradition of what David Roediger calls "Fordized Taylorism," Hoskins drew intricate "performance records" graphs and analyzed the situation at Kellogg in terms of "mid-morning swings," "luncheon let-down," and "mid-afternoon peaks," concluding that average worker efficiency per hour had improved substantially with the introduction of four shifts per day. "The conquest of fatigue [might be] cumulative," he suggested, given that "83 cases of shredded whole wheat biscuit used to be packed in an hour (under the eight-hour day). At the time of my visit, the number was 96." Meanwhile, the "pest of so many manufacturing plants, unnecessary overtime that somehow takes on the appearance of necessity," had been eliminated at Kellogg's. Under the "long hour regime," when their lives were dominated by work, workers tended to resist a production bonus. But under the six-hour system, most workers were showing that they preferred to work harder for premium pay rather than longer, for overtime.

Like Brown and the editors of *Factory and Industrial Management*, Hoskins observed that the depression had raised the "familiar specter of technological unemployment"—as Karl Marx and the Socialists asserted, capital and machines were steadily replacing labor. There were but "two ways out" of the mass unemployment and economic chaos that loomed: "New industries, the large-scale fulfillment of new wants, . . . must absorb the men and women released from older employment. Or hours of work must be shortened, so that more workers will share in the jobs that do exist. This, of course, not merely in 1931 but for the years to come."

Industry's future rested on the early realization that both paths were necessary. What "thinking men in industry [were] saying is shorter hours for men and longer hours for machines." The six-hour shift was destined to become "one of the important shock absorbers of American industrial advance."[23]

Like *Forbes*, most publications that ran stories about Kellogg's experiment in the early 1930s simply assumed that shorter working hours were a benefit of industrial progress, on a par with higher wages, and that workers shared this view. Unlike present-day historians, however, few journalists felt compelled to explain why Kellogg workers apparently supported shorter hours. Many had been covering labor's fight for "progressively shorter hours" for years and found it natural that workers would want to work less and would consider shorter hours with the same pay a good deal.[24]

During the spring of 1931, *Factory and Industrial Management* updated its earlier story, finding that Kellogg's six-hour day had "won its spurs." Envisioning a new future for industrial capitalism, the editors wrote that the six-hour day opened up

> a new way of life, and . . . [showed] that production is a means and not an end, that our national increase of productivity makes it practical to devote a greater share of life to living. [The six-hour day] recognized the *changed balance between leisure to live and productivity to supply the means of living* . . . and recognize[d] increased leisure with security as the most logical increase in the standard of living. [It was] the forerunner of a general movement aimed not only at meeting the widespread unemployment . . . but at providing a saner utilization of our resources of man power and machinery. (Emphasis added)[25]

Most business and financial publications agreed that Kellogg's scheme offered a permanent solution to technological unemployment based on "elimination of the work, not the worker." Journalists responded to *Factory and Industrial Management*'s criticism that "we have not sufficiently realized in the past the value to the employee and to society of leisure, freedom, and opportunity to enjoy life in one's own way" and begin to sketch out the broad outline of "Liberation Capitalism."[26]

THE THEORETICAL ORIGINS OF "LIBERATION CAPITALISM"

"Liberation Capitalism" did not spring fully grown out of the imaginations of managers like Lewis Brown or journalists like Chapin Hoskins.

It had a long history. The theorizing and research that went on before the depression deserve some historical articulation beyond the exuberant rhetoric of journalists and the practical concerns of industrial managers. Intellectuals and theorists do occasionally make a real difference. When they do, it is only fair to let them have their say.[27]

Economists such as John Stuart Mill and Simon Patten had long speculated that human needs for things the marketplace provided were finite, reasoning that as industry advanced, it was possible for humans to get "enough." Such theorists tended to divide economic goods (or utility) between "necessities" and "luxuries," and to divide the world between "free" and "utilitarian" realms. Needs for basic economic goods and services, being finite, tended to decline as industry advanced. As the most pressing material needs were met in a condition of "abundance," other "nonpecuniary" human needs, desires, and activities outside the market would become relatively more appealing, and might be given more time and attention. Mill wrote that after "necessities" had been provided for the masses, the nations of the world *should* accept that condition as constant and embrace what many feared—the economic "Stationary State." In such a condition, human progress would take place in realms outside economics, in "mental culture, moral and social progress . . . and the Arts of Living." In a situation in which "no one is poor, no one desires to be richer," people would have "sufficient leisure, both physical and mental . . . to cultivate freely the graces of life." Such free activities would flourish and expand because industry, increasingly productive, would provide more and more leisure instead of more and more unneeded (or less needed) goods and services.[28]

But the picture was not entirely rosy. Economists had been drawing "backward-bending" supply curves for labor since the days of the Mercantilists, predicting that leisure would automatically grow as wages and wealth increased. Mill and Patten, however, later joined by Thorstein Veblen, warned that economic abundance could just as easily produce another, less promising result. The danger lay in a nation's trying to expand wealth and maintain economic growth after the "basics" had been taken care of.[29] Mill predicted that if the western world tried to continue economic growth forever, beyond the point where people had enough, the natural world would be destroyed: "the earth must lose that great portion of its pleasantness which it owes to things that the unlimited increase in wealth . . . would extirpate from it" and humans would be left "con-

CHAPTER ONE

suming [more and more] things which give little or no pleasure except as representatives of wealth."[30]

In the 1920s Rabbi Abba Silver, Monsignor John Ryan, Stephen Leacock, Stuart Chase, and other writers added to the catalogue of horrors uncovered during the nation's scramble for more and more in an age of abundance. Responding to the birth of consumerism, the rapid increase in advertising, and what Edward Cowdrick called the "New Economic Gospel of Consumption," they expanded Mill's list to include waste on an unprecedented scale, exploitation of humans, increasing disparities in wealth and power, and the commodification and degradation of free human exchange and activities (a favorite metaphor has always been prostitution, the ultimate form of commercialization and thus destruction of the human potential for free action).[31]

Arthur Olaus Dahlberg emerged as the most widely read and influential theorist of Liberation Capitalism during the 1930s. He tried to lay out the full significance of the nationwide experiment in work sharing, its history, and its place in economic and social theory. Responding to charges that work sharing was a harebrained fad, he was at pains to show that the theory behind the project had been extensively discussed by economists for years.[32] Dahlberg updated the traditional themes of writers of the 1920s such as Stephen Leacock and David Friday, applying them to the national politics of work sharing and industrial experiments like Kellogg's six-hour day. For Dahlberg, the most important economic and social question facing the western world was "whether we take . . . leisure in the form of shorter hours . . . or in the form of unemployment and lose it."[33] Unless that question was answered correctly, "capitalism would fail" and be replaced by authoritarian government. AFL President William Green turned Dahlberg's argument into a slogan: "Free-time *will* come, the only choice is unemployment or leisure."

Dahlberg suggested that an "Age of Leisure" under capitalism would mean unprecedented freedom from work and material concerns, unlimited opportunities for the masses to live outside the marketplace. More time spent with family, friends, the community; in nature, learning, teaching, worship, appreciation, and play would invigorate working-class culture and lead to a different kind of progress and a new understanding of human and national achievement.

With Mill, Dahlberg thought that the key failure of capitalism was its resistance to the natural decline of the importance of the marketplace, a resistance based on inflated egos, flawed values, and short-sighted beliefs, not on objective, rational economic analysis. For ideological or psychological reasons, most businessmen and economists rejected long-term work reduction as industry's best, last achievement, for such a consummation would set the economy and business in second place, as a servant to other kinds of human needs and purposes. They feared the loss of their status as providers of the primary and most pressing needs of human beings. For them the business of America was and should always be business. Or as Ford put it, "What else is there to do?" but work and create more wealth.

Accordingly, most economists and businessmen and a growing number of politicians embraced that fantastic project that Mill, Patten, and others had warned about: eternal economic growth. Moreover, they were beginning to enshrine this insane idea as an absolute, unquestioned economic principle and to establish it as the ideological foundation of the modern state. According to the Gospel of Consumption, the social expectation that people could reduce their working and curtail their buying to do something "better," this old yearning for an age of "abundance," had to be rooted out. Language that consigned work and wealth to a subordinate role in life had to be replaced by appeals to a "higher standard of living" and a proper regard for "new products" and for work as life's permanent center. This was "serious business." It was the responsibility of what Rexford Tugwell called "workers on work" to find new, "important," "useful," and "necessary" work for the nation to do, for the alternative was aimless drift toward chaos.

The fundamental value attached to everlasting economic expansion entailed several corollaries: government support for (and thus control of) economic growth, the eternal creation of new work to replace work "lost" to machines, a new definition of "full-time" work to counter the century-long social acceptance of work reduction, and the rejection of the notions of "basic necessity" and "enough."[34]

Dahlberg used the metaphor of a "new religion" to attack these ideas. (Stuart Chase used that of industry's "squirrel cage.") The "Calvinistic worship of toil" had become a new, secular religion in which economic growth was "an end and a world of itself," where "we automatically anoint our business men as the high priest of our religion . . . [and] the manufacturer . . . becomes the modern shepherd . . . [seeking] some human frailty which he can cultivate into a new demand."[35]

CHAPTER ONE

Salesmen were continually trying to "convert" the buyer to the true faith:

Consuming more physical goods is spiritual expression. Advertising campaigns are his sermons. "Consume More" is his text. . . . Our long day, then, forces our producers to lead us into a commercial religion and materialistic philosophy. Energetic salesmen, impelled by selfishness, determine the course of our spiritual expression and become the priests of our religion. They impel us to worship wants. . . . When selfishness can turn nowhere else, it wraps our soap in pretty boxes and tries to convince us that is solace to our souls. (224)

Leaving its proper place, the satisfaction of "basic necessities," and embarking into nebulous realms of "psychic need," cultural "meaning," and "human relationships," capitalism was making the nation "spiritually poverty stricken." And therefore "we labor and die. For poverty is more than a matter of bread. But as things stand now, our energies are so completely devoted to economic ends and concerns which have no [authentic] spiritual meaning for us—we have no energy remaining"(233). Capitalism was unmatched in its capacity to produce "necessities," but produced awful results when it tried to manufacture "spiritual meaning" and "cultural values," and when it began to commodify "free activities."

Disagreeing with Chapin Hoskins and other industrial managers, Dahlberg concluded that the only way to check the political momentum behind work creation and federal support of perpetual economic growth for "full-employment" was by "*federal statutory enactment*" of shorter hours (243). It was unfortunate that the state would have to intervene; it would have been better if individual firms and workers continued, as they had been doing for over a century, to agree on work reduction. But government-supported capitalism was emerging as a new political reality that had to be countered politically. According to Dahlberg, at least statutory work sharing would "not make our capitalism into socialism," as would other kinds of government interventions to "stimulate the market" to create more work (ibid.).

Still, the practical, day-by-day implementation of work reduction would have to come from "technicians and managers." With or without shorter-hour legislation, they would have to be "the prime movers," encouraging local support for shorter hours and dealing with the many practical issues that would arise. The danger lay in the seductive appeal of mass advertising, the machination of politicians, and the wily rhetoric of the true believers in the Gospel of Consumption. The new ideas and rhetoric about "standard of living" and the need to work full-time could thwart the healthy desires for both higher wages and shorter hours that workers had been expressing for generations. Managers therefore had to remain "professional" and resist the rhetoric and aggressive values of the Gospel, employing "sound management techniques" dispassionately. This would allow working hours to be "adjusted" in a continuing process (243–44). History suggested that balance would automatically be achieved between higher wages and shorter hours. This natural evolution would "undoubtedly decrease the *cultural subservience* of the . . . workingman. The spunk which has oozed out of him in recent decades might return [resulting in] a *cultural revival* the like of which the world has never seen. It would be a revival untrammeled and free." (235, emphasis added).

Shorter hours, growing locally, would act as a prophylactic against a new cultural imperialism. It would provide a new freedom, empowering workers and setting them again in control of their "culture"—those areas of life that should be outside the marketplace, the process of industrialization, and the modern discipline of work. Thus the industrial manager could help to save "worker culture" and further the "regeneration of . . . the workingman."

> For by the mere act of shortening its hours of labor and constantly maintaining a genuine scarcity of labor, capitalism can eliminate unemployment and the fear of unemployment; it can eliminate industrial wastes and inanities of consumption; it can eliminate exploitation of personality and the corruption of values; it can eliminate insecurity and get at the kernel of all economic evil by giving economic power to the mass of the people; it can remove the brakes from its marvelous machine, give engineers a free rein to spin the wheels of industry, and rekindle the American belief that the material world can be molded to our will. (244)

The industrial managers Dahlberg had in mind, people like W. K. and Paul Litchfield, probably saw only the broad outlines of Liberation Capitalism. But Lewis Brown was exceptional. He knew enough to claim that "we are going to start something that has been talked about for years," and to boast that only Kellogg's had the "courage" to put welfare capitalism's avant-garde theories into operation. A local reporter from the *Moon-Journal* was infected by Brown's enthusiasm.

> Kellogg . . . today set the world pace for humanizing industry. . . . Inauguration of this revolutionary change in working policy, discussed by leading economists and industrialists of both England and America for more than a decade as a palliative for labor surplus resulting from the mechanization of industry, . . . continues to keep Kellogg . . . among the very leaders in the industrial life of America in the consideration of its employees. It is generally believed that the effect of this unusual and extraordinary move . . . will be far-reaching—setting a precedent for large manufacturers throughout the country and attracting attention of leading economists and social scientists. . . . Battle Creek [is] in the very fore-front in America as one of the finest communities in the consideration given to the working man and his right to a substantial working wage and with it, the opportunity for pleasure, happiness, and enjoyment.[36]

LEWIS JOHN BROWN:
LORD LEVERHULME IN BATTLE CREEK

Born in England in 1891, Lewis Brown went to school there but claimed that his "real education" as an engineer and industrial manager was gained "on the job" in "some of the leading industries" in the United States. He began his career in 1907 with the Emerson Manufacturing Company in Rockford, Illinois, moving up from "office boy" to "assistant general work manager and in charge of plant engineering." Brown remembered that he had been taught the fundamentals of "scientific management" at Emerson.[37]

In September 1929 Brown "became connected with The Kellogg Company . . . as personal representative of Mr. W. K. Kellogg."[38] Brown wrote:

> Mr. Kellogg who was not very active in the business spent a good deal of his time in California and wanted someone to straighten out some conditions in the business that were not satisfactory. November 1st of the same year he left for California making me president and general manager. During the next two years a complete study was made of the business, wage payment plans revised, sales problems

studied and the complete system of budgetary control installed. . . . [On] December 1st, 1930, under my personal supervision, the six hour working day plan was devised and successfully installed. In 1931 the profits of many millions were double those of 1928.[39]

Brown maintained his ties with England through letters and visits, however. One of the greatest influences in his business life was Lord William Hesketh Leverhulme, the Lancastrian soap king who was a founder of Liberation Capitalism. Brown kept a copy of Leverhulme's book, *The Six-Hour Day & Other Industrial Questions,* marking passages and writing notes in the margins. He quoted Leverhulme often in his speeches and drew directly on his writings about business management, the advantages of shorter hours, gardens, recreational services, and city planning.[40]

William Hesketh Leverhulme made his fortune from Sunlight Soap, Lux, and Vim and then turned to social causes. He founded one of the first modern suburbs, Port Sunlight, for workers in his company as an experiment in city planning. Detached houses were the rule, each with its own garden. He designed the town to include a hospital, library, church, concert hall, swimming pools, and gym, and paid special attention to community leisure services such as choirs, silver bands, and a bewildering assortment of literary and scientific societies—he took almost the whole town to see the Paris Exposition in 1900.[41]

Leverhulme's detailed, practical innovations gave Brown a sound business foundation for Kellogg's six-hour day. Brown underlined several of Leverhulme's observations about the increased productivity that resulted from shorter hours, including his conclusion that "working shorter hours with lessened fatigue does not reduce output, but generally, and with very few exceptions, tends to increase output." He also underlined Leverhulme's claims that shorter hours would help create more jobs and would prove to be the *"only"* possible long-term response to technological advance open to companies and nations in the "age of the machine." Brown even highlighted Leverhulme's observation, reminiscent of Mill: "To get the work condensed into six hours would enable us to produce . . . everything that we require"(24).

But Leverhulme's central vision of Liberation Capitalism had the biggest impact on Brown and thus indirectly on Battle Creek. Introducing the book, Viscount Haldane linked Leverhulme's work to the intellectual heritage of John Stuart Mill:

Men and women, relieved from the grinding pressure of poverty, and having enough to live on, may well prefer, as the main thing that counts in life, to know more rather than to have more wealth. The possessions of the millionaire may, in days to come, count for less to the average man than under existing conditions. And here comes in the real point of Lord Leverhulme's ideal of a six-hour day. The labour of such a day must be concentrated if it is to bring a sufficiency in wages. But if it does bring such a sufficiency it leaves leisure for the things of the soul. (xii)

After a discussion of public schools, adult education, and military service, Leverhulme described his version of Mill's dream:

Now, human beings who have received [education and military training] at the age of thirty can be trusted to make the best use of their spare time. They will usually have a hobby. The man at thirty will perhaps keep a garden. . . . We should gain vastly in all directions by the introduction of the six-hour day; the worker would have opportunities for recreation, for education, and for the achievement of higher social standing. The term "factory hand"—that most hateful of terms, as if the "hand" possessed no intellect, and no ambition in life at all—that term would go. The factory employee, no longer a "hand," would go for six hours a day to the factory in the true spirit of service. He or she would receive for that six hours at least the same pay that he or she now receives for eight hours.

   Out of all this wreckage of [World War I] must ultimately come better and more ideal conditions of living for all classes. . . . Kindly Nature will reward our labour with enough and to spare, and with lengthening life, deepening joy, and happiness for all. (34–35)

Lewis Brown spread this message to audiences throughout the Midwest and Canada and did his best to make Leverhulme's vision a reality in Battle Creek.

LOCAL CONCERNS: KELLOGG'S SIX-MONTH EVALUATION

While Dahlberg was appealing to industrial managers to apply the theories of Liberation Capitalism, Kellogg's, Goodyear of Akron, Ohio, and other businesses were testing whether shorter hours worked locally, fine-tuning their experiments, and struggling with numerous practical problems.[42]

On 14 April 1931, Kellogg's decided to make the six-hour day permanent. Brown published a report concluding that shorter hours had proven to be a rational response to mechanization. The practical, financial foundation of the experiment was holding up, for workers on shorter schedules were working more efficiently and harder. Brown noted that employees worked with a will and with spirit in anticipation of the early quitting time; they willingly accepted the "speed-ups" and production bonuses because of the lure of leisure. Except for a few malcontents who used to take the lion's share of overtime, most accepted "working harder instead of longer" for premium pay.[43]

Brown admitted that most jobs at Kellogg's were repetitious and "tend to become monotonous." He concluded that this was increasingly true of all work in the new industrial state; since the advent of the assembly line, romantic notions about enlarging worker control on the job and providing joyous work were dangerous pipe-dreams. In order to stay competitive, Kellogg's (and all other firms as far as he could tell) were having to *tighten* work discipline and increase specialization. Moreover, the jobs that required the most skill and training were among the first to be mechanized. The increased likelihood of boring jobs made work reduction even more important. Since modern work was bound to be increasingly geared to the dictates of the machine, the best the worker could hope for was less of it.[44] Like athletes in a relay race, production workers of the future would perform their task at top speed for shorter and shorter periods and then be relieved before they used up their energy; the pace, not the work itself, would be the focus of interest. The shorter the burst of work, the better the work.

Brown was convinced that workers on the line were ready to turn from work to leisure to gain more control over their lives, individual self-expression, fulfillment, creativity, craftsmanship, community, fellowship, conversation, and all the other things that romantic dreamers were hoping somehow to put back into modern jobs.[45] Leisure had turned out to be a powerful motivator at Kellogg's. If workers were rewarded for good, hard work by a bonus and by the right to leave work earlier, the added incentive of freedom would move them at least as effectively as cash. Brown believed that few workers found their work as interesting and "rewarding" as their time off. On the contrary, work was still a means to an end for most Kellogg workers. "Leisure" for Brown had matured into an opened-ended idea, akin to "Freedom" and encompassing rest, family life, recreation, "education, music, . . . cultural studies [sic], . . . resulting in a more healthy, ambitious, alert, and aggressive working force."[46] He was sure that the six-hour day was the answer to workers' discontent with speedups, loss of craftsmanship, boredom, and repetition. Shorter hours was a lightning-rod, attracting and dissipating worker dissatisfaction, and also energizing them.

Governed more and more by the machine, work was bound to become machine-like. Brown concluded that the best solution was to eliminate more of it for the individual worker. Constant work reduction and higher hourly wages would resolve the issue of job control, at the bottom of most worker discontent and the basic reason for union successes. Brown and other Kellogg managers predicted that plant workers would exchange control at work for constantly expanding control over their lives—especially if life's center was shifting to leisure. Control at work would always be limited—work by definition involved a loss of freedom and the control compared with time off. Work discipline, the foundation of industrial capitalism, was increasing. Realizing this, workers were making the rational choice of leisure's greater freedom and the control offered by the enlightened personnel manager over the piecemeal efforts to modify work discipline offered by the unions.[47]

Brown concluded that by shifting the issue of freedom/control from work to leisure, he reconciled workers' basic concerns about their jobs with the production needs of the company. Shorter hours would henceforth be the foundation of lasting worker–management agreement.

FROM THE POLITICS OF WORK SHARING
TO THE POLITICS OF WORK CREATION

From the beginning of the six-hour experiment, Lewis Brown had seen its national political implications. He wrote in the company's paper: "I believe the time has come to admit to ourselves that we [as a nation] cannot expect consumption of manufactured products to equal the productive capacity of our industries. . . . [I]t is a fundamental fact which we must learn to live with." In a letter to James Couzens, U.S. senator from Michigan, Brown objected that a bill Couzens was about to introduce looked like "a modified arrangement of the Dole [sic] system as now in effect in

England, and which has proven to be so unsatisfactory." Brown urged the senator to fight to get people back to work, and to find a way to do on a national scale what Kellogg had successfully accomplished in Battle Creek.[48]

After Brown's departure from the company, Kellogg's remained, in *Newsweek*'s words, "the outstanding exponent of the six-hour day."[49] Other businesses in Battle Creek and in Michigan followed suit as work sharing became a national movement in 1932–37. The movement had strong business support initially and militant labor support through 1938. After W. K. visited Hoover in the White House, lawmakers cited the six-hour day in Battle Creek as a model for the nation to combat technological unemployment.[50]

Between 1930 and 1934, support for work reduction reached its high-water mark in the United States. Hoover's secretary of labor, William Doak, declared that "industry, in general, favored" shorter hours. Several major industrial firms voluntarily cut weekly hours to forty and then to thirty in 1930 and 1931. Some, such as Kellogg's and Remington Rand, tried to maintain weekly wage levels, while others expanded their total payroll expenditures while cutting per capita wages proportionately. The Industrial Conference Board surveyed 1,718 business executives late in 1932 and estimated that 50 percent of American businesses had shortened hours to save jobs.[51]

In April 1931 delegates to the national Chamber of Commerce convention proposed a voluntary, national effort to follow Kellogg's example. Secretary of Commerce Robert P. Lamont told the convention that Kellogg's "has been fortunate enough to be able to continue its production at a high rate [and] has adopted a working schedule of four six-hour shifts. As a result of this experiment, this corporation has not only found it possible to lower working hours and maintain a fair wage rate, but also . . . reduce costs of production."[52]

For a while labor seemed interested. In May 1932 William Green contacted Kellogg's through Lewis Brown and instructed H. B. Hayden of Market Street Bank in Philadelphia to contact Harry Haas, president of the American Bankers Association. Haas agreed to "see President Hoover regarding" the formation of some "committee" composed of labor, business, and government officials "to consider the [national] inauguration of a six-hour day or of a thirty-six hour week."[53] Hoover himself finally threw his support behind these efforts. In a speech to the National Conference of Business and Industrial Committees in August 1932, Hoover called shorter hours the fastest and most efficient way to create more jobs. Responding to Hoover's encouragement, the conference created the Teagle Commission for work sharing, headed by Walter Teagle, president of Standard Oil of New Jersey.[54]

The "Share-the-work" drive opened in September 1932 and grew immediately into a national force with strong business support. Even though the National Association of Manufacturers supported the drive primarily as a hedge against labor's push for national shorter-hours legislation, public response to the idea and business cooperation were impressive. The Department of Labor estimated that 25 percent of American workers "held jobs on the plan."[55]

The movement built momentum during the 1932 campaign. Both major parties included a shorter-hours plank in their platforms. During the campaign, shorter hours was the most important unemployment remedy discussed. Prominent supporters were to be found along the entire political spectrum, including most major labor leaders and prominent businesspeople.[56] But after a few half-hearted overtures to the Teagle Commission in September and a lukewarm endorsement in October, the American Federation of Labor (AFL) Executive Council rejected the Teagle campaign. Accusing business of cutting workers' pay whenever hours were cut, labor argued that business was forcing workers to shoulder all the cost of the nation's unemployment.

For two months the New Hampshire Plan to "share the cost of shorter hours" equally between management and labor seemed to offer a compromise. But that promise was cut short when Hugo Black introduced to the Seventy-second Congress the AFL's bill to prohibit, in interstate or foreign commerce, all goods produced by establishments where workers were employed more than five days a week or six hours a day. After the election, legislation rapidly replaced wage cutting as the issue separating labor and business.

In the face of labor's threat to legislate a thirty-hour week, business support for work reduction receded and changed into full-scale opposition. Labor abandoned its hopes for a compromise along the lines of the New Hampshire Plan and focused its efforts on legislation. With some important exceptions, most notably Kellogg's, business abandoned work sharing and promptly forgot about work reduction as a management strategy or business philosophy. Discounting Chapin Hoskins' "two-ways-out" solution, business emphasized economic expansion as the only way to "re-employ" workers and embraced Roosevelt's new policy of work creation by government action. Rapidly, business interest in managing the declining amount of work to be done in the new industrial state was replaced by a recommitment to save work from further erosion and marshal the resources of industrial management and government to ensure all Americans "full-time work."

In direct response to the threat posed by labor's thirty-hour bill, Roosevelt and his advisors developed rhetorical, ideological, and policy alternatives to work sharing that they consistently put forth as better unemployment remedies. Work reduction was dividing a shrinking "lump of labor" (an economist's phrase that was given a new pejorative, rhetorical life) and "redistributing the unemployment"; after 1934 Roosevelt became more interested in increasing total work effort and creating new jobs by stimulating the economy (deficit spending and liberal Treasury policy) or, if necessary, public employment. Where supporters of shorter hours saw increased leisure as a basis for individual freedom and progress, FDR's administration envisioned the government acting to ensure everyone the "right to work" a "full-time" job and looked to secure work, not the freedom from work, as the basis for national progress.

The political contest that raged over the Black–Connery measure and experiments like Kellogg's reflected an ideological division of the first importance—a division between views of progress and views about the fate of work in the depression. With the ascendancy of Roosevelt's views and rhetoric, supported by business, the vision of increased leisure as the basis of culture and a healthy social order waned. With government support for the "right to work full-time," the politics of shorter hours faded. With the emergence of the "second" New Deal, the shorter-hours movement ran up against its first successful coalition of adversaries and the salvaging of work from the steady erosion of shorter hours began.[57]

Business abandoned its voluntary work-reduction experiment to support Roosevelt's work-creation efforts, and the nascent vision of Liberation Capitalism faded. Attacked at first as wasteful "make-work," FDR's ideas about work creation have become political orthodoxy throughout the industrial nations—so much so that in the last decade of the twentieth century it is unusual to hear politicians speak without hearing "JOBS, JOBS, JOBS."

Roosevelt's rendezvous with work creation was arguably the most important political watershed of this century. Taking the long view, one may observe that the rise of work creation and the fall of work reduction or sharing, together with the eclipse of Liberation Capitalism on the national level, left those companies that had advanced on the shorter-hours front exposed. Roosevelt's discovery of work creation thus provides a larger, political context for the failure of Kellogg's experiment, and indeed a good explanation for the end of the shorter-hours movement in the United States.

KELLOGG'S SIX-HOUR SALIENT

At the Kellogg plant, support for work reduction continued after FDR discovered "JOBS, JOBS, JOBS." The rapprochement between management and workers that Brown had forged strengthened after he left the company. Through most of the 1930s, management's shorter-hours strategy matured and became the outstanding example of work sharing and Liberation Capitalism in the United States, an example that W. K. offered as an alternative to FDR's failing effort.[58] After 1935, management–labor agreement receded in Battle Creek, but so slowly that it is easy to observe how business support turned into full-scale opposition, and how workers and the unions responded. Since the six-hour day at Kellogg's was the nation's (and indeed one of history's) shorter-hours salients, it is also possible to determine how and why the rhetoric of "JOBS, JOBS, JOBS" thrived in this century while shorter hours and increased leisure were rejected.

In 1935, after "five years under the six-hour day," Kellogg's recommitted itself to the short schedule, finding that the "burden [or overhead] unit cost was reduced 25% . . . labor unit costs reduced 10% . . . accidents reduced 41% . . . the severity of accidents (days lost per accident) improved 51% . . . [and] 39% more people [were] working at Kellogg's than in 1929." "This isn't just a theory with us," W. K. boldly maintained. "We have proved it with five years' actual experience. We have found that, with the shorter working day, the efficiency and morale of our employees is [sic] so increased, the accident and insurance rates are so improved, and the unit cost of production is so lowered that we can afford to pay as much for six hours as we formerly paid for eight."[59]

Kellogg's even used the six-hour day in its advertising. "A Message from W. K. Kellogg" ran in newspapers nationwide, often as a full-page ad. Set in the midst of a corn field, and signed with Kellogg's famous signature, the message was:

> Everyone is interested in the country' improvement. We will have found economic recovery only when every one does his share. As we see it our duty is threefold: first to provide the American farmer with a fair market value for his crop; second to give employment to as many people as possible; and finally to supply a wholesome food at a low cost. . . . Two years ago before NRA [National Recovery Administration] we adopted a six-hour working day for our twenty-six hundred employees at good pay. This meant four shifts of six hours and enabled us to give employment to twenty-five per cent more people than in pre-depression times. Kellogg Corn Flakes are enjoyed daily by millions of people."[60]

At the end of 1935 (and again in 1939), W. K. Kellogg boasted that the six-hour day was "an unqualified success" and continued to insist that if it were put into general use, "employment would increase 20%" nationwide.[61] The *Moon-Journal* reported that "W. K. Kellogg . . . reaffirmed his belief in the social and economic advantages of the six-hour day," adding that he was convinced by his company's experience and the "failure of other methods" that the "shorter work day without cuts in pay [was] the only permanent and workable solution of the unemployment problem." Opposing FDR's work creation, Kellogg concluded, "We are going to have to come to something like this [shorter hours]. . . . We shall never solve the unemployment problem by 'made work,' by the dole, or appeals to patriotism and to other methods that have been tried and found wanting."[62]

Kellogg's extended other basic worker benefits during the 1930s, tailored to fit its work-reduction strategy. Just after his 15 April 1931 announcement, Brown initiated a vacation with pay plan, linking it to a "waste saving campaign" that he claimed would pay for the vacations.[63] In December 1933 the company introduced "Kellogg's Security Plan," an amalgam of life, disability, and accident insurance and a retirement plan. Underwritten by the Metropolitan Life Insurance Company, the plan insured each worker's life for a thousand dollars and provided the best available disability and accident insurance. Kellogg's paid the entire cost of the insurance and matched employee retirement payments. *Factory and Industrial Management* called the security plan "a measure supporting the six-hour strategy [and] . . . a logical complement to the six-hour day." Like the six-hour day, it was designed to "assure the maintenance of purchasing power which is essential if the output of industry is to find customers." Moreover, Metropolitan offered lower rates because of the plant's excellent accident record and low rate of sick days claimed—both, according to Kellogg's, partially explained by the six-hour day.[64]

The company started to prorate fringe benefits. Vacation pay, for instance, was calculated on the basis of the average weekly pay of each worker. The company also began to prorate insurance and retirement payments, so that the firm's "fixed costs" were stabilized as a fraction of its total payroll, rather than growing in proportion to the number of workers. Kellogg's was working out the details of "shorter hours and more workers," trying to contain its "fixed costs."

Further implementing management philosophy, the company began to contribute to the workers' leisure. Kellogg's provided elaborate facilities and devoted substantial personnel resources to planning and promoting company activities. It erected a gymnasium and a $15,000 recreation hall equipped with a the latest sound and motion picture equipment. During dedication ceremonies, Brown said that the recreation building was "a good investment" and would be used for "Dances, Meetings, Athletics, Civic Activities for the betterment of our City, Conventions, Public Entertainment, Educational Lectures." He spoke of "the necessity of play as well as work" and concluded that the recreation hall "has been created as a part of the various Kellogg social features to add further happiness and enjoyment."[65] The "Personnel Division [has] recently organized to assist in the planning of these various activities." N. D. Huff, director of the Personnel Department, took his responsibility seriously: "We are dealing with human materials and our purpose is to produce healthy, intelligent, and interested employees."[66]

The company also provided a "social hall" for dancing over the noon hour and for company events, an outdoor athletic park, and a ten-acre "recreation park" at the plant. W. K.'s estate at Gull Lake was frequently used for company picnics and parties. The company baseball and softball teams were popular, as were the singing groups. Perhaps because of Lord Leverhulme's passion for worker-gardens, the company divided a seventy-five-acre farm adjoining the plant into garden plots for employees. "In view of the increased amount of leisure time provided by the six-hour day," Brown wrote, "Kellogg employees will welcome the opportunity to utilize their spare time in gardening." The company also offered $250 in cash prizes, instruction, and instructional literature, and for a while ran a feature in the *Kellogg News* called "The Kellogg Gardener."[67] But Kellogg's Band received the most attention. It played every Monday evening over the local radio station, WELL, operated by The *Enquirer,* and played at fairs, festivals, and in parades all over the state.[68]

Workers remember that the company encouraged social functions even more when the union was formed in 1937 and "contributed prizes and time off in an effort to keep any union movement on a 'old friends' basis." One worker who began working at the plant in 1931 recalled "elaborate parties with professional music . . . free entertainment for employees as well as the public, . . . baseball and basketball teams that were among the best in the Mid-West."[69]

Undeniably, Kellogg management was interested in keeping the workers content and in line, and used recreational programs to further this aim. But it is not possible to reduce Kellogg's efforts entirely to this self-serving aim. Kellogg's recreation programs were consistent with its larger management philosophy and with an attempt to build détente with workers on the basis of shorter hours. And a good deal of the company's interest in recreational activities was due to the personality of W. K. Kellogg.

"W. K."

Through much of his life, W. K. Kellogg was interested in improving work through expanding leisure and providing for the "worthy use" of free time. The policies he promoted at the company and through the Kellogg Foundation often coincided with his private views.

In November 1931 he wrote his grandson, John Jr., a letter full of wonderfully mixed metaphors and "Suggestions for One Who Wishes to Hit the Trail Successfully, Make the Grade, Play the Game, and Win." "First of all," he advised, "get plenty of sleep and recreation," since properly used leisure and relaxation were essential for a sane life. Work could never be a life in and of itself. He advised his grandson not to fall victim to the common youthful belief that work was the end-all and be-all of life, as W. K. himself had.

He watched in alarm as his grandson ignored his advice, overburdened himself with work and responsibility, and fell ill. Again W. K. lectured

John Jr. to slow down and work less. He finally resorted to cutting off the young man's salary "until such time as you curb your enormous energies and concentrate on getting well."[70]

Throughout his life W. K. observed, "I never learned to play," and he profoundly regretted his shyness and isolation, his inability to enjoy life and people. He told his biographer, "I would give the world to be able to get along with people as well as you do." A psychiatrist who was related to W. K. and spent some time with him observed that he was "deeply unhappy and frustrated. In all my long practice of psychiatry, I don't know of a more lonely, isolated individual. . . . Possibly by the time he gained success at middle age, the capacity for enjoyment of a rich life had atrophied. He had few vices and only short-lived hobbies so that he had practically no escape . . . for his nervous tensions." One of his few pleasures was giving his money away, but he argued, "I love to do things for children because I get a kick out of it. Therefore I am a selfish person and no philanthropist."[71]

W. K. often speculated that his views and opinions were influenced by his family and his upbringing. His mother and father were leaders of the Seventh-day Adventists in Battle Creek when the city became a publication and organizational center for that church, and for most of his mature life he still felt ties to it. He shared the Adventists' strict opinions about alcohol, "promiscuousness," and tobacco, and spoke of them as "our people."[72]

The Adventists grew out of the "Millerites," a mid-nineteenth-century sect most famous for predicting the second coming of Christ between 21 March 1843 and 21 March 1844 (postponed to 22 October 1844). The sect was led by the visionary and seer Ellen G. White through most of the nineteenth century. Still centering on preparation for Christ's imminent return, the group began to embrace a variety of public health causes: "water cures," simple diet, and abstinence from tobacco, coffee, spices, tea, profanity, and eventually meat. Sister White led the way, exhorting her people to be "even more stubborn" in their efforts to improve the health and purity of their communities in preparation for the Rhapsody: "We have a duty to speak, to come out against intemperance of every kind—intemperance in working, in eating, in drinking, in drugging, and then point to God's great medicine, water, pure soft water, for diseases, for health, for cleanliness, for luxury."[73]

W. K.'s elder brother, John Harvey Kellogg, focused on the public health and fitness aspects of these teachings, devoting his life to the Battle

Creek Sanitarium and to his own particular brand of health maintenance and restoration. John Harvey transformed the Sanitarium from a small Seventh-day Adventist retreat to a world-famous institution—arguably the most famous health spa in the United States during the period from the 1890s to World War I, which was the heyday of spas, water cures, health resorts, and mineral baths.[74]

John Harvey branched out from hydrotherapy, abstinence, and vegetarianism to explore ways of processing grains and cereals to make them taste like coffee and meat. He also sought to treat people with "nervous conditions" or "neurasthenia," a malady that had become something of an epidemic. This "condition" was then thought to be caused by the lack of physical exercise and relaxation associated with the ending of the frontier and by the sedentary and stressful occupations and habits of modern life.[75]

Much of John Harvey's treatment involved rest. But he also prescribed activity-based relaxation, reasoning that the vigorous exercise of parts of the body and mind neglected in ordinary life and occupations could provide a kind of release and restoration that simple immobility could not. Indeed, he believed that simple inactivity could make a person's nerves worse. Consequently, a large gymnasium was at the center of the "San," and relaxation punctuated by exercise became as important as diet and water in the treatment of "visitors."[76]

Active recreations, picnics, theater presentations, and cooking classes were also offered as an antidote to the stress of modern work and the "over-stimulation" of the brain and nervous system. Through 1903, at the height of the "neurasthenia" plague, when hundreds of the best and brightest in American cities suffered from overwork, nervous exhaustion, or breakdowns, the Sanitarium at Battle Creek thrived. Its regimen of waters, relaxation, exercise, and diet combined the nostrums most in vogue, and people scrambled to book rooms. John D. Rockefeller, Henry Ford, Harvey Firestone, Billy Sunday, Will Durant, Lowell Thomas, Eddie Cantor, Roald Amundsen, and Richard Byrd visited the Sanitarium.[77]

W. K. was caught in the rush. He had taken a job as factotum for John Harvey, who worked him nearly to death. Famous for his energy and untiring devotion to work, John Harvey cultivated the image of a superman, dictating to secretaries for eight hours at a stretch, performing operations through the night, conspicuously working at meals and on trains. John Harvey expected W. K. to live up to this myth, and berated him for being lazy if he stole some time at home. Later in his life W. K. wrote, "Dr.

[John Harvey] Kellogg was a prodigious worker. He worked long hours and . . . insisted that others work with him. . . . One week I was on duty 120 hours. . . . For many years we worked on Christmas and New Year's Day and . . . the Fourth of July. . . . I was so overworked that I am conscious that very little, if any of it, was performed satisfactorily."[78]

W. K. dreaded such chores as interviewing destitute patients and being his brother's errand boy. He was also sensitive to the price he paid for overworking. On 6 February 1884, John Harvey, without warning, told him to stay at the Sanitarium in order to take a visitor back to the train station—a task that stretched through the night and into the next day as the visitor and doctor droned on in conversation. "Puss [his wife] came up to the office about half past seven to see why I hadn't come home," he recorded in his diary. "She was so scairt that she cried." He remembered that he seldom saw his young children awake. He wrote to his eldest son, Karl, "I have always regretted I did not spend more time with you and Lenn and Beth when you were little, but the pressure of work was such that it seemed almost a physical impossibility." He also remembered that overwork made him sleep badly, and this affliction stayed with him the rest of his life.[79]

The contrast between the pressures of his thankless job and the rest and recreations of the well-to-do patients at the Sanitarium must have struck the young W. K. He was persistently ambivalent about work, alternately proud of being a self-made man and sad because he had devoted his whole life to the job. But his trademark saying, "I never learned to play," was an indictment of overwork more than a boast. W. K. attributed the isolation, shyness, insomnia, and ennui that tormented his later years to youthful overwork.

In response to patients' complaints about the blandness of meals at the "San," John Harvey assigned W. K. the task of making cereal grains more palatable. W. K. began experimenting. He soon offered patients zwieback, caramel cereal coffee, and "granola," a biscuit made from various grains that was baked, fed through a pair of rollers, and crushed into pieces.

Then came the breakthrough that is legend in the city. John Harvey insisted that the idea for the process came to him in a dream in which individual grains of wheat became little pieces of toast. In any case, he sent some boiled wheat to W. K. and told him to find some way to improve the taste. Dutifully, W. K. remembered, he took the wheat to the "San's" kitchens after his standard fifteen-hour work day and conducted experiments through the night. After boiling the wheat, the brothers fed it through the "granola" rollers and pressed the mixture flat, producing an oatmeal-like sludge. According to the fable, the brothers eventually neglected a batch of boiled wheat long enough for it to become moldy, and they discovered that each individual, aged wheat-berry emerged from the rollers as a perfect disk, forming flakes that when toasted had a wonderful taste and texture. The secret of "tempering" the grains for a uniform moisture content had been revealed, and "Granose," the first flaked cereal, was born. Three years later flaked corn cereal followed.[80]

The popularity of flaked cereal spread rapidly as "San" patients took samples home with them. C. W. Post and others recognized the marketing potential of the cereal and during the first decade of the century established forty-two companies in Calhoun County to manufacture cereals and coffee substitutes. After founding the Sanitas Food Company to manufacture cereals and health foods, John Harvey and his brother separated rancorously, beginning a feud that dragged through the courts for years. W. K. finally bought John Harvey out and began advertising on a massive, unprecedented scale, eventually driving out all but the most powerful competitors. Through the 1920s, W. K. led the company to first place among cereal producers and turned his company and town into something of a national legend. Advertising made Battle Creek as well known as any major city in the United States.[81]

As he was building his company, W. K. became increasingly concerned with worthwhile ways to spend his money, and he began to look for ways to help people at the plant and in the community and state. Consistent with his family's longstanding interest in the health of the community and his brother's work at the Sanitarium, Kellogg promoted his own version of health care, based in part on public provision of recreation and exercise. He gave substantial sums of money to build public recreational facilities, and he provided leisure services in the region that promoted family activities and healthy styles of life: building the $194,245 Youth Center in Battle Creek, donating land for Camp T. Ben Johnson and the Boy Scout camp at Sherman Lake, and miscellaneous gifts (totaling nearly $14,000) for recreation projects from 1916 to 1941. The day care W. K. provided for workers' children, the playgrounds and parks on the plant premises, public parks, nature centers, and community recreation facilities reflect his interest in what he understood as the public welfare.

A life-long bird fancier, he donated land to establish a popular bird sanctuary at Wintergreen Lake near Augusta, Michigan, and the Kellogg state forest expressly for the purpose of wildlife conservation and public recreation, defined as family picnicking, hiking, nutting, trout fishing, hunting, trapping, bird watching, and Christmas tree cutting.

In 1925, he established the Fellowship Corporation, and through that agency donated over a million dollars to such projects as the Battle Creek civic auditorium. Five years later, in June 1930, the Kellogg Foundation grew out of the first agency. Although it devoted most of its resources to education and health, the foundation continued to support numerous local and state recreation projects, such as camps, public swimming pools, parks, playgrounds, and libraries during the depression.[82]

According to W. K. Kellogg, the "public sector" needed to expand, not only for social welfare and public health, but for the future of freedom. While private industry (certainly not government) had to provide the necessities, work and wages, private foundations and government should provide for leisure—free people with free time required free places. Indeed, Kellogg believed that government's main business was freedom, protecting life and liberty first, and then providing for parks, libraries, community centers, and swimming pools for the pursuit of happiness.

His concern for public welfare extended to the Kellogg Company and the institution of the six-hour day. There is a good case to be made that his experience at the Foundation and working for his brother, treating victims of overwork and "neurasthenia" directly influenced his support of shorter working hours.

As part of the six-hour initiative, W. K. encouraged Kellogg workers to make good use of their time by maintaining contact with the Michigan soil—to remain on their farms as long as possible or at least tend one of the garden plots he offered free to workers in the city. Kellogg felt that close, active contact with nature, long a part of the Sanitarium's treatment program, had a restful and healing quality that was an antidote to modern life.[83]

He kept farms of his own, ignoring the expense, chiefly for the joy of raising horses and watching nature. The six-hour day allowed a few farmers to save at least part of their farms and stay out of the city, and W. K. made a special effort to hire marginal farmers. As a result, a number of rural residents found jobs at the plant. Many kept farming only as an avocational activity—gaining their livelihood and the wherewithal to farm on a reduced scale from their job at Kellogg's. A curious group of gentlemen farmers grew up around Battle Creek, worker amateurs who, like the English gentry of the nineteenth century and W. K. himself, engaged in farming more for the sake of the activity and as a way of life than for hard-headed economic reasons.

Like Lewis Brown and Chapin Hoskins, W. K. Kellogg was apparently intrigued by the possibility of mass leisure and the utopian future lying at the end of the process of work reduction. From his point of view, the family, community, and personal and public health should be the first beneficiaries of the new time wealth. Therefore he made an effort to influence workers to spend their time in "worthwhile" activities and to discourage commercial, passive amusements and what he saw as harmful recreations, such as drinking, "carousing," and gambling. A story has endured in Battle Creek that W. K. once scheduled a company picnic at Gull Lake but was dismayed to discover that an enterprising businessman had opened a saloon on a nearby hill, festooning the establishment with such bright banners and large signs that the picnickers could hardly fail to notice. When W. K.'s efforts to buy the man out were rebuffed—"You don't have the money to keep me closed that day," the man is supposed to have replied—Kellogg circulated a memo to all employees at the plant, discouraging them with veiled threats of dismissal from patronizing the saloon while extolling the benefits of healthy recreation. The strategy apparently worked well enough to send the saloon keeper packing.[84]

Until W. K. left the direct management of Kellogg's in 1937, the company continued to support six-hours. Kellogg was convinced that for the overwhelming majority of Kellogg workers, the shorter the shift the better. If they were able to maintain their standard of living, they would be only too happy to share their jobs with others because they would be getting something of value in return—free time.

W. K.'s life, words, and deeds strongly suggest that his vision of freedom was consistent with that of Lewis Brown and Lord Leverhulme. His vehement rejection of the "socialist trends" he saw in American politics, and his visionary attempts to make private enterprise work to improve the lives and enlarge the freedoms of Battle Creek workers, placed him in the forefront of Welfare Capitalists, enlightened managers, and exponents of Liberation Capitalism.[85] The editors of *Factory and Industrial Management* may well have been quoting or paraphrasing W. K.'s down-to-earth rhetoric when they wrote that the six-hour day represented "a new way of life, and [the fundamental truth] that production is a means and not an end, that our national increase of productivity makes it practical to devote a greater share of life to living."[86]

Chapter Two

The Struggle about Time

In what is probably his best-known short essay, E. P. Thompson wrote about the coming of industrialization to England. "As the new time-discipline is imposed," he concluded, "so the workers begin to fight, not against time, but about it."[1]

The struggle "against time" occurred in the early days of the Industrial Revolution when workers resisted the coming of work discipline and industrial capitalism. They resisted, in part, because the process was purifying and concentrating work, removing the irregular and "irrational" effort that characterized "preindustrial" labor.

Traditionally, work was an integral part of community life. Workers came and went through the day, trading stories and gossip and generally following a leisurely pace that allowed them to do all sorts of things that were not "on task"—activities having as much to do with the ordinary details of family and community as with "the job." Bursts of concentrated work alternated with long periods of milling about. Moreover, skilled artisans enjoyed considerable control over their trades. Not only were they able to set their schedules and control their work rhythms; they had the chance to perfect traditional skills and designs and often incorporated their own creative ideas into their work. The things they produced were as much a part of the community's culture as the songs and stories, arguments and gossip that surrounded them in the workshop.

But industrialists could not afford to have workers doing "other things" at work—contaminating the effort that they were paying good money for. For industry to be productive and capital to prosper, jobbers and managers had to persuade workers to work, and work only, when they were "on the clock," and to accept a clear separation between their jobs and their lives. The craftsman's relative autonomy had to be replaced by tight organization and coordination, a process that gave increasing authority to the industrial manager and foreman and further removed work from its place in the community and role in local culture.

A struggle ensued as workers tried to hold onto traditional craft skills and crazy-quilt work patterns while industrialists and managers tried to streamline production and instill the necessary work discipline and regular habits. "A quite sharp attack upon popular customs, sports, and holidays" during the last years of the eighteenth century was followed by the steady erosion of worker control and crafts through the nineteenth.[2] Thompson, in masterful style, tells how workers resisted with absenteeism, work "breaks," drinking bouts, celebrations, holidays, fairs, and festivals; how managers cajoled and punished with fines and firings; and how the rhetorical battle was joined and new idioms were deployed—"Saint Monday," "soldiering," "my time" versus "company time." When church and school weighed in on management's side, supporting industry's time requirements, workers grudgingly accepted the new work discipline as the best of a bad bargain. But the worker's "struggle against time" did not just end. It was transformed into the "struggle about time."

If work was to be a daily experience of helplessness in which even conversation was frequently forbidden, and the job itself was grueling and fatiguing, then it had to be reduced. In order for workers to have any life at all, any "free time" with family and friends and to themselves, it was essential that industrial work be tamed and put in its rightful place as life's servant: "The first generations of factory workers were taught by their masters the importance of time; the second generation formed their short-time committees in the ten-hour movement. . . . They had accepted the categories of their employers and learned to fight back within them."[3]

SHORTER HOURS AND THE HISTORIANS: A REVISIONIST VIEW

A struggle ("against time") to preserve work as an integral part of worker culture became a struggle ("about time") to win enough free time from the new, acculturated work to maintain community traditions and worker culture. This transformation began a century-long campaign that spread throughout the industrialized nations and lasted well into the twentieth century—the international shorter-hours movement. Workers' concerns about their culture and their lives *outside* the modern industrial order remained constant; only the form of their resistance changed.

Previous historians had agreed that labor fought for fewer hours mainly for economic reasons *inside* the industrial order: namely, to win higher total wages and to reduce unemployment. The labor economists at Wisconsin and their followers assumed that workers could be best understood as modern economic creatures, primarily interested in getting "more" of what industry was producing, rather than as beings preoccupied with cultural matters. Labor leaders like Ira Steward and Samuel Gompers represented workers' fundamental economic interests by pressing for shorter hours, repeatedly pointing out that the supply of labor had to be regulated to fit the demand. Mechanization was throwing more and more workers out of their jobs and creating a pool of workers on the street underbidding those on the job. As machines replaced men, wages suffered. Only if the labor supply was constantly regulated by shorter hours could market forces be balanced. Therefore, labor had to engineer a permanent scarcity of labor to ensure that workers were paid their fair share of the wealth they created. As the twentieth century began, these economic concerns became increasingly important, and, the labor economists concluded, by the 1930s they "crowded out all the other . . . motives" that lay, somehow, *outside* the realms of wages and specific job concerns.[4]

The labor economists also focused their attention on the job, assuming that it had always been the workers' central concern as well and concluding that shorter hours were important for workers because a shorter work day made the experience of work better. Even today, many labor historians and economists assume that shorter hours were just one of several job reforms, like safety and work conditions, that labor pursued in the service of "good jobs." Prominent historians still insist that "the Job" is the proper focus of labor history, and that cultural historians have strayed so far from "men and women at work" that the discipline is losing its coherence and identity.[5]

But Thompson and, in the United States, Herbert Gutman, planted the seeds for an alternative, cultural interpretation that is only now beginning to emerge. Several recent histories of work time, while still relying heavily on political and economic explanations, have expanded the cultural interpretation of shorter hours that Thompson began.[6]

In *Our Own Time,* David Roediger and Philip Foner demonstrate that "the demand for additional leisure differed fundamentally from that for greater pay." Whereas the labor economists tended to dismiss worker leisure as trivialized by capitalism and a consumer culture, Roediger and Foner demonstrate that workers actively sought leisure to achieve their own "legitimate goals" and values: worker culture, political participation, control in the workplace, family, and a host of nonpecuniary interests. Whereas for years historians understood the hours question as a wage derivative and thus a rather narrow concern, Roediger and Foner show, on page after page, that shorter hours was in fact the broadest and most inclusive of all labor issues, encompassing or "symbolizing" concerns about "health, education, steady employment and political participation." Roediger and Foner also show that the demand for shorter hours, not wages or organization issues, gave birth to organized labor, was the dynamic issue at the heart of labor's growth throughout the nineteenth and early twentieth centuries, and was the major source of worker solidarity. The campaign for shorter working hours was the fountainhead of labor organization and success. Wages divided unskilled workers from craftsmen, women from men, ethnic group from ethnic group. More than any other issue, shorter hours brought workers together, even in international cooperation.[7]

Roediger and Foner give substance to George Meany's oracular statement that "the progress toward a . . . shorter work week is a history of the Labor movement itself."[8] The lens of shorter hours transforms the history of labor from a dull story with one refrain, "more," to an epic search for freedom. Exploited, trivialized, and dismissed, leisure remains today as a monument to workers, a reminder of their struggles and the embodiment of their yearnings for an escape from economic concerns and the liberation of their time for life outside their jobs.

In *Quest for Time*, Gary Cross works out the historical implications of work reduction in France and Britain, showing how the struggle to free time from work entailed working-class responses to important political, cultural, and ideological issues and concerns—not merely economic ones. Seeking a "relinkage of political and social history," Cross shows how the workers initiated and sustained the movement, and how the movement influenced the politics of the two countries for a century. He also demonstrates that the work-reduction movement was not a derivative of wage concerns or driven primarily by economic motives. Even though "labor historians have argued that hours demands were little more than 'circuitous means of getting a raise,'" this approach "is one-sided and blinds us to the important dimensions of the meaning of time."[9]

Cross does not deny that wages and unemployment were factors in the shorter hours movement; he asserts only that "leisure" or "freedom from work" was also a factor. This seems a modest enough claim, one made originally by Helen Sumner in the 1920s. Yet the implications of this simple revision are earth-shaking.

By demonstrating that the demand for shorter hours was not merely a wage issue, historians show that workers had nonpecuniary aspirations (what Cross calls a new "leisure ethic") alternative to and even diametrically opposed to work and the marketplace. Cross finds that the desire for shorter hours represented nothing less than workers' desire for freedom from the discipline of work and bosses—a distinctive idea of freedom from economic concerns. As such, shorter hours represented an authentic working-class vision of progress based on nonpecuniary advance in areas such as the family, community, worker control and culture, religion, education, and amusements. As Cross puts it "This redistribution of time toward leisure represents a concrete reduction of authority and compulsion, a personal realization of liberty, and even the democratization of opportunity for personal choice."[10]

Like Roediger and Foner, Cross demonstrates that work reduction was one of the broadest of worker struggles, encompassing important working-class aspirations and acting as a lightning rod for a number of their grievances.[11] One of their most remarkable findings was the movement's strong ties to the late eighteenth-century revolutionary period and to subsequent revolutionary developments in the nineteenth century. Quite simply, workers adopted revolutionary rhetoric and visions and applied them to their own daily life. Since for them the chief source of repression and barrier to personal freedom was found at work, workers used the rhetoric of liberty (natural rights, the rights of man and Englishmen, the pursuit of happiness, and equality) in their shorter-hours campaigns. Parading through Boston under French revolutionary banners, workers believed that they were continuing a struggle as old as the Declaration of Independence. The language of Chartism and the Republican revolution in France in the 1840s, and even ante-bellum rhetoric about the evils of slavery and the need for emancipation of industrial workers, also found a place in the shorter-hours movements of the United States, Britain, and France.[12]

Roediger observes that the demand for increased leisure, although bound tightly to practical concerns over fatigue and wages, nevertheless "evoked broader, even visionary, hopes for a radically reshaped society" among the middle-class reformers who became the dominant spokespersons for the ten-hour movement. "Add another two hours to the liberty term," wrote Richard Trevellick, a nineteenth-century organizer for the National Labor Union, "and we shall increase the ratio of progress threefold . . . laboring men and women educated to a standard of physical, mental, moral and social excellence that will be its own security against idleness, vice, degradation and misery."[13] Workers used the iconoclastic rhetoric of the revolutionary period to press for shorter hours during the Jacksonian era. Roediger cites the Boston carpenters who in 1825 assailed the "despotic servitude" enforced on them by dawn-to-dusk schedule of the summer. Philadelphia journeymen carpenters, striking for ten hours in 1827, resolved that "all men have a just right, derived from their Creator, to have sufficient time each day for the cultivation of their mind and for self-improvement." The famous "Boston Ten-hours Circular" of 1835 attacked long hours as an offense against God and natural right: "The God of the Universe has given us time, health, and strength. We utterly deny the right of any man to dictate to us how much of it we shall sell."[14]

The waves of religious revivalism before 1866 worked both for and against work reduction. Protestantism certainly strengthened the work ethic and promoted sobriety, prudence, and gain, but long hours in pursuit of materialistic aims that damaged morals and interfered with religious observances and spiritual advance were condemned. People like Charles Douglas, Seth Luther, and Frederick Robinson, held up increased leisure as a legitimate avenue for human improvement—a realm of free action especially suited to spiritual advance.

Such revolutionary rhetoric and logic continued for the life of the shorter-hours movement and carried it along. The movement came to represent a distinctively working-class kind of liberalism, which Cross is at pains to distinguish from the standard laissez-faire liberalism of France and Britain. Roediger and Foner also point to the opposition to shorter hours by those more interested in property rights and economic growth.

Cross notes that this radical vision weakened in the early twentieth century. Coincidentally, the work-reduction movement lost momentum: "Despite steady economic growth since World War II, there has been little change in working hours in recent years; in fact the eight-hour day has been the norm for seventy years." Although he speculates that free time has increased in the forms of vacations and retirement, Cross concludes that without a radical vision and rhetoric supporting "freedom from work," the shorter-hours movement became dormant or simply died.[15]

Clearly, the movement for shorter hours was the reform issue of the working classes. It stood on its own and was not a wage derivative. It is also clear that it was driven by a radical vision of freedom from the industrial order and economic concerns, and freedom for cultural matters in nonpecuniary realms. Finally, one may now conclude that both the vision behind work reduction and the reality of work reduction have been blocked for over half a century.

The implications of the new history of shorter hours are still being worked out, but they may be sketched in broad outline. In the first place, the scope of the revision is quite large, affecting an issue that lasted well over one hundred years and engaged the United States, Canada, Great Britain, and France—and probably some of Central Europe, even Russia, in the first decades of this century. Moreover, work reduction involved the mass of workers in most of the Western, industrial world and addressed a critically important part of their daily life: the intersection of work (the pecuniary use of time) and leisure (freedom for other things).

Helen Sumner identified the pursuit of shorter hours for leisure as "the origin of the Labor movement in the United States." Recent histories confirm this observation and find further that the issue was a constant source of strength in labor organization, politics, and strikes. Without the fight for shorter hours, the movement has become moribund, torn apart by competition for jobs and wages. An excellent case can be made that the end of shorter hours is directly related to the decline of the Labor movement.[16]

STILL ANOTHER REVISION

These new histories raise questions that have a distinctly revisionist ring. Since workers were also interested in shorter hours for cultural reasons, how important were organized labor's abstract economic theories and complex market strategy for ordinary, non-union workers? Since workers were also trying to find time for life outside the job, how important was labor's attempt to improve the workplace relative to workers' desire to escape it altogether? Since workers' interests included cultural matters that transcended their economic concerns, were the working classes composed primarily of the "economic man and woman" that the labor economists assumed?

Even though such questions appear to challenge the labor economists' basic assumptions, so far historians have been exceedingly modest in their conclusions about the history of work time. The new forces of cultural history have not made a direct assault on the traditional economic interpretation, using the central issue of shorter hours as the point of attack. Instead, historians have tended to accept the older interpretation and tack on their cultural analyses, putting a bit more stress on the workers' desire for leisure for cultural goals relative to their desires for higher wages and "good jobs," never venturing to claim that cultural, nonpecuniary concerns shaped workers' economic, political, and work behavior. But seen together, these recent histories of work time outline a fundamental revision of labor history that may lead to the replacement of the older, primarily economic interpretation (represented by Irving Bernstein's claim that "the economic argument crowded out the others") with a cultural explanation (E. P. Thompson's "struggle for time").[17]

Local studies are beginning to undermine the labor economists' interpretation. Apart from the two familiar nineteenth-century maxims—"As long as there is one worker unemployed, the hours of labor are too long" and "Whether you work by the piece or by the day, decreasing the hours increases the pay"—historians have produced little evidence that ordinary workers knew about organized labor's long-term market strategy or cared about its philosophy. On the local level, most workers, organized or not, faced bosses who resisted both higher wages and shorter hours. When industrial managers were pressured to shorten the work day or week, they invariably insisted that the workers take a pay cut, or at least give up the prospect of a raise. In the long process of negotiation and compromise, whenever the shorter-hour issue was raised, local workers were nearly always presented with a choice between wages and hours— the more of the one, the less of the other. This point was driven home by the Kellogg worker who told the author, "Only an idiot would think you can get as much working less instead of more hours a week." Workers' experience differed fundamentally from union theory and rhetoric on this point.[18]

Workers' concerns about unemployment also tended to be local. Little evidence has been produced to show that rank and file union members, let alone unorganized workers, believed so strongly in labor's campaign to regulate the national labor supply that they were ready to fight for shorter hours locally and to trade other benefits, such as raises, to strengthen labor's strategic, national advantage. On the contrary, workers were much more concerned that family members and friends in the community were about to be laid off, or that they might lose their own jobs. Work *sharing* at the local level, rather than labor's broadly based market strategy, seems better able to account for workers' longstanding interest in shorter hours. Workers' concerns about unemployment had as much to do with moral conviction and a willingness to give up some of their own work to help others as with principles of political economy. They were more interested in preserving local jobs than in achieving an abstract, long-term economic advantage in a national marketplace.

Moreover, recent histories of work time have found that workers were at least as interested in improving their lives outside work as they were in improving their jobs. The older emphasis on workers' concerns about "good jobs" has been updated by analysis of the content or use of the time won from work. The historical narrative, shifting its focus from "men and women at work" to workers' lives away from their jobs, has altered the conventional interpretation. Leisure may now be understood less as a way for workers to perfect their work or gain economic advantage, and more as a cultural asset, allowing expression of traditional values and customs, formation of class consciousness, and maintenance of family, church, and community. Free time has been shown to be the primary cultural medium in the industrial state, opening up a range of "free activities" outside industrial discipline and the marketplace. Leisure allows workers to express the range of nonpecuniary, cultural motives and concerns that historians, anthropologists, and ethnologists have recently emphasized, and which Thompson suggested was originally at the heart of workers' long drive for shorter hours.[19]

Notwithstanding management rhetoric about "improving work" and "good jobs," jobs continued to be characterized by declining worker control and craftsmanship throughout the century of shorter hours. Steven Ross summed up historians' findings when he wrote: "Although work was the central focus of daily life, it did not produce a single working class experience" for workers in nineteenth-century Cincinnati. "Good jobs" remained a dream well into this century—and largely a dream of people who were not workers. Ross's conclusion recalls a story James Truslow Adams told about a Yankee reformer speaking about "good jobs" to a gathering of urban workers in Boston early in this century, and predicting that everyone would soon find fulfillment and satisfaction in work. When he soared too high and spoke rapturously of "the joy of work," as Adams told it, the house rocked with laughter for several moments.[20]

Johnny Paycheck's popular country ballad "Take This Job and Shove It" has a more authentic ring than the management expert's verbiage about "job satisfaction" or the politician's blather about "good jobs." Observers have found continuing, widespread dissatisfaction with modern work through most of this century. James Gilbert and Daniel Rodgers, for example, conclude that work and the "work ethic" underwent a "crisis" around the turn of the century in the United States, when utopian dreams of work perfection were widely rejected by both workers and intellectuals.[21]

"Most critics of industrial monotony came to a . . . simple answer: if modern industrial work was soulless, then men should do less of it." Rodgers notes. By the early twentieth century, "a sizable number of Northern Protestant moralists had begun to argue that it was not in self-discipline that a man's spiritual essence was revealed but in free, spontaneous activity."[22] Such "critics" and "moralists" found strong support among workers in their communities, discovering a "passionate interest" in free time that did not spring from "all the complex intellectual rationale behind [labor's] eight-hour campaign" but from an "essential . . . obvious appeal: the promise of the relief from toil."[23]

Other historians have investigated more overt forms of work resistance. Writing about workers in Barcelona and Paris during the Popular Front era in *Workers against Work,* Michael Seidman finds that rejection of modern work characterized workers' response to class issues and radical politics: "Workers expressed their class consciousness by avoiding the spaces, time, and demands of wage labor." Instead of embracing the Marxist vision of liberating work, workers in the two cities "expressed" their own, characteristically working-class utopian vision: liberation *from* work, by absenteeism and even sabotage of the workplace. Investigating the Russian Revolution, William Chase and Lewis Siegelbaum make similar findings: in the major political upheavals of this century, the mass of workers found liberation in escaping from the tyranny of modern occupations rather than overturning political orders.[24]

If leisure was largely a cultural asset and "good jobs" a remote, unrealistic dream for most workers, surely it is reasonable to suggest that the shorter-hours campaign was as much about leaving work as about making it better—that the century-long campaign to reduce working hours, like the more extreme worker revolts, may be best understood as a widespread *critique* of modern work and work discipline, even a *rejection* of industrial capitalism (and other authoritarian work regimes) in the form most immediately experienced by most workers: the daily job.

Cross concludes that shorter hours formed the basis for a distinctive working-class ideology. But taking the workers at their words and deeds, one might go further and suggest that the shorter-hours campaign represented the rejection of what Gutman calls the *sine qua non* of capitalist culture, the Protestant work ethic. Rejecting life centered in and valued primarily through industrial, acculturated work, workers turned away from the job to find their own cultures; building new, alternative, and distinctive institutions on traditional and ethnic foundations.

Increasing leisure rather than political change may well have provided the primary relief from industrial work and the capitalist order—a daily respite outside the marketplace. As such it posed a direct threat to industrial culture and the marketplace, offering liberation from the modern economic order. Free time was freedom *from* modern work discipline, indeed, but it also represented freedom *for* something outside—for an existence beyond the marketplace, "outside" working, buying, and consuming and the control of owners, managers, advertisers, and professionals.[25]

David Montgomery, contrasting the historians John Commons and Herbert Gutman, notes: "Commons has taught us to study workers through the behavior of their unions in the labor market while Gutman scrutinized their activities in a broadened social context. Commons had analyzed the worker as economic man, and Gutman [and one might add Thompson] showed that the basic thrust of the 19th century workers' struggle entailed a rejection of economic man."[26]

The history of work time presents an excellent opportunity to write a more complete history of the worker as the antithesis of "economic man and woman." Shorter hours may be shown to have contained a historical possibility outside modern economies, representing an extra-economic, cultural reality that motivated the majority of workers, and thus the majority of the populations in the industrial nations, to act in the marketplace (by leaving it) for over a century. The history of labor and workers can no longer be confidently summed up in economic and political terms simply as "wanting more." Labor history may be better understood as a century long "quest for time"—the pursuit of freedom from industrial work discipline for life (for culture, civil society, community, family, solitude, etc.) *outside* the modern industrial order and political realms.

The history of the quest for time shows that workers understood work as the *means to other ends* throughout the nineteenth century and well into the twentieth; and that the century of shorter hours was as much about leaving work for something better as it was a "quest for good jobs."[27]

UNIONS AND THE SIX-HOUR DAY

Interpretive issues notwithstanding, there is broad consensus about the historical facts. Nearly everyone agrees that workers thought increasingly shorter hours were a good thing, roughly on a level with higher wages, and were willing to fight for them for over a century. This was the quintessential worker cause and labor goal, and yet, somehow, it was sidetracked during the second quarter of the twentieth century.

Seen in this broad historical context, union demands for shorter hours during the late 1920s and early 1930s, and Kellogg's workers' response to the six-hour day, are logical developments.

During the first decades of the twentieth century, unions stressed the practical, "serious" benefits of shorter hours, such as increased productivity, reduced fatigue, health, and safety.[28] As part of its five-day-week initiative during the 1920s, organized labor reemphasized leisure as a primary justification for shorter hours. At its 1926 convention, the AFL recommitted itself to the "progressive shortening of the hours of labor," noting the increasing stress and strain of modern occupations. As the decade wore on, unions turned more and more to the positive benefits of leisure.

Unions in the clothing industries were among the first to reassert the cultural advantages of shorter hours. As part of the campaign to restore their Sabbath, the Jewish community in the Northeast pressed for Saturday holidays and the easing of Blue Laws. Unions in New York, Boston, and other northeastern cities with large Jewish memberships took up the Sabbath issue during the campaign for the five-day week, and broadened it to include nonreligious cultural benefits. *The Advance,* the *Clothing Worker,* The *Lady Garment Worker,* and other union publications promoted the five-day week for its "humane" benefits—"rest and life." Such journals, as well as the *Monthly Labor Review,* observed that workers were willing to give up wages or postpone wage demands for progress toward the forty-hour week. Letters from workers and the published statements of local and national union leaders linked increased free time to spiritual, family, and community concerns.[29] The Education Committee of the International Ladies Garment Workers cited the "dramatic" increases in attendance at the union-sponsored education programs, union social centers, and public recreation facilities as "clear evidence" of workers' desire for increased free time to "improve the mind and spirit." The "flowering of Yiddish culture" Irving Howe describes may well be connected to the unions' push for a five-day week.[30]

Other national labor leaders and unions followed the clothing workers' lead, adding criticism of "devitalized" jobs. AFL President William Green wrote that modern work was "meaningless, repetitive, boring," without "creative expression," providing "no satisfaction of intellectual needs," and increasingly stressful. "Devitalized" work resulted in "nervous disorders" and mental health problems—working-class versions of the elite nervousness that animated John Harvey Kellogg. Green contrasted the workers' lot in the 1920s with that of "our ancestors," who "were at liberty to rest during the day, to take moments of refreshment." The modern worker, amid the "grinding roar and noise of modern plants" and forced to keep pace with the machine, "if he is to live at all . . . must reduce the number of hours."[31]

Green urged that in order that "our social and human values may not be overwhelmed in the general mechanizing process and the lives of workers may not be merged with the machine until they, too, become mechanical . . . there must be a progressive shortening of the hours of labor . . . to safeguard our human nature . . . and thereby [lay] the foundation . . . for the higher development of spiritual and intellectual powers." He predicted "the dawn of a new era—leisure for all" and a "revolution of living." "The leisured proletariat" now should have free access to "good music, the fine arts, literature, travel, and beauty in all guises." Shorter hours meant "a greater probability of the cultural use of leisure. . . . It is in their leisure that workers find themselves . . . sharing in the common life of the community . . . and are heirs of the knowledge and culture of past generations." The family, the community, and traditional cultures would be revitalized—progress in these areas would catch up with technology and the advance of capitalism. Those things which work used to provide, such as craftsmanship, creativity, worker control, purpose and meaning, now must be regained in freely chosen leisure activities.[32]

Green concluded in the *American Federationist*, "The human values of leisure are even greater than its economic significance."[33] This set the tone for labor's rhetoric about shorter hours. On another occasion,

Green remarked, "Two fundamental factors determining the life of any person are income and work hours. Income furnishes the key to [economic] opportunity. Work hours conditions physical well-being as well as personal contributions to community life."[34]

But Matthew Woll, vice president of the AFL, issued a warning in words reminiscent of Mill and Patten. "Unfortunately, our industrial life is dominated by the materialistic spirit of production, of work and more work, giving little attention to the development of the human body, the human mind, or the spirit of life. . . . All the finer qualities of life are entirely ignored." The dehumanized nature of modern jobs was complicated by the "materialistic spirit" of the business community and the government's willingness to expand "make work." For Woll, increasing leisure was a "restraining influence," a way to control the material values rampant in the Gospel of Consumption and the expansion of meaningless work; "constructive recreation" for physical, social, cultural, and spiritual purposes was the alternative to "work and more work."[35]

The Great Depression, of course, intensified the unions' interest in shorter hours. Organized labor set out to make the five-day week universal and opened a new work-sharing front, the six-hour day/thirty-hour week. This reform, had it succeeded, would have been the largest single reduction of working hours in history. As part of its campaign for national thirty-hour legislation, a campaign that dominated organized labor's political agenda throughout the Great Depression, labor fully supported Kellogg's experiment. Green reiterated his early support, first published in *Factory and Industrial Management,* several times in correspondence with the company, prompting Lewis Brown to brag about labor's "enthusiastic endorsement."[36] Throughout its losing legislative battle to reduce the work week during the depression, labor held up Kellogg's six-hour day as a practical model of work sharing, providing profit for industry, free time for workers, and additional jobs for the unemployed. With Kellogg management, organized labor continued to talk about shorter hours as a job benefit on a par with wages. Industry would offer shorter hours and workers would naturally accept them as a reward for productive, hard work—just as they had been doing for over a hundred years.[37] Like Brown, W. K. Kellogg, and most of the press, labor envisioned work continuing to contract and workers devoting larger parts of their lives to what both William Green and W. K. Kellogg called "finer" activities.

Chapter Three

Seize the Day: Leisure in

Battle Creek

In 1932 Donna Holser, a Kellogg worker, spoke for generations of workers when she compared her happiness about six-hours to "how wonderful we thought it was when we changed from 9 to 8 hours." For Battle Creek workers and the national unions, the six-hour day was a continuation of a one-hundred-year process. Holser, like most workers at the time, assumed that work hours would continue to decrease as industry advanced, and they expected to "feel wonderful" each time it happened.[1]

Grace Lindsey started working the six-hour day at Kellogg's in April 1932. Asked in 1989 what she did with the two extra hours a day, she was somewhat at a loss. There "wasn't much to do. . . . [Y]ou visited with your neighbors and went noplace . . . just your family and relatives—no TV or shopping. . . . I mean entertainment like we have today."

But as those days came back to her, so did the language workers used in those days. First, she remembered the "social part" of working at Kellogg's in the thirties: that Kellogg's frequently organized activities at the plant, "a picnic or a potluck and softball twice a week, but we had our own groups and stayed together." She also remembered that "you got all your [house]work done before you went to work" and that "husbands could work their shift and take care of the children" and "help out at home." With a bit of help at home, the two "extra hours" a day gave her a little time to "do more of what I wanted to do." She was "able to do" a variety of things "outside" both work and housework, such as evening trips to Kalamazoo and walks around the town. Toward the end of the interview, she began to talk about ping-pong, apologizing for talking about something so unimportant. She remembered with obvious pleasure the days when she played the sport, and associated playing with the shorter shift at Kellogg's:

Ping pong. I played ping-pong. Some of these newspapers [mentioning her accomplishments] I [still] have—we played Ping Pong all the time. . . . I won the state, we traveled all around. I did a lot of things. . . . I forgot about that. . . . [I]t was important to me then. . . . [T]here's all the newspapers I have [kept]. . . . We had a ping-pong table right in the lobby [of Kellogg's] . . . playing ping-pong. I forgot that . . . I played one year after [her daughter] was born. I got beat once in the [state] championship and I came back [the next year] to get the championship. . . . It was a family thing. That was with all the family. We'd get together. We had a ping-pong table and all my relatives would come for dinner and things and we'd all play ping-pong by the hour. That's what I did.[2]

Her timidness in telling the story of her skill and success, her awkwardness in revealing the pleasure she took in the sport and its meaning in her life, and the fact that she nearly forgot about it speak volumes about the cultural changes, particularly the trivialization of amateur sport, that took place in Battle Creek during her lifetime.

Leroy Despins remembered roller-skating at "the Palace," and he spoke at length about his accomplishments. Located on Goguac Lake at the south end of town, the Palace skating rink grew out of a recreational complex that once included a "circus," a two-story dance and recreation hall, and a Ferris Wheel close by the power station. By the mid-thirties, the skating rink was a major local attraction and, like ping-pong, enjoyed a popularity that lasted through the war. Despins talked most about his brother's skills—"twirls . . . those things you see them do on ice at the Olympics, my brother could do on roller-skates." He spoke of Bill Cosier, who revived the rink, as a local benefactor. Despins himself had time to play softball and basketball at Kellogg's during the thirties; the company provided uniforms and facilities, including Building Number 5, a gymnasium complete with showers and coaches. Kellogg's would hire two or three "semi-pro" players (from a group of now-vanished itinerant players who once existed because of local interest in *playing* ball) and would pay them the same wage for working at the plant and for time spent playing with the company team.[3] In a scheme perhaps unique to Kellogg's, winning players got extra time off the assembly lines—additional evidence that free time had become a unit of exchange between management and labor and that management understood that freedom from work was a powerful incentive, perhaps as adaptable and effective as cash.[4]

"Everybody played," Despins recalled. When you got back to the plant working, we would chew the fat about the games. . . . Why wasn't that guy [who played softball well] playing hardball. . . . It brought us together and gave us something to talk about." With the six-hour day, Despins "had a car . . . and [was] free to do lots of things. . . . I had the world by the hand." Blanchard, Despins, and Lindsey all contrasted those more relaxed days with the pace of recent times. "Now it's work, work, work for everybody," Despins complained. "Nobody has any time anymore to do anything—to even be with the kids."[5]

Such anecdotal evidence strengthens Lewis Brown's claim that most Kellogg workers were in favor of the six-hour day and that they agreed with him that additional leisure meant additional control of their lives.[6] Journalists add credence to Brown and W. K.'s claims. A reporter from the *Battle Creek Enquirer* talked informally with workers at the plant gate between the midnight and 6 a.m. shifts on the first day of six-hour operations. Most, he wrote, were looking forward "eagerly" to the additional free time and had "varied ideas for spending their extra two hours. This morning it was the favorite topic of conversation about the plant between shifts. For the first time they have real leisure. Some declared that they were going to make much needed . . . improvements at their homes. Others intended to study. The hunters were looking forward to . . . getting out in the woods and fields oftener."[7] No mention of worker dissatisfaction appeared in the two Battle Creek papers through 1936, even though the local press was usually ready to print bad news about Kellogg's.

In April 1932, reporters from *Factory and Industrial Management* visited the Kellogg plant and talked to "about a dozen employees and supervisors of various grades." Like Brown, they noted that when six-hours was originally adopted, "some objections were raised, especially by those who were earning a good deal of overtime under the old arrangement." But overall, they observed, Kellogg employees "preferred six-hours," and several, like Brown himself, condemned the "work-hogs." For most, the additional leisure helped compensate for the little that was lost from the weekly paycheck. The reporters found that the "much appreciated . . . new leisure" gave some a chance to "hunt and fish—the 6-hour day has been hard on the game near Battle Creek." Workers had time to "putter around the house . . . keep a garden or run a farm." Women workers had more time for "home duties." Correspondence courses and the com-

CHAPTER THREE

pany's industrial management study group were popular. "Altogether," the reporters concluded, "the additional leisure is being put to good use, whether economic or merely as an increase in freedom and happiness."[8]

Henry Goddard Leach, editor of the *Forum and Century,* wrote that "the visitor sees" workers at Kellogg's delighted with the six-hour arrangement and a community "enriched" by the additional free time. "The visitor also sees . . . a lot of gardening and community beautification . . . athletics and hobbies . . . booming . . . libraries well patronized, . . . and the mental background of these fortunate workers . . . becoming richer." Health was improving and accidents were decreasing at the plant. Kellogg's had made what to some was a "utopian fallacy profitable alike for workers and owners and a boon to the community." Chapin Hoskins of *Forbes* reported that "an entire organization was sold on the idea," and *Business Week* described employees as "completely sold on the plan."[9]

Reporters sounded common themes: more people had jobs; the workers seemed to *prefer* having "more life" outside for "their own," and thought that their family life was better; there were more community activities, better lawns and gardens, homes spruced up inside and outside, parks and recreation facilities filled, more sports being played, more hobbies, reading, and "studying." They used similar words when they described the workers: "delighted," "completely sold," "excited." No mention of six-hours as unexpected or excessive or out of the ordinary may be found in the press of the day—after all, reporters had been following the story of work's decline for years. Some even spoke of workers' "cultural interests."[10]

THE WOMEN'S BUREAU SURVEY

The best evidence of worker opinion is a survey done by the Women's Bureau of the U.S. Department of Labor in the summer of 1932.[11] Because of the Hoover administration's interest in work sharing, the Women's Bureau dispatched a research team to Battle Creek. Led by Ethel Best, the "agents" visited 434 female Kellogg workers in their homes. They were careful to tell the workers that the survey was a government rather than a company effort, and that the company would see only a summary of the results; individuals would not be identified.[12]

Best found that of the 404 women who expressed an opinion, nearly 85 percent "preferred" the six-hour shift over the eight-hour one. Most women (121) said that they "preferred" six-hours primarily because it gave them "more time for home duties." But according to Best, nearly as many (119) gave "more leisure" as the principal reason: 31 talked about "less fatigue," while 27 spoke of "leisure and less fatigue."[13] The 46 women who "preferred" eight-hours all mentioned "less pay" under six-hours as the main reason. Eight added that with the increased pace at work and no lunch break, they were hungry or felt more fatigued.[14]

Contradicting company claims, Best's team found that most women had lost wages. Comparing the September 1930 payroll records of 196 workers with those of April 1932, Best concluded that 77 percent received less under six-hours. In half the cases the decrease was 10 to 20 percent, and in one-third the decrease was less; only 45 workers had larger paychecks. But more importantly, almost 90 percent of the women said that they were making less.[15] Nevertheless, "little dissatisfaction with lower earnings resulting from the decrease in hours was expressed, although in the majority of cases very real decreases had resulted." Best's primary explanation was that "the workers seem to feel that ... after all they were being given time off for their reduced pay."[16]

Workers' Words

Best concluded that the women who "much preferred" or expressed "enthusiasm" for the six-hour day were mostly new workers, hired because of the added shift. In paying close attention to the way the women spoke about shorter hours, she and her agents were well ahead of their time, moving beyond simple statistics to an analysis of language patterns and even to an evaluation of mannerisms: "shows enthusiasm," "is delighted."

But Best did not venture beyond her observations about "strong preferences" to remark about what one may term a dominant "idiom of freedom." Even though 90 percent felt that they had lost money, nearly a third had husbands who were unemployed or employed part-time, and over 10 percent had "broken marital ties," and even though most of the women were spending the "extra time" doing "home duties," the Kellogg women talked most often about "freedom" or used related language when the agents asked them to "compare the 8-hour and 6-hour shift."[17]

The most common words or phrases used involved "free" or a compound: "freedom," "free time," "free evenings," "free to ..." Nearly as common were phrases such as "give[s] time for." Many women also spoke of time "outside," referring either to time outside the job or to time outside both the factory and home, time *for* other things. Other representative phrases include Anna Olson's observation that she now had time "*to be* at home" and Nellie Nustell's comments that she "has more time *to be* out-of-doors" and that she "and her mother *spend* a good deal of time in the garden."

"Necessity," "have to," "can't afford to work less," and the like were also occasionally used (24 cases). A few of the women who "preferred" to work eight hours went to some lengths outlining the press of circumstances, the "need" or the "necessity" that compelled them to work more. Some who favored six hours spoke of need in relation to home duties—for example, "I need to be at home." But such need-language was rare, limited to 24 of the 434 workers.

The second most commonly used construction had to do with control and possession: "my work," "my own" work or time, "[have] time . . . for," "time to [one's] self," "enables" or "am able to." Several women told the agents directly that they preferred time at home doing their "own work" over time on the assembly line doing work for Kellogg's, and described the extra time specifically in terms of increased ownership, possession, or control.

When speaking about the constraints they felt in their lives, the women spoke frequently about the confines of work at the plant; they seldom spoke about the constraints imposed by finances or "home duties." The agents reported that the women said that working eight hours left "nothing but work" in their lives, no "chance" to do what "they wanted to do." Some spoke of eight-hours as having "spoiled the day," "broken up the day," "taken my evenings [or days]," or required them "to work all day" or "all the time." Several said that they would "hate" to go back to eight-hours or that they could "not stand" it. For example, Ritha Hale said, "I'd hate to go back to 8 hrs. . . . It's wonderful having your evenings free." Henrietta Showerman declared that she "would hate to go back to 8 hrs now. The old shift broke into" her evenings. Pearl Peasley, forty-one years old with an unemployed husband, said, "I'd die if I had to go back to eight hours." Marcelle Evans vowed, "I'd never work 8 hrs or longer again if I could help it."[18] Others told the agents that working six hours gave them "all morning [or evening] free [or to myself]," "plenty," "lots," or "so much time," "the best part of the day," "the day clear." Still others used related language such as "it's more like living" and "it does not feel like [I am] work[ing]."

In light of recent scholarship, such language is somewhat surprising. Sociologists and others have recently maintained that women in the industrialized world have had little or no leisure in the modern sense, being required to do the housework whether they have an outside job or not.[19] Moreover, on first glance Best's study seems to support this conclusion—most of the Kellogg women said they returned to "home duties" in the extra time. Best noted that some women used "more time in which to do the same [house]work as formerly," and others were doing washing and heavy cleaning that had been farmed out or delegated to others. Altogether, 121 of the 434 women, mostly older women, said they preferred six-hours because it gave them "more time for home duties," and 224 women—"well over one-half" of the women, according to Best—said that performing "home duties" was their principal use for the new leisure. Thus, a good deal of the extra time, probably most of it, was reabsorbed at home.

One is left with an apparent inconsistency between the women's dominant idiom of freedom and what seems to be their return to housework. It is tempting to follow critical fashion and discount what the women were saying, explaining away their rhetoric of freedom as denial, or a masking of the real repression going on behind the scenes. But by analyzing the women's language carefully on its own terms, and comparing its various components, one detects more congruity than inconsistency.

In the first place, the idiom of freedom was not absolute or used in isolation. The women used words like "my time" and "free time" comparatively, usually with reference to their jobs. When they compared work at the plant with work at home, they tended to describe even unpleasant and unrewarding housework as "my work." Nothing is clearer from the interviews than that the women spoke uniformly of being more in control of their "extra hours" than of their time at work at Kellogg's, whether they were doing housework or recreation. "My time" versus "company time," the rhetorical division that began with the Industrial Revolution and that historians like E. P. Thompson and David Brody have described thoroughly, persisted at Battle Creek.

In the second place, "home duties" was a complex term, with a number of different meanings. The 224 women who talked about doing more "home duties" referred to such things as "housework," caregiving, gardening, home projects, and "time with the children." Moreover, the women often distinguished "housework" from other "home duties" on the basis of choice and desirability, describing a continuum that ranged from major chores (typically washing and ironing) to ordinary cleaning-up to canning to sewing to needlework. Using the women's syntax, one could speak reasonably of being "free from" the job at Kellogg's to do "my work" at home, "free from" ordinary housework to do a little gardening, after which one might "find a chance" to read to the children, and still characterize the whole range as "home duties."[20]

Finally, one may begin to reconcile the women's idiom of freedom with their return to "home duties" by observing that many did not meekly go back to doing housework they had somehow neglected or delegated when they had to work eight hours. When they made a strong claim to extra time as their own, it may very well be that they meant what they said.

Explaining why they preferred six-hours, 119 women said directly that they wanted more "leisure." Describing what they did with the "extra time," 141 women told Best's agents the same thing that plant workers told the *Enquirer* reporter the first morning of the six-hour schedule: that for the first time they had some "real leisure." They said that they were "able . . . to take care of" ordinary "housework," or got it "out of the way" before they went to the plant, and, working only six hours there, afterward had a purer kind of freedom in the "extra time," less combined with servitude and drudgery than traditional housework.[21]

The women's dominant idiom of freedom and ubiquitous use of possessive pronouns ("time of my own") and verbs such as "to have" (e.g., time) and "to be" (e.g., with the children) show that a strong minority, arguably a majority, were not about to surrender all their extra time to housework.

There was a major division within this strong-willed group. For about half (69), "freedom" "was found mainly in traditional family and community settings and activities—in "home duties" that transcended housework. For the others (72), "freedom" and control were found mainly in leisure activities opening to them outside the home—in sports, hobbies, radio, movies, travel, and friends.

Traditionalists

Sixty-nine women told the agents that they were "spending" most of their "extra time" around their homes: sewing, crocheting, canning, gardening, being with the children, helping out in the neighborhood. They spoke of such home-based activities as freer and having more to do with their own choice, control, and self-expression than other kinds of housework they were called on to do, such as washing and ironing (these they "got out of the way" before going to work). As the women described them to the agents, "home duties" ranged from unpleasant, necessary chores to activities that combined freedom with useful pursuits and required high levels of personal skill, creativity, and involvement.

Myrtle Ostrander, for example, distinguished between different kinds of housework by degree of freedom, choice, and control. She told Best's agent that since she was working only six hours, she "does all her own sewing and takes care of a large garden, . . . but not housework as her [unemployed] husband does that." Ostrander also distinguished gardening and sewing from major household "tasks" such as the laundry and ironing. These, along with routine "housework," she persuaded others to do.[22]

Like Ostrander, several women spoke of a change in the allocation of home duties and talked about sharing work with their spouse inside as well as outside the home. Women whose husbands were unemployed or employed part-time and "Kellogg Couples" (husbands and wives working six hours at Kellogg's) were more likely than others to report sharing some home duties. In other cases, responsibility for various tasks became a point of contention. The six-hour day often created a fluid condition at home, opening up issues about the division of labor by gender and leading to vigorous renegotiations about housework and home projects.

Best and her agents showed up during the summer months of 1932, at the height of harvest season for fresh fruits and vegetables. Several women were busy canning. Asked how they were using the "extra time," these women simply pointed to the obvious. Putting together the Kellogg women's words and stories from the 1930s and recent interviews, it is possible to reconstruct canning as a remarkable example of "home duties," and demonstrate how complex the phrase was.

Canning was in part utilitarian, in part a family activity, with strong aesthetic and craft components. Typically the fruits or vegetables were gathered in the morning or the day before, the rule being "the fresher the better." Kettles of water were set to boiling while jars and new lids were washed and sterilized (sterilization having become a "scientific" and highly technical matter learned from journals and extension home economists). The kitchen or back porch came alive with the comings and goings of those who were gathering the vegetables from the garden and those who were getting them ready for canning. The activity naturally be-

CHAPTER THREE

came the medium for something more important than preserving food. Stories, jokes, teasing, quarreling, practical instruction, songs, griefs, and problems were shared. The modern discipline of alienated work was left behind for an older, or at least more complex and convivial, kind of working together. The women who told about canning tended to be at the heart of the process: organizing, encouraging, and directing; without them, the enterprise would not have happened.

The women spoke of pride in creating something at once useful and beautiful; some entered their goods in local contests and fairs. They displayed their canned goods to Best's agents and to other interviewers, and spoke at great length about technical points and features that distinguished their efforts from those of the neighbors: of the clarity and color of the jellies, the taste and texture of the fruits and vegetables, and usually of a specialty—each had some unique product or process that she had made her own. Because they were "homemade," the canned goods had a special appeal to family and neighbors. It was commonly agreed that "store-bought" was far inferior in taste, looks, nutrition, and appeal—a poor substitute. Interviewers who took a special interest were sometimes given a sample, an act that was at once a token of hospitality and a symbol, a physical representation of the "good" the woman had made out of the extra time and her willingness to give it away.[23]

The president of Local No. 3 in Battle Creek, Paula Swan, spoke enthusiastically about canning at home during her early days at Kellogg's, remembering that it was "a family project" and that "we all cared for it," "we all enjoyed it." She strongly denied that it was work in the same way that her job at Kellogg's was work. Certainly it required effort—great effort in some cases to get her unconvinced sons involved. But it became a family activity that provided a number of important benefits, the most important of which was that her family was doing something meaningful together. Once they were recruited, Swan recalled that her "sons opened up to talk freely," and that during such projects "we were most a family." Unlike commercial recreation or family trips, "working" together, sharing a common purpose, was "special." She could give her children a glimpse of what her childhood was like and could experience again the smells and tastes of old times. It also gave her a chance to teach the children discipline and responsibility and give them some confidence in their ability to plan and see a project through—to be a responsible part of a complex, important process. Because of things like canning, Swan concluded, "we were better parents." She contrasted such complex, work/leisure activities with the silly kinds of leisure pastimes (television and video games) that have developed over the years and the coming of long-hour jobs. She believed that vapid leisure and overdevotion to work have taken nearly all the time from the family, separated parents and children, and left children alone at the mercy of mass, passive amusements that "mean nothing" and "go nowhere."[24]

Several of the women in Best's study specifically mentioned sickness in the family or among their friends when the agent asked them how they used the "extra time"; the response is hardly one that a modern observer, more accustomed to trivialized leisure, would expect. One spoke of being "grateful" that she was "able to take care of" her dying husband over the last year of his life; another was glad of "being able to care for" a grown daughter recovering from a serious automobile accident. Four spoke of their own illnesses that would have prevented them from working eight hours, and of "being able" to care for themselves. Antoinette Hatter's child had suffered a "slight attack of infantile paralysis." She observed that six-hours gave her "the chance to take care of" the child at home. Such caregiving was hardly a "leisure activity" in the modern, trifling sense of that phrase; even less was it a mere "job" in the sense that work at the plant was a job. Caregiving required great effort, energy, and self-giving, yet the women spoke regularly of doing it freely. One asked, "How could you ever set a price on such a thing?" The modern tendency to identify time outside of jobs, and effort without paid remuneration, as meaningless and foolish had not yet come to Battle Creek.[25]

The sixty-nine women spoke of "being able" to return to some of the traditional crafts and activities they had to give up after they got a job. But they were careful about which ones to restore.[26] None said they were interested in additional ironing, washing, and cleaning up. Instead, they talked about resetting their caregiving, volunteer efforts, and home projects in the context of freedom, in their "extra time." They claimed these activities as their own by choice, giving added dimension to phrases like "my work" and "free to." Even though they frequently defended canning, sewing, and so on in terms of saving money, none spoke exclusively in terms of "having to" or only in terms of function or utility. On the contrary, most spoke of having "the chance" or "being able" to do them, and often described them (as well as "church work" or "working down at the children's school") as important, meaningful parts of their lives that were "free" to them and that they in turn "gave" away. Best's agents frequently used phrases such as "she is enthusiastic," "heartily enjoys," "much appreciates" to describe how the women talked about such activities.[27]

Instead of giving up their new-found hours to be a house-servant, the sixty-nine claimed a margin of freedom for their home, caregiving, and community activities. Phrases such as "free to," "able to," "have the chance to," and "lets me," distinguished such activities from industrial work and unrewarding "housework," to be sure. But such language also transformed previously unalloyed utilitarian activities into another realm—what Giovanni Gentile describes as "the cultural."[28]

Crafts and skills that had once been an integral part of economic survival and governed by the press of circumstance were transformed into free activities, projects, and pursuits done as much for themselves as for utilitarian purposes. The products were occasionally sold but more frequently given away. Preserving food to ward off starvation during winters on the Michigan frontier was hardly the same thing as canning when canned goods were cheap and readily available at the neighborhood store; raising vegetables on a pioneer homestead was one thing, flower gardening in a modern city was quite another. The forms of such activities were similar, but the substance was profoundly altered. They had been transformed by a language of freedom from task and ordinary utility into a realm where beauty, enjoyment, conviviality, giving and being with other people were of primary importance.

Just as the activities were transformed by the language of freedom, so were the products and services that resulted. "Home-made" ice cream and bread, "home-grown" vegetables and caregiving, were useful and comparatively inexpensive, but special. One regularly depended on the "store-bought," of course. Often one had to seek professional help from doctors and others. But such products and services were not the same as those that were crafted and given in freedom. Because the activities were done primarily for their own sakes, the products were "free." As Gentile describes them, such "cultural goods . . . have this special attribute, that he who shares them with others does not lose them but increases his own pleasure in them. By dividing them he multiplies them."[29]

For the women, the canning, gardening, and caregiving they were doing in their "extra time" were on balance free and meaningful because they chose to do them and to give them, not because they were forced by economic necessity or because they were helplessly playing some "social role."[30] Preparation for holidays and special family occasions, time with the family and friends around the kitchen table and on the porch, even the hours spent with a dying mate transcended what Joseph Pieper describes as the modern presumption of "universal utilitarianism" and all-absorbing necessity. His generalizations about the historical "rise of the world of total work" and the modern "inability to accept anything as given" do not apply to these Kellogg workers.[31]

The defining historical feature of the women's activities, the thing that distinguishes them from work for money alone, from pure social or family role, or plain housework, was the workers' claims to freedom, choice, giving, and control. These women were fully aware of taking a step beyond utility and function into an emerging realm *outside* and *better than* mere work in their two extra hours.

Time Outside

Of the women who talked about having some leisure for the first time, at least seventy-two spoke about freedom as "time outside" both work and home. Such "time outside" clearly transcended utility, traditional family role, and function, and opened potentials and problems they had not been used to. Like the sixty-nine women who chose to return to home-based activities, most of the seventy-two had a positive view of the life opening for them, but several were ambivalent or rejected it.

The *Enquirer* reporter who wrote that "for the first time [workers said] they have real leisure," also wrote that "not a few dismissed the [reporter's] question" about what they planned to do because they had no idea. Best's team made similar findings. For a definite, small group, the freedom of six-hours was too free. They told Best's agents that they were at loose ends, bored, restless, or sleeping too much and would rather be at work—not because of the money but because work offered them "something to do."[32]

Lyvernie Newhouse (Best's questionnaire, no. 131) brushed aside the extra time with a causal remark—"[I] just [get] up [later] when [I have] to go to work." Cornelia Mitchell said the extra time "doesn't make much difference" because she "just loafed around more." Clara Hayward (Best's questionnaire, no. 229) had "nothing to do with the extra time. No one needs 18 hours of rest." Hayward, a widow with grown children, roomed and ate out, and was somewhat at loose ends. She said she would rather work longer to be with her friends at work, but she also felt guilty about working long hours when others needed the work so badly and expressed her willingness to share her job. Evalyn Jones (Best's questionnaire, no. 261), twenty-nine years old and single, was also "rooming out" and had "few friends in town," and so had "nothing she wants to do with her extra time. Gets lonely and would rather work longer hours . . . does not like 6 hours."

Others, mostly younger but just as unoccupied, were upbeat. Even though they had no specific use for the extra time, they "wandered around town," "visited," "went riding," "went downtown"; they were confident in their freedom, telling the agents that they had "a good time," or "it's great to have time to myself," "so much time to myself!" They indicated that the extra time was good on its face, and that whatever came was bound to be better than long hours at the Kellogg plant.[33]

But most of the seventy-two women had definite ideas about how to use their extra time. Best observed that they were trying a wide variety of "outside" activities: sports, hobbies, music, travel, "driving around," "friends," "socialization," "study," "art," even "flying lessons." Like the sixty-nine women who turned back to their homes in the two extra hours, they also spoke of having time free from both the job and "housework" and of freedom and choice as the distinguishing feature of outside activities.[34] But few in the larger group were concerned even marginally with the practical aspects of sports or hobbies. For them, the extra time was not only "outside" the factory and the home; it transcended function and utility. The adjectives and phrases they used to describe their activities are revealing: a "good time," "fun," "pleasure," "amusement," "an evening out." They spoke often of their skill and accomplishments in terms of the activity itself (e.g., "I enjoy playing the piano," "I was really good at ping-pong"), rarely in terms of a utilitarian purpose or product.

For the seventy-two, the boundary between the world of commerce and work and the "cultural world" that Gentile described was more clearly drawn. For them, the chosen activity was more clearly "outside" and for itself, even more than for the sixty-nine. The extra time, as the seventy-two used it, conforms to Gentile's definition of "culture" even better.

> Work differs from culture in two vital qualities. Work . . . by its use
> of nature as a means to satisfy human needs, creates wealth, the
> value of things. Value depends wholly on such human necessities. . . .
> Economic value is therefore always relative, a means to an end. This

end by its very nature is something apart from economic value, apart from the material object in which that value is incorporated. Economic value being thus always relative, so is the work which creates it. Culture on the other hand . . . [has] true and absolute value, because its end is not outside but inside itself. . . . Culture is an end in itself, not a means to an end, since it is not useful, [and] serves no ulterior purpose.[35]

Grace Lindsey's story, retold at the beginning of this chapter, is a good example of this sort of claim to cultural creation outside work and utility. An obvious transition in Lindsey's way of talking was noticeable in several of the interviews done in the late 1980s and early 1990s. Like several others, she began by talking about how "hard things were" during the Great Depression and how there was room for nothing in her life but trying "to make ends meet." But as she and others talked about the extra two hours a day, they stopped using the modern idiom of absolute necessity and began to talk about being "able" to do things that were important to them outside factory work and housework, using the idiom of freedom recorded by Best's interviewers. Lindsey would occasionally shift back and forth rapidly; she once began, "We didn't even have a radio . . . nobody could afford to travel or do much of anything," and ended the sentence with an observation about how much more time she "had to spend" with her relatives and nuclear family and an affirmation of support for shorter hours: "I assure you that [the six-hour day] wasn't temporary for me."[36]

Marcelle Evans used the extra time to take flying lessons and expected that her "outside activity" might develop into a "career"; two others hoped to give music lessons, and another pair who took business courses had career aspirations. But most of the women explained their leisure activities in terms of the activity itself and the social interaction and personal relationships involved, not the prospect of future work or "career."

Free from Work

Both groups of women talked about their free activities as outside ordinary work, utility, and function, as the ends for which work at Kellogg's and housework were the means. They made it clear to the agents that they were working, in part, so they would "have the chance" to do outside things. Like generations of workers throughout the industrial nations, they welcomed industrial advance for the "free time" it offered rather than the "new work" or "better work" that might or might not come along.

Only one of the 434 women (a woman with seven young children) even hinted that her job was freer, more desirable, or, to use a current rhetorical pattern, more "essential for the fulfillment of her human potential" than her "time off," and only nine spoke about the extra time in terms of finding better work or improving job skills for a "career." Their aspirations for enlarged freedom, self-expression, or control hinged on reducing work, not on finding a better career or improving their jobs down at the plant. Although a few of the younger women had career aspirations, the overwhelming majority still believed that a shorter working day was more likely to free them for a better life than what one worker scornfully called "a Prince-Charming-job."[37]

Even though they spoke of their job as necessary for their freedom and some measure of autonomy at home, it was not nearly sufficient. The Kellogg women remained skeptical, even cynical, about modern work and—with their fellow workers in Barcelona and Paris at the time—occasionally expressed profound dissatisfaction. But rather than taking the more extreme measures against work discipline (overt resistance, absenteeism, and sabotage) seen during the Popular Front era in Europe, they settled for the traditional and moderate bid for the "progressive shortening of the hours of labor."[38] Like generations of workers in Europe and the United States, the Kellogg women continued to hope that work and "necessity" would absorb less of their lives. And as John Maynard Keynes observed at the time, as work and necessity withered, freedom appeared to be emerging as life's primary challenge and concern. Struggling for shorter hours and for a life increasingly under their own control and centered in their leisure, Kellogg workers were far from believing that a "good job" was the best they could hope for.

The modern utopian dream that work ("career," profession") might somehow be transformed into a place of freedom and for the "realization of human potential" for the majority of workers (the romance of a "Prince-Charming-job") had not yet obscured the original, clearer worker vision in Battle Creek.

KELLOGG MEN

What did the men think of the six-hour experiment? How important was the hint of opposition that Brown, Hoskins, and Best spoke about? The "uniform six-hour day" was the local union's first demand when it organized Kellogg's in 1937, and the men in the few remaining eight-hour departments voted three to one for six-hours in a union-conducted ballot in June of that year, even though they were, according to the company and the union, the group most in favor of longer hours. Yet the historical record leaves room for some doubt, at least for the years before 1937. Because the "disgruntled" workers and "work-hogs" that Brown and the women spoke about were apparently men, it may well be that the fraction of men who "preferred" eight-hours was larger than the number of Kellogg women.

Best's agents left some hints about the men's opinions by recording the comments of a few women who told them what they thought the men were doing and saying. For example, Diane Buroker told the agents that her "husband likes [the] six-hour shift, . . . does painting and repairing around the house," but Donna Holser complained that her "husband doesn't know what to do with himself, now that he has extra time. . . . [I]n summer he goes fishing every day." Cora Pallett quoted her husband as saying that "the 4 hour day is coming"; Louise Worthington, whose husband was unemployed, said that he "was very enthusiastic over it (6 hrs) and hopes more industries will go on it."[39]

Best's agents also reported that six-hours caused some disagreements within families, dividing the women who defended shorter hours from other family members who were interested less in time at home and more in money. When Grace Otto observed that she "preferred 6 to 8 hrs-a-day," her husband (who was also employed at Kellogg's) told the agent that he "would rather have the money," adding that "what people need nowadays is money, not less work" and that "women don't notice it as much as men." It is unclear whether he was referring to the loss of money or the importance of work.[40]

Following up Best's report, Kellogg's did a survey of the men's opinion in December 1932, but this survey offered little improvement on Kellogg's earlier effort. Even though the ballot was secret, the workers were asked to choose between "six-hours at the present wage rates" or "eight-hours under the old wage rates." It was hardly a surprise that 95 percent of the men voted for six-hours, opposing a cut in hourly wages.[41]

Recent surveys and interviews with surviving Kellogg workers help to supplement the sparse and unreliable historical records and answer the questions at the beginning of this section. The author conducted a series of personal interviews (replicating parts of the Women's Bureau study) and mailed questionnaires to former Kellogg workers from 1988 through 1994. The surveys were designed so that workers could answer in their own words. Almost 100 of the 241 workers who returned the survey wrote narratives about what they remembered.[42]

The author also interviewed dozens of workers, Kellogg managers, union officials, community leaders, librarians, newspaper reporters, and others in Battle Creek itself, recording the interviews or taking notes. In most cases the visits were followed up by telephone. The people in Battle Creek often provided new leads that resulted in dozens of new interviews. A total of 124 workers were interviewed by phone or in person, for a total survey base of 365 Kellogg workers (241 letters and 124 interviews).

Seventy-four Kellogg workers who worked during the depression either responded to the survey or talked directly with the author; 28 of them were male. All but seven (3 women, 4 men) remembered that they were in favor of the six-hour day; most remembered that they were strongly in favor of it. With one exception, every worker who expressed an opinion remembered that the great majority of Kellogg workers, men as well as women, supported shorter hours in the early days. Still, nearly half remembered that wages suffered. Dab Ferrall, who began working at Kellogg's in 1923, wrote the author: "There was *no* complaints, even though it was a cut in pay . . . as there were so many needy people—I think perhaps, people as a whole were more human then."[43]

Over 70 percent thought six-hours was good for job security and helped unemployment in Battle Creek. Some (14) mentioned the "speedup" of the line, but they seldom remembered that they objected and never used terms such as "raw-hiding" or complained about increased management control. Asked why they liked the six-hour shift, most often they repeated what Kellogg workers told Ethel Best in 1933: they had more time for family and leisure and experienced less fatigue; in most cases they also added that "more jobs were created." Asked why they disliked six-hours, most replied, "Less money." Workers alive today thus still share the opinion Best discovered among the women workers of the 1930s: they fully realize the price of shorter hours, yet they were certain about their preference for the extra free time.

Best's 1932 conclusions apply to surviving workers from that decade, both male and female. They remember that there was, in Best's words, "little dissatisfaction with lower earnings resulting from the decrease in hours . . . , although in the majority of cases very real decreases had resulted." Moreover, the explanation Best offered for the women's willingness to give up some of their pay—"after all they were being given time off for their reduced pay"—is supported by interviews with surviving workers of both sexes nearly sixty years later. Kellogg workers in the 1930s, like workers throughout the previous century, still considered time off work to be a primary benefit of working, comparable in importance to wages. Best's finding stands upon reexamination today.

The surveys and interviews the author conducted revealed a few additional points. Nearly all the workers contacted by the author mentioned "more jobs" as the reason Kellogg instituted the short shift and a major reason they supported it. Moreover, surviving workers still used some of the same phrases workers and managers used during the depression to describe the deviant group who opposed six-hours: "work-hogs" or "overtime-hogs," "selfish" or "money hungry." Surviving workers still think badly of those who were "greedy for work" and agree that this group was a minority, an "outcast group" of "misfits," at least during the depression years.[44]

W. K. Kellogg is still a kind of folk hero in Battle Creek. Surviving workers recalled Kellogg's vision of the future of work reduction and the importance he put on leisure for the benefit of the family and health. All who remember the thirties credit "W. K." for starting the six-hour day to create more jobs even though, as one retired worker remarked, "he got condemned for it . . . just like people condemned Henry Ford when he started paying five dollars a day." Others remember that W. K. was as interested in life outside the plant as in the production and marketing of Corn Flakes. His interest in wildlife conservation and sanctuaries, his feelings about the importance of having a farm or at least a garden at home, his enthusiasm for community sports, libraries, culture and beautification—in short, his support of the free, public sector in Battle Creek—has become part of the city's "W. K." legend. His is a paternalistic legend, to be sure, but one that still reflects some of the old hopes about work and leisure that the workers shared with W. K. for years.[45]

More than half of the group of workers from the 1930s, male and female, remembered thinking of work reduction as an ongoing, open-ended process; they answered "yes" to the questions: "At the time, did you think that shorter hours of work were inevitable?" and "Did you think that because of machines, everyone would work less and less in the

CHAPTER THREE

years ahead?" (one-quarter could not remember). Half of the group also remembered thinking that the "six-hour day was a natural development," a logical next step after the five-day week. Three-quarters remembered that they believed that Kellogg was a national leader in the share-the-work movement in the 1930s and that the six-hour day would spread to other firms. Well over one-third reported that they were aware that "the new leisure" was a topic of national debate during the 1930s, but less than one-quarter followed the political developments having to do with shorter hours (for example, few remembered anything about the Black–Connery Bill or the Fair Labor Standards Act).

The author's survey and interviews are also evidence that Kellogg men shared many of the rhetorical tendencies of the women. The men who spoke or wrote about the Kellogg's experiment frequently alluded to "freedom" and "control," seldom mentioning "necessity" or "need." Echoes of the same rhetoric of freedom Best heard may still be detected among the male old-timers from the plant.

"My enjoyment was being home," one wrote. Because of six-hours, "employees got less tired and worked better—more interest" in the work. Another liked working six hours because it gave him "more time at home with the family." Time with the family was the most common way that the men said they used the extra time. An eighty-eight-year-old man remembered: "I liked the 6-hour shift. . . . I could go home and have time to work in my garden . . . big garden, fruit trees and flowers." Another remembered that "the idea of the six-hour day was Kellogg's so that people could have a garden to help for a better life and free time for employ[ees]."[46]

Other representative phrases include "gave me extra-time for myself," "I loved it . . . because we had more time to ourselves and was not tired all the time like other people working 8 hrs," and "6 hrs was sure great . . . gave you time to do other things." One of the retirees had a cousin who worked the six-hour shift for Goodyear in Akron, Ohio, and naturally assumed that the six-hour shift was going to spread to other companies. Another said that "everyone talked more leisure time" during the depression because they assumed that it was here to stay. One of the men had his wife write that he "liked the six-hour shift . . . [the wife's] 8-hr day plus 2½ hr. extra for transportation allowed [her] little time beyond care of home and 5 children. And his six-hr shift put him in Union City & fitted [her] schedule and let dad be with 4 boys at ages it was important."[47]

Ralph Parrish wrote that "in the thirties very few workers had any surplus money, so the only way he could enjoy the extra time was to do something that required no extra funds." Several other workers, like Grace Lindsey, noticed that the mixture of free time and money changed. During the earlier years there was an abundance of time and little money, so the leisure was more traditional or do-it-yourself, but now people were pressured for time ("time-hungry"), even though they had more cash.[48]

Only when the men talked in abstract terms about the hard times of the Great Depression, or spoke about Kellogg's transition back to eight-hours during the 1950s and 1960s, did they employ the current, dominant idioms of need. By the time they spoke to the author, the old idiom of freedom had become fragile and timid, easily obscured by current ways of talking. The men who used the old language spoke as hesitantly and apologetically as Grace Lindsey. One man who began working at Kellogg's in 1936 wrote that he liked the six-hour shift and "really welcomed the time away from work," but closed his letter with "what I write now will differ from many of the answers I have made." He then explained away his positive views of six-hours: he was young and foolish then, there was a depression on, W. K. was an idealist. He concluded with a revealing comment: "I *learned* six hours a day was not enough," adding wistfully, "We have to wonder about the man that thought we should have four hours a day."[49] Such language and stories reveal a profound change in the way workers talk about work and leisure in Battle Creek, a change that was "learned" as much as it was a spontaneous and "natural" response to "economic conditions."

Direct evidence about what the men did in their extra time is scanty. According to journalists who wrote at the time, second jobs were as rare among the men as among the women, while "home projects," gardening, and "farming" were among the most common activities. There were reports that some of the extra time was spent at bars and clubs; certainly the bars near the plant flourished after the repeal of Prohibition and the advent of shorter hours. Like some of the women, a few of the men had no place to go and nothing to do outside the plant and so were at loose ends, preferring to work because it gave them something to do.

According to most contemporary accounts, hunting and fishing were popular. Like canning, these were traditional activities that had been partly lifted from the realm of utility and function into the realm of leisure or play. Several of the workers wrote or spoke to the author about hunting and fishing, and what they meant to them.

The hunters and fishermen, like the canners, talked most about the process—the doing of the activity rather than its utility. As with canning, the product was regularly given away. Discussing the use of his extra time, one man told about a "sportsman club" that was located just outside town on Fourteen Mile Road between Battle Creek and Marshall. This "camp" or "club" was an "unofficial organization," made up of workers from the plant with a common interest in the outdoors. Even though the wives were invited to some of the dinners (a controversial decision), it was definitely an all-male group with a somewhat shady reputation. Another recalled the hours that he had fished and hunted at the club as "the best of his life." The peace and solitude, "being out of doors," the old challenge—these were what often moved him to get up before dawn to fish in the mornings before his afternoon shift at Kellogg's.[50]

By Battle Creek's and Kellogg's strict standards, the camp was a ripe place where alcohol, tobacco, and bad language were tolerated more than usual. But it was also full of ritual and stories. During the season, the men would eat together once a week. The meal, often venison or a smelt dinner, was the occasion for gossip, political discussion, and many stories. Delayed at a store, one man insisted impatiently that he had to rush off to the club because he and his friends had "a lot of lying to catch up on." Stories were a center of the group's activities, anecdotes as old as the Michigan frontier, tales of Indians and wars, of strange deaths and mysterious changes. Raconteurs would also rework local gossip, "lying" to order events into a narrative with at least a little plot. Other rituals were perhaps vestiges of better-organized male frontier institutions. A new member had a sort of initiation to go through—a simple introduction and the trial of being the center of attention and of having to tell about himself before the group; there were occasionally reports of hazing. The act of hunting itself was full of rituals, some idiosyncratic, a few shared. Jargon about hunting equipment and the like gave the "club" its own language.

While the "sportsman's club" did not play as profound a cultural role as the male institutions and ritual places Victor Turner described for nonindustrial cultures, it retained some echoes of the liminal place and time. It was definitely outside both the town and ordinary convention, offering the men an enclave to be "apart, together"; they were free to act in less than dignified ways. Hunting itself had the appearance of an escape from the modern world in which the Michigan frontier forest seemed to live again.

Newspaper and magazine reporters in the 1930s frequently mentioned that the men were doing "home projects" in addition to hunting and fishing. Helen Hartwig told one of Best's agents that she and her husband "decided that instead of using their money to pay rent . . . they would build a small house of their own. They . . . built the front part of a bungalow and . . . will finish it later." Leroy Despins told the author that he and his wife also built a house, though "only average carpenters." He distinguished work at the plant from his carpentry, speaking of it as a "fun and creative thing to do. . . . [I]t was downright fun, making something. . . . She'd read [the blueprints] and we'd both do the work. Working at Kellogg, you have got to be thinking ahead all the time, pressured . . . but building, it was peaceful and rewarding—something my wife and I could do together."[51] Major do-it-yourself projects were popular during the thirties, and critics of industrialization such as Helen and Scott Nearing and Ernest Flagg offered advice about how to use increased leisure and simple technology to become self-reliant. The Hartwigs and Despins had some of the same ideas as these well-known, popular writers; it is impossible to conclude more than that.

THE NEW LEISURE

Many who worked at Kellogg's in the 1930s were unsure what the "new leisure" would mean for the city or nation. Even though some had made up their minds over the succeeding years, rejecting further work reduction as unnecessary or harmful, they still remembered taking a "wait-and-see" attitude during the depression and afterward. Unlike recent critics, these workers found nothing natural, or given, about the eight-hour day and five-day week as a "full-time job"; neither did they think the six-hour day (or even less) was somehow unnatural or inconceivable as an economic possibility. Rather, they tended to feel that the six-hour day was an reasonable experiment that failed.

One of the best accounts of what workers thought of the new freedom was given by the *Enquirer* reporter who interviewed workers on the morning of the first six-hour day. His observation that workers were bemused and unsure about the new leisure squares best with the surviving historical record and the remembrances of living workers. His conclusion

CHAPTER THREE

that for the "first time they have real leisure," agrees with what workers still report: that the added two hours a day of free time were novel, and workers had little direction and few preconceived ideas about how to use them. Even though some workers still remember the old visions of a future of leisure expressed by Lewis Brown, the AFL, and the Technocrats, few remember accepting any such vision or prescription as their own.

Instead they remember that their day-to-day existence was changed by the six-hour day. In the decade before the war and Kellogg's return to the eight-hour day, workers began to experience a more refined kind of freedom in their daily lives, a freedom that was neither political nor moral. Several reported that the balance of their lives shifted from being centered in work and "having to do things" to being centered in freedom, with its attendant, often fearsome possibilities. "It was like being at Summer camp all year long," one woman remembered, and she meant her words to convey her ambivalence.[52]

In their experience of the "new leisure," Kellogg workers were virtually alone; their formal education had certainly not been about leisure. A few visionaries such as Lewis Brown and W. K. Kellogg offered limited help and guidance, but the "public sector" that Kellogg talked about was a poor one in Battle Creek, and political interest in expanding leisure services and facilities was sparse. The void was rapidly filled with mass leisure's commercial amusements.

Still, fewer than one in six workers whom this writer interviewed or corresponded with said they were bored or had more chances to "get into trouble." More than 80 percent remembered that six-hours allowed them to spend more "time with the family" and "work around the house"; more than 70 percent said they "enjoy[ed] life more" and spent more time with friends. Over half said they spent more time and effort at their churches, on community affairs, or "appreciating nature."[53]

It is reasonable to conclude that traditional working-class activities began to absorb the extra time: gardening, hunting, storytelling, gossip and conversations, going to local ball games and to church more frequently, participating in neighborhood clubs (Staffan Linder's "time-intensive" leisure).[54] Even though these were years of grim depression, workers remember an overall sense of relaxing into an easier and freer life—a life that was less work-absorbed and less caught up with things to buy, with "getting and spending." Despite concern about keeping their jobs and worry about the nation's economic health, they recall their experience on the frontiers of work reduction fondly and as an important part of their lives.

These workers experienced lives that were less work-centered than ever before or since in the industrial world. Those experiences produced a variety of deeply felt opinions, ranging from vehement rejection of the "extra time" to visions of a worker future centered at home and in free participation in the community. Those experiences left a lasting trace in Battle Creek, a resilient memory that was expressed clearly in the tenacity with which Kellogg employees held on to their six-hour day.

Chapter Four

Erosion of the Six-Hour Coalition: Unionization and Division

From 1936 to 1937 the National Council of Grain Producers (NCGP) negotiated contracts with six major milling companies that had previously been without unions. Kellogg's, the largest manufacturer of ready-to-eat cereals in the world, was NCGP's prize. Union officers J. Lyle Sage and Meyer Lewis went to Battle Creek in late 1936 to help organize the company. Just before Christmas they applied to the AFL for a charter, which was issued 30 December 1936. Thereupon Local No. 20,388 of the NCGP was born, officers were elected, and negotiations with the company began.[1]

The first direct meeting with management was held on 18 May 1937. Confident of their rapprochement with workers based on the shorter-hours scheme, W. K. Kellogg and his managers were shocked by the union's rapid success. Evidence exists that W. K. was not in control of the situation that day, weeping during the meeting and repeating, "If only they had come to me, I would have given them what they wanted."[2]

W. K. had good reason to be upset and puzzled. For over a dozen years, Kellogg's had taken pride in being in the forefront of welfare capitalism, employing the latest developments in scientific management and paying what management considered the best (hourly) wages in Battle Creek. The company was also leading the way in the battle against unemployment, providing its workers with the shortest working day in the country.

The historian David Brody stresses workers' acceptance of welfare capitalism during the 1920s, but notes that the depression "shattered" industrial paternalism. Irving Bernstein insists that notwithstanding all the benefits it offered, welfare capitalism foundered because it did not address workers' fundamental desire for democratic participation in, and shared control of, the workplace. In the case of Battle Creek, both interpretations have merit.[3]

Brown and Kellogg had extended welfare capitalism to its limits in their attempts to defuse the job-control issue. Trying to shift control issues from work to leisure, arguing that increased rationalization of work was inevitable and that freedom and control would expand to everyone's satisfaction in their time off, Kellogg's management built on an idea the AFL had developed during the late 1920s. For a while Kellogg's succeeded. For a while increased worker control in the form of expanding leisure competed with job control for the workers' allegiance—facts that lend support to Brody's interpretation. Why, then, if management–worker relations were so good, did the union find it relatively easy to organize Kellogg's?

From management's point of view, the principal reasons appeared to be the vigorous work of the NCGP and the AFL organizers and, judging from the first union demands, the workers' desire for a plant-wide six-hour day. The reasons for the union's coming to Kellogg's were, of course, more complex. Among them were previous union successes at other Battle Creek plants, notably neighboring cereal plants, wildfire union activity in the region following passage of the Wagner Bill and the National Industrial Recovery Act, and the dramatic events in nearby Detroit and Akron. But more important was the workers' desire for a voice in the operation of the workplace, as described by Bernstein.

Brown's coalition had succeeded in the sense that workers embraced the basic idea behind his plan: that is, that shorter hours meant more freedom and control over their lives. But shorter hours could not completely compensate for other job benefits. Best's survey and the author's interviews show that whereas a large majority accepted the production bonus in exchange for overtime and conceded the night bonus, the lunch period, increased line speed, and so on as part of the deal, an important minority clearly still wanted those benefits as well as shorter hours, and welcomed the union because it promised both. Moreover, the new, broader job-control issues such as the union shop, collective bargaining, and grievance procedures stood on their own, transcending the six-hour coalition Kellogg's tried to sustain.[4]

Notwithstanding Kellogg's best efforts, an important group of Kellogg workers remained as concerned with control of their time at work as they were in increasing control of their lives outside the plant. Management failed to define the two freedoms as mutually exclusive before 1937, and Kellogg workers, wanting both, simply turned from management to the union to guard and expand their freedoms, both at work and off-work.

CHAPTER FOUR

The pinnacle of welfare capitalism Kellogg had achieved was thus swamped by the tide of interest in work-control issues that swept the region during the depression.

FIRST NEGOTIATIONS

By the time contract negotiations began in June 1937, membership in the union was substantial. Dale Lovelace, an AFL representative sent to Battle Creek for the negotiations, told the local press that 90 percent of Kellogg workers had joined the union. Local newspapers also reported that over a thousand workers, half the plant labor force, attended a union meeting to vote on a strike. The principal issue in 1937 was the union shop, but as Lovelace explained to the press, the union had two other "main objectives": higher hourly wages and "a standard six-hour day for all departments in the factory." The company was willing to negotiate wages and hours, but stood firm in opposition to what it called the "closed shop." After negotiations deadlocked, the union took a strike vote on 10 June, but did not count the ballots when negotiations resumed immediately. The company continued to refuse the union shop, even rejecting a union counter-proposal that would have made union membership mandatory only for new employees.[5]

With the AFL's blessings, negotiators then postponed demands for the union shop and turned to the standard six-hour day as a compromise. The union position was that in order to protect the majority's six-hour day, the plant should be on a uniform schedule; the existence of eight-hours in any department represented a threat to the majority. Meyer Lewis noted that this stand was consistent with labor's national campaign for "progressively shorter hours," and William Green had identified Kellogg's six-hour day with labor's national strategy. Local union members and officers firmly supported this position. During a marathon sixteen-hour meeting of the membership on 12 June, they demanded a plant-wide six-hour day as the major concession for giving up the union shop.[6]

Shortly afterward, W. K. Kellogg withdrew from the day-to-day management of the company and turned over negotiating responsibilities to August E. Johansen, manager of industrial relations, and Power Custer, factory personnel manager. He also appointed the Chicago banker Watson Vanderploeg as director and in less than two years turned over the presidency to him. The new management team was not lumbered with W. K.'s paternalism, but it also lacked his vision of Liberation Capitalism. Not sharing his insights and commitment to work reduction, management ignored Kellogg's experiment. But instead of developing its own coherent labor policy, the new leadership reacted to the union.[7]

For a variety of practical reasons, Kellogg's had never scheduled six-hours for a few employees—those in the Mechanical Department, janitors and window washers, watchmen and painters, yards and grounds workers, and the Miscellaneous Packing and Shipping Department. Consequently, the company refused the union's request for standard six-hour shifts, insisting that it needed the scheduling flexibility and arguing that the few workers affected preferred eight-hours and the additional income, and that workers at Kellogg's who wanted to work eight hours had been gravitating to these five departments. The union countered that these workers, like all the rest, preferred shorter hours but had been forced to accept eight.[8]

Battle Creek's mayor, R. J. Hamilton, active in the negotiations since the threat of a strike had arisen on 10 June, proposed polling the members in the five departments. Perhaps on behalf of management or workers in favor of longer hours, perhaps on his own, he introduced a rhetorical form that was to became dominant in the years to come. As though it were not apparent to all, he "explained" to the workers in person and in the press that "an employee voting for a six-hour day, [does] so with the understanding that he or she would receive the same wages per hour as for an eight-hour day. . . . Thus the six-hour day would result in a reduction in aggregate weekly earnings for those working longer shifts."[9]

The union conducted a secret ballot under Mayor Hamilton's "supervision" at the union hall on 16 June (the very day that William Connery, chair of the House Labor Committee and sponsor of the Black–Connery Bill for a national thirty-hour week, died suddenly of food poisoning in Washington—both stories were on the front page of the *Enquirer*). In order to determine department preferences, each craft had a ballot of a different color. The *Enquirer* reported the next day that nearly two-thirds voted for six-hours.[10]

By their vote, the majority of workers in the five departments demonstrated that they were willing to "buy" shorter working hours, thus adding credibility to the conclusions that Ethel Best had based on hypothetical questions. The vote is strong evidence of male workers' "preferences" during the 1930s. All of the workers in the five departments were probably male and, according to all reports, were the strongest supporters of eight-hours. The vote is also an indication that the new "no-nonsense," reductionist formula "Shorter hours means less wages" was not yet widely accepted. Best's observation that the workers seemed to feel that "after all they were being given time off for their reduced pay" was still valid.[11] Certainly, the affected workers later pressed for a higher hourly rate to compensate for lost wages. But the hourly wage figure settled on after 1937 was a compromise, a sharing of the cost of shorter hours between workers and management, and thus similar to the New Hampshire Plan of the early 1930s.

On 18 June a negotiated settlement was announced. The union gave up the union shop, accepting instead recognition of Local no. 20,388 as the sole employee representative. On the two other major negotiating points, the union won only a six cent per hour pay raise for women (and the promise of a "complete survey of the wage structure for men within sixty days") and the six-hour day for the Mechanical Department, for janitors and window washers, and yards and grounds workers. But the settlement fell short of the "standard" six-hour day. In accord with the color-coded vote, a few watchmen, painters, and the Miscellaneous Packing and Shipping Department remained on the eight-hour day over the objections of the union. Management insisted that "minority rights" be protected, and that the few who voted for eight-hours must be allowed to work longer.[12]

The union also won the reinstatement of night-differential payments, the return of fifteen- to twenty-minute "relief periods," and overtime pay (time and one-half) for work over six hours a day and over thirty-six hours a week, for Sunday, and for six major holidays. These "secondary" issues were to have a direct, negative bearing on Kellogg's long-term six-hour experiment.

A NEW COALITION

At the beginning of the six-hour day, Brown and Kellogg had put together a package of worker benefits (higher hourly wages, shorter hours, and more workers) balanced by concessions (elimination of overtime and shift-differential pay, institution of the bonus system, etc.). They attempted to gain the employees' good will through this package and were convinced that their policies resulted in extremely good relations with Kellogg workers through the depression.

Elimination of a night-shift pay bonus was one of the more important concessions. Brown reasoned that since the short night shifts were attractive to some workers (who had the daylight hours free), a free bidding procedure would take the place of forced assignment or night bonuses. But after Brown departed and W. K. stepped down, management gave no sign of linking shorter hours and differential pay. Therefore, responding to the minority that had opposed Brown's package through the 1930s, the union demanded higher night-work pay in line with what were later called "standard" eight-hour industries. The demand for the return of "relief periods" further eroded Brown's original program and diverted attention from Kellogg's other job-improvement innovations, such as hourly job rotations.[13]

Moreover, the new management neglected Brown's most important innovation, the replacement of overtime with the bonus system. The production bonus was left in place after 1937, but at the *workers'* insistence. A significant number of workers still preferred Brown's "relay race" of intense work and an earlier quitting whistle to the mind-numbing boredom of long, slow hours. Indeed, the union tried to improve the bonus system in 1937, pressing management to prohibit "foremen and foreladies" from participation, for obvious reasons. Agreement was also reached in the first contract that "suitable work . . . be provided for older employees unable to handle heavy or fast work." Furthermore, in the computation of vacation pay (and other compensation, such as reinstatement pay), the "average bonus" (a term carefully defined in the contract) a worker received over the year was added to the weekly base rate; unlike overtime, premium pay under the bonus system was in effect even on vacation. Just as the company had offered a package of benefits based on shorter hours (e.g., pro-rated insurance and retirement premiums), the union was beginning to build a structure of benefits on the basis of the production bonus.[14]

But without Brown and Kellogg promoting the package of concessions and benefits, workers saw no reason why they should not receive overtime as well, and the union pushed ahead with demands for time and one-half pay for work over six hours a day and over thirty-six hours a week. It is clear that by 1937 the union no longer thought of the production bonus as an alternative to overtime pay, choosing instead to support both as the option producing the largest paycheck; it is equally clear that management, willy-nilly, went along. More than any other union demand, this position would come to haunt Kellogg workers, eventually jeopardizing management support of the six-hour day and dividing workers favoring higher wages from those favoring shorter hours.

With Brown's shorter-hour strategy thus eroded, Kellogg management soon began to look for a basis of labor–management agreement other than Liberation Capitalism and work reduction. Management started to extend other, "tangible" benefits and to forge a new alliance with a segment of the union leadership and with a vocal minority of senior, male workers who had fought the hardest for overtime and night differentials. Quite simply, the new coalition was based on higher wages and "tangible" benefits for the senior, secure workers in exchange for management's getting a smaller workforce working longer hours. With the ascendancy of the new coalition at Kellogg's, Brown's management strategy, his vision of Liberation Capitalism, and labor's traditional shorter-hour philosophy were gradually eclipsed, and the six-hour workers lost influence.

AN INCIDENT IN THE CONTAINER DEPARTMENT

In 1938 an incident in the container department showed how management was exploiting divisions over wages and hours, searching for a way to further weaken the "standard" six-hour day. The company proposed that during occasional periods of heavy production, when weekly schedules required more than thirty-six but less than seventy-two hours in the Container Department (operating only one shift per day), the company should be allowed to schedule an eight-hour day, and a forty-hour week. Only in the summer, during peak production, when more than seventy-two hours were needed, would two six-hour shifts be used and workers laid on: "by working 8 hrs. instead of 6 hrs. the employees in this dept. would be sure of 40 hrs. pay instead of anywhere from 18 to 36 hrs. as will be the case if the company puts in two 6 hr. shifts."[15]

On the surface, this seemed a reasonable enough proposal. The company made a strong case for "flexibility," arguing that the six-hour rule forced it either to pay excessive overtime in the Container Department or, during slack periods, to pay workers to stand around with nothing to do. But it was the major issue that arose for the union in 1938.

Employees in the Container Department pressured the union to accept the company's proposal, demanding that the president of the NCGP be called in and then pushing through a vote for eight-hours in the Container Department during a poorly attended union meeting on 18 April 1938. Opponents quickly called two special meetings the following week, voting to rescind the call to the NCGP and to keep six-hours. By the end of April, the issue had become so controversial that Meyer Lewis, president of the NCGP, finally came in from the national office to meet with the membership and management. Lewis asked two questions, "Would everyone . . . be affected the same way?" and "How many people would be put out of work?" Thus, initially, Lewis followed the AFL's general policy, which William Green had outlined during the 1937 negotiations: the union should keep up the pressure for "standard" six-hours for the sake of employment stabilization.[16]

Lewis also reported that the membership feared that management was trying to hinder progress toward the "standard six-hour day." After a series of meetings, the union made a counter-offer, insisting that before members considered work-rules concessions for the Container Department, the company must formally agree that "the flexible six and eight hour day arrangement was not offered for the purpose of undermining the six hour day or the first step in its gradual elimination" and that "it is not in the mind of the company to use this arrangement as a precedent at a later date to force a permanent eight hr. day."[17]

The union and management finally accepted the two-part agreement Lewis proposed. He noted the suspicions of workers outside the Container Department and observed, "This problem will have to be met when such an attempt is made." But he recommended that the company's proposal "be granted with the following provisions: 1. That it may be withdrawn at any time. . . . 2. When it is withdrawn, the department is to revert to the six-hour day."[18]

During the Container Department incident, the company also claimed that the bonus system was no longer working. The division between longer-hour and shorter-hour workers had surfaced again over the issue of bonuses versus overtime. Because of the new overtime payments, some senior workers had lost interest in the production bonus; few were working both harder and longer to get both bonuses. Moreover, because overtime was allocated by seniority, the older workers who preferred overtime saw the production bonus as a direct threat. Friction developed between those who wanted to work faster for shorter periods ("rabbits")

CHAPTER FOUR

and those who wanted a more leisurely but longer work day ("work-hogs"). Less than a year after it had started, the combination of premium pay plans was proving to be a major headache for management.

Thus even before the war, Kellogg's management found six-hours and its corollary, the bonus, expensive, troublesome, and at odds with its business philosophy. Somewhere between 1935 (when Kellogg management enthusiastically endorsed the six-hour day) and the 1938 Container Department episode, management's shorter-hour strategy unraveled.

Clearly, even though a large majority of workers jealously guarded their six-hour day, an important minority wanted more work and more money. In a revealing note, Lewis wrote that he recommended granting the company the eight-hour day, forty-hour week temporarily in the Container Department because "I feel that the people working in the department who have seniority, are entitled, when business warrants it, to get *a full week's work*" (emphasis added). Senior workers in the department, expanding the rhetorical formula that Mayor Hamilton had used publicly, made a strong case to Lewis in terms of "a full week's work" and began to question whether a shorter work day was a "tangible" benefit at all.[19]

THE STRIKE OF 1941

In 1941, when the union struck Kellogg's for the first time, the long-hour/higher-wage minority found leaders among union officers and gained strength in numbers. The principal issues were once again the union shop and an *hourly* pay raise. But a segment of the local union leadership accused Kellogg's of "propaganda" during the initial skirmishes because management claimed that Kellogg workers were the best paid in the cereal industry. Even though management had neglected W. K.'s shorter-hours strategy since 1937, it still tried to use the benefits of 7the six-hour scheme (higher hourly wages) to court public opinion and workers' favor. The claim made sense only under Brown's management philosophy, which understood that leisure was a job benefit with a cost. This position, in turn, depended on workers' endorsement and support.

Until 1937, the local union as well as the AFL accepted this logic, endorsing experiments that shared the cost of shorter hours between workers and the company. In 1941, however, a faction in the local union begin publicly to question whether the six-hour day was worth the price.

One union "officer" suggested to the *Enquirer* that the weekly paycheck and "tangible" benefits such as insurance and paid vacations were the only true measures of employee compensation and downplayed shorter hours as a reemployment strategy. Responding to the company's claim of "the highest wages in town," this unnamed officer told union members, "At the end of a week compare your checks with General Foods or Wheaties—and figures don't lie." The implication was clear; since workers in the other cereal plants were "able to work longer" each week, they received more "tangible compensation," even though they made less per hour.[20]

This rhetoric signaled a change in organized labor's shorter-hours policies and philosophy—a change that was to engulf the entire Labor movement after the war. The idea that shorter hours were not a real benefit on the same level as wages, and the idea that work reduction at the "expense" of total weekly pay and "cash benefits" was by definition exploitation of workers, were just emerging in the early 1940s. A direct challenge to labor's longstanding support for the "progressive shortening of the hours of labor" and the "eight-hour philosophy," such language spread, causing workers in the United States to abandon shorter hours. According to the new rhetoric, a shorter work day with the same weekly pay was no longer a step forward; nothing substituted for more money. The unidentified union officer in Battle Creek who said "figures don't lie" was an early convert. As the new rhetoric spread to become a dominant idiom, it became a primary cause of the death of the six-hour day in Battle Creek.

Company officials concerned with scheduling flexibility had raised the issue of the cost of six-hours to individual workers in 1937 and during the Container Department incident, only to see the eight-hour day decisively defeated by employee vote in the first case and carefully circumscribed by the union in the second. Heartened by the local union official's support in 1941, management seized on the question of total weekly pay and began its long campaign against the six-hour day in earnest. Again and again it asked workers to compare an eight-hour paycheck with a six-hour one. Workers, however, would resist this cash-only logic for the next forty-three years.

The 1941 contract also contained practical measures that strengthened the emerging union–management coalition. Even though the 1941 strike was mainly about the union shop, issues related to the short schedule figured prominently. In addition to the union shop, the union won an hourly wage increase based on a new cost-of-living provision in their contract and a two cents per hour increase in night pay (for the "two night shifts," bringing the total differential up to five cents per hour), and double-time pay for holidays—a provision that strengthened the position of overtime supporters.

Moreover, the longer-hours faction pushed successfully for a contract provision to lay off employees with less than five years' service "before reducing the hours of work for the balance of the employees in that division to less than 30 hours." This strongly indicates that influential union members, especially men from the Mechanical Department and the Container Department, had given up on work sharing, at least beyond six hours, and that the union was beginning to tilt toward the wage interests of established, senior workers over the employment needs of younger workers in danger of being laid off. This provision also set an important precedent that was used later to justify protection of forty hours and overtime.[21]

After the 1941 strike, the union also agreed, orally, to establish a committee composed of union and company representatives to study the possibility of abolishing the bonus system in favor of straight hourly wages and overtime. Additional problems had arisen when new machines were introduced and new production quotas had to be established; the "bonus situation" was a constant source of discontent and worker grievance after 1937—so much so that the union had already formed its own "Bonus Committee" to oversee the changing bonus criteria. Management was constantly trying to readjust baseline production standards so that workers would not be paid for all the increases in production that followed the introduction of new machines but would still receive some incentive. Younger workers were often confused and others complained about the constantly changing standards. Moreover, because workers continued to be divided between those who supported the production bonus and those who supported overtime (and who regularly raised the specter of a "line speedup"), the bonus was a prime target for company attack.[22]

As early as March 1939, the production bonus was eliminated in the Mechanical Department, composed mostly of senior male workers who were known for their interest in overtime and who formed the nucleus for the longer-hour insurgency. The 1941 contract provided for "the company . . . to work out an arrangement whereby all the present production bonuses will be eliminated and hourly rates installed comprising the former base rate and average bonus." The company was finally able to exploit worker division and confusion on this issue and persuade the majority who still favored the production bonus to give it up in return for an across-the-board pay raise and the promise of more overtime after 1941.[23]

But the company negotiators were worried that workers would no longer have a reason to keep up production levels; indeed, overtime would give them a powerful incentive to work slower and stretch out the work. After the elimination of the bonus, worker incentives remained a thorn in management's side well into the 1950s. The best that it could do at the time was ask the union to promise that "present standards of . . . performance will be maintained and that the company has the right . . . to install better methods and . . . more efficient equipment and . . . the efficiency of . . . operations will not be hindered . . . by the Company's not having an incentive bonus plan in operation."[24]

The 1941 strike and settlement seemed to be full of bad news for six-hour supporters. Still, the large majority held fast and, opposing the eight-hour faction in the union, refused to accept language that measured compensation only in terms of the weekly paycheck. Continuing to speak about shorter hours as a concrete benefit of working at Kellogg's that they were willing to "pay" for, the majority demanded that the union represent their views. Consequently, through the 1940s, the shorter-hours majority remained the dominant voice in the local union.

As the minority asserted itself with company support, the majority became increasingly wary of the company's intentions. Even though Kellogg's had published a "bulletin" in 1941 stating that management had no intention of abolishing six-hours, the union leadership pointed out with alarm that management "still maintains that each division should have a right to vote on the issue—six or eight hours." Since 1937, when the first color-coded department votes were taken, the company had insisted on protecting the rights of the minority who wanted eight hours, even if it resulted in the confusing operation of six- and eight-hour departments. The majority of union members pushed hard for elimination of department-by-department voting and insisted that votes be taken company-wide, a process sure to return a heavy majority against the eight-hour day. Ironically, as the eight-hour day gradually returned to Kellogg's in the 1940s and 1950s, the company and union positions on "minority rights" and voting procedures reversed.[25]

With the coming of World War II and manpower shortages, Kellogg's returned to three eight-hour shifts per day on 28 February 1943, citing Franklin Roosevelt's executive order as authority. The union initially opposed the move, giving in only after the company agreed to amend the 1941 contract to read that "adoption of the eight-hour shift is effective only for the duration of the existing national emergency and does not represent an abandonment of the six-hour work day inaugurated at Kellogg's in 1930."[26]

The war produced a wage bonanza at Kellogg's. With the promise of flush times and in the midst of a national emergency, some workers lost sight of shorter hours temporarily. The forty-eight-hour week with eight hours overtime became so common that the company had to publish a memo stating that "a guarantee of 48 hours per week cannot be made." The experience of the war drove home the point that some union leaders had recently made, and that Kellogg's management had been making for years: work longer and be paid more money.[27]

Nevertheless, most workers were ambivalent about the long hours. Some resisted or refused the forty-eight-hour week. Some who remember the war days still talk about having "lived in a dream"—nothing but work, the days rushing by, no "time to themselves," job stress that pulled families apart. Some speak of the change from thirty or thirty-six hours a week to forty-eight as a shock. Even though "the money was good," the transition from the "relaxed" and convivial atmosphere of prewar days to the stress and strain of wartime production was difficult, according to most accounts. Some remember that they worked long hours more for "duty" than for the money. The workers whom the author contacted said that they were glad to see the wartime production schedule end. Most talked about "things returning to normal," and "getting back" to their lives, referring to the end of the war, of course, but also to the end of "too long" work hours.[28]

Chapter Five

After the War: The Rise of the Eight-Hour Coalition

At the end of the war, Kellogg workers took stock of their long wartime hours and fat paychecks and pressed the company to live up to its 1943 agreement. Unemployment was a major concern; as soldiers returned many feared another depression and saw shorter hours as a proven, local unemployment remedy. Both the union and the company were committed to giving Kellogg workers who had gone to war their old jobs and seniority. Finally, the feeling was widespread that a forty-eight-hour week was only an emergency measure; it was now time to return not only to peace, but to sane living and to the benefits workers had won over the years. Bowing to the majority's wishes, the union made recovery of six-hours its primary postwar goal.[1]

Few events in the history of the Kellogg plant are more dramatic than the workers' reaffirmation of their commitment to six-hours. The cost to the individual workers was clear—the difference in paychecks during and immediately after the war drove home the lesson that leisure had a price. Certainly they tried to soften the blow. Even though their contract was not up for renegotiation until August 1947, the union asked for a 22.5 cent an hour raise (including a 5 percent cost-of-living raise) beginning 30 January 1946, "in order to *partially* off-set the decrease in take-home pay" resulting from the return to six-hours (emphasis added). Using the same reasoning that led W. K. and Lewis Brown to add a fourth shift in 1930, the union maintained that the "gain in efficiency . . . that resulted from the change to a 6-hour day" would pay for the raise and for the expanded payroll.[2]

The company replied that any raise above the contractual cost-of-living increase was out of the question: because "there was no reduction in hourly rates on the occasion of the change [to 8-hours] . . . in 1943, . . .

there [is] no justification in increasing hourly rates upon the return to the 6-hour day."[3] Furthermore, since the union had agreed to abolish the production bonus in favor of overtime, the company dismissed claims about increased efficiency due to reduced hours as contradictory: "It has not been the policy or agreement of the Union and the Company to establish a lower schedule of job rates in recognition of any differences in efficiencies [between eight- and six-hour departments]. . . . In the case of the container department which has a flexible 6 and 8 hour day, there has been no agreement to pay a higher hourly rate while on 6-hour shifts, or a lower hourly rate for an 8-hour day." The company had no intention of reopening the question of how worker efficiency might be tied to shorter hours, having long since abandoned the idea of paying a premium for shorter, more productive work to discourage longer, inefficient routines.

On the contrary, Kellogg management contended that "if [employees] want more 'take home pay,' [they] should work eight hours instead of six hours, as most plants are now working"; and the company was willing to reopen contract negotiations ahead of time to make the eight-hour day permanent. Moreover, management added a hefty incentive in 1946, proposing that if workers agreed to make eight-hours permanent, the company would grant an additional ten cent an hour raise above the 5 percent cost-of-living raise provided for by the 1941 contact (for a total raise near the twenty-two cent an hour increase demanded by the union).[4]

The company did not object to a six-hour schedule because it would have to pay more overtime. On the contrary, it agreed with the union that a return to six-hours would mean less overtime for the average worker and a definite cut in the average weekly paycheck. The company was more disturbed because it would have to lay on a fourth daily shift, hire more workers, find new foremen and supervisors, and pay more worker benefits.

But Local No. 20,388 refused to forget the company's six-hours promise. Edward Pilsworth, president of Local No. 20,388, wrote to William Green and raised the question of a strike for a return to six-hours before the August 1947 contract-renewal date. While he still fully endorsed shorter hours, Green replied that a strike was illegal under the contract, and sent J. N. Cummings, an AFL operative from Detroit, to help the local negotiators.[5]

The company repeated its offer to raise hourly wages ten cents in exchange for the eight-hour schedule, and Cummings took the offer back to the rank and file. The union then held two meetings in mid-April 1946, voting on the company offer by secret ballot. Again the union used color-coded ballots, this time for men and women. Of the 1,917 votes that were cast, 1,477 (77 percent) voted against the eight-hour day, and 440 voted for it; 87 percent of the women and 71 percent of the men voted for six-hours. From this vote and other evidence, it is clear that factions were solidifying; highly paid men with seniority in areas such as the Mechanical Department and the power plant voted for more work and more pay, while the vast majority of the women and almost three-quarters of the men in danger of being laid off or loosing seniority because of returning soldiers voted for six-hours.[6]

Cummings was nonplused. As one of the newer union operatives in Michigan, he was apparently unaware that shorter hours had been a primary concern of organized labor through the depression, and he struggled to explain to Green and to himself why workers would turn down more money. He wrote to Green that he "told the company that their employees had been forced to go on the six-hour day, . . . and now a large percentage . . . did not want to go back to eight-hours." At the same time he "pointed out" to management that by "demanding" that workers accept six-hours, management "had hurt them financially." Workers were "forced" to find second jobs, and therefore opposed eight-hours for purely financial reasons.[7]

Cummings' letters are notable not only because of his ignorance of the facts, but also for his rhetoric. Unlike the women who talked to Best's agents during the depression, Cummings spoke exclusively of necessity: of workers being "forced to take a second job" and the "tragedies" caused by the loss of potential wages. As eight-hours returned to Kellogg's, this rhetoric spread, obscuring but not silencing the women's claims about freedom and control.

Cummings' analysis and rhetoric represented a new attitude toward work reduction that was gaining ground among labor leaders. Like Cummings, the newer breed of leader could not conceive of workers giving up higher wages for anything as intangible as "leisure" or "freedom from working"—or even to make room for another worker to find a job. They focused on the job, wages, and tangible benefits (*paid* vacations and holidays, insurance, retirement) to the exclusion of shorter hours, which they saw as a drain on "real" benefits. Organized labor turned increasingly from local, voluntary work sharing to government efforts to expand employment and to marshal political support for new government work-expansion programs.

As far as Cummings was concerned, the only reason Kellogg workers could possibly want to go back to six-hours was to take a second, part-time, intermittent job with few benefits and a considerably lower hourly wage. Leisure was of little value to Cummings, a thing to be exchanged automatically for meager wages. His overriding reality was more money; thus the company must have "forced" workers to work less than "full-time."

But William Green "was much interested in" Local No. 20,388. Because of the widespread fear that the depression would return, Green wanted shorter hours to remain a viable labor issue after the war, and tried to restart the momentum that had built through the 1930s. Through the year immediately following the war, Green encouraged union members in Battle Creek to continue their national leadership in "the progressive shortening of the hours of labor."[8]

1947: RESTORING THE SIX-HOUR DAY

Following the first postwar vote, Kellogg's began "restoring" six-hours. But a few of the predominantly male departments delayed the process, and the issue was far from settled from management's point of view. Contract renewal negotiations began early in 1947 with the local union officers E. Levitt, G. Gulledge, A. Bilson, and C. Hammon back at the table. Cummings had been recalled to Detroit, perhaps because of his disagreement with Green over shorter hours.

The company continued to urge a return to eight-hours, launching an "information" campaign to show how much more employees would make and pressing the union in negotiating sessions. During the 12 June meeting, the union resisted, arguing that with the return of Kellogg employees who had been in the military, "a large number of employees . . . would have to be laid off" if the eight-hour shift was retained.

The company replied that this would not be a "serious problem," since a "very large number of short service employees" were working at the time. These wartime "temporaries" could be let go, soldiers rehired, and the workforce reduced without threatening most "regular" employees: "only 200 or so" workers would lose their jobs. It proposed that another vote be taken—department by department, because it "was only fair to permit a minority to have a schedule of hours which is most suitable" for them. Workers who had voted for eight-hours in 1946 strongly endorsed management's proposal. But the majority of the membership throughout the union insisted that the six-hour changeover continue and "if the 8-hour day was to be considered it should be effective for all or none of the employees." The union insisted that if another vote had to be taken it should be company-wide, similar to the 1946 vote, and be binding on all employees.[9]

Through June and July, the company pressed for the department-by-department vote, published notices on the company bulletin boards comparing eight-hour and six-hour paychecks, and kept up the pressure for "minority rights," contending that it "was not fair that employees whose persnnal [sic] arrangements are such that they favor a 6-hour day should override the rights of others who may be in the minority." Moreover, management pointed out that "in most of those departments on a 6-hour day the employees do not have the same opportunity for overtime work, and therefore the same opportunity for the highest possible annual income, as do the employees in" eight-hour departments.[10]

In order to placate the union and not "prejudice the vote," the company withdrew the offer it had made the year before to raise hourly wages ten cents if workers would vote for eight-hours. But in spite of its claims of fairness, the company made other promises to departments that voted for eight-hours: it would provide a minimum of four hours overtime to workers called back to the plant after or before their regular shift, and it would pay departments double time for Sunday work if they voted for eight-hours, but it refused union requests to provide six-hour departments the same benefits.[11]

Management pressure widened the split in the union. Strengthened by company support, the minority was able to force the six-hour majority to compromise. In return for giving up its demand for a department-by-department vote, the minority proposed that a minimum of thirty-six hours a week be guaranteed "older employees." The membership accepted, and the union took the proposal to the negotiating table. The company representatives refused. R. S. Poole and Power Custer, both from the Personnel Department, called the new intra-union compromise an "annual wage guarantee," and branded it "definitely impractical on a 6-hour day, which permits no flexibility of scheduled work hours." Moreover, the company argued that the "present system of laying off employees with less than five years of service before the hours of work in a week are reduced to less than thirty for older employees is a sufficient safeguard against attempting to spread employment too far." Continuing to exploit the divisions within the union, management pointed out that such a wage guarantee would also mean laying off more "young employees . . . than would retention of the 8-hour day."[12]

This exchange is additional evidence that, along with management, some workers and union leaders had lost interest in work sharing and in trying to deal with unemployment in Battle Creek at the local level. The company was increasingly interested in reducing the number of workers at the plant, and the union was increasingly interested in guaranteeing workers with seniority a "full week" and overtime.

After the company rejected the union's compromise proposal, the minority again insisted that it had a right to vote on eight-hours by departments and not be bound by the 1946 membership vote. The union negotiating committee finally gave in and agreed to take the department-by-department vote proposal back to the membership on 16 July. But the membership modified the plan, agreeing to the department-by-department vote only if it was limited to those departments that had historically demonstrated strong support for eight-hours, among them the Power Plant, Print Shop, Miscellaneous Packing and Shipping, and the Mechanical Department. Because this modified vote did not directly threaten the six-hour standard for the majority in other departments, the membership accepted it on 25 July 1947.[13]

THE NEW COALITION GAINS GROUND

After the 1947 vote, a majority of Kellogg workers were still on six-hour shifts. But an important watershed had been reached: nearly half of the male workers were on eight-hours.[14] Subsequently, the company identified six-hours with "women's work" or "girls' departments" and eight-hours with "men's departments," hiring new employees accordingly. Kellogg jobs had, of course, always been assigned by gender, and women had been hired mainly for the poorly paying line jobs. But after the war, management began to use the six-hour shift to excuse the poor wages of the women, obscuring the real culprit, the *hourly* wage difference between men and women. The feminizing of shorter hours began in earnest after the 1947 vote.[15]

Older, sick, and infirm employees began to be reassigned to the "light work" in the six-hour departments. The union accepted these developments as fulfilling the contract clause that called for finding "suitable" work for weak or disabled workers. The resulting segregation of older men, disabled workers, and women in the six-hour departments further discredited shorter hours. In a new procedure implemented in 1947, moreover, individual six-hour departments could initiate a department vote by collecting names on a petition. This allowed for votes to be regularly taken and led to most departments changing over to eight-hours during the 1950s.[16]

Clearly, management was winning the union over to "work longer for more money" and away from its traditional concern for the unemployed or laid-off worker. By pitting senior workers against junior, males against females, the employed against the unemployed and laid-off, and by rewarding senior workers who gave up six-hours, management extended the foundation of the new coalition and undermined the shorter-hours rapprochement that had united Kellogg workers and management for over ten years.

A select group of established workers won higher wages and fringe benefits and the "exclusion of further work reductions." In return, the union accepted, tacitly and then openly, management's "need to trim the workforce." In the closing years of the 1940s, new provisions to protect the "full-time" work of male, senior workers were added to the union contract. For example, section 710 of the 1941 contract was modified in 1948 to provide that workers with less than five years seniority be laid off "before reducing the hours of work for the balance of employees in that division to less than five days" a week, thereby increasing the lay-off threshold from thirty hours a week (under the 1941 contract) to forty hours in the eight-hour departments.[17]

Management forgot W. K.'s concern about local unemployment and, denying the individual firm's responsibility, looked to the government to deal with the "unemployed"—an abstract, national problem. More concerned with guaranteeing workers with seniority a "full week" and overtime, the union acquiesced in a policy that reduced Kellogg's total payroll. Kellogg and Brown's rapprochement with Kellogg workers in the 1930s had been based on the elimination of the work instead of the worker; the postwar agreement was based on the elimination of jobs and the maintenance of "full-time" work for the established few. According to one woman who was an employee at the time and still remembers these events: "The work-hogs won."[18]

THE NEW COALITION FALTERS

Now that the bonus had been eliminated, labor and management disagreed about how best to motivate workers. In the 1950s, acrimonious disagreement about productivity and work rules threatened to wreck the coalition. Six-hour workers remained a vocal and critical minority, taking the union to task for its lack of concern with laid-off workers, criticizing senior workers for their greed, and tenaciously holding on to their extra time and to labor's traditional shorter-hour philosophy. They continued to challenge the détente based on higher wages for fewer workers. The older vision of industrial progress they offered remained a source of embarrassment to the union and a thorn in the side of management until 1985.

The spread of the eight-hour day resurrected old problems of job control and discipline that had been less bothersome under six-hours. Because the work day was longer, workers were more concerned with breaks and the work pace, pressing in 1947 and 1948 for longer lunch periods and two five-minute relief periods, one before and one after lunch, that could "be used for smoking, personal relief, etc." The company was increasingly concerned with the rise in "lost time" and began closer supervision, insisting that "additional time cannot be taken for personal relief except in emergency [and only as] determined by the foreman." R. S. Poole wrote a memo "To Kellogg Men and Women" outlining a "new policy . . . based on the principle that everyone must work a full period of actual time on their particular job."[19]

The union admitted that "some employees have been abusing the rest period by taking extra time away from their jobs than really necessary" and, gratuitously, listed specific examples: workers smoking a cigar or a full pipe of tobacco in the toilets and "a good many employees" leaving their jobs to move their automobiles in the parking lots. Concluding that "we cannot defend such violation," the union promised to help assure Kellogg's a "fair day's work for a fair day's pay," maintaining that "the union *is not* and *will not* be for the purpose of supporting any employee who violates the principles of fair play."[20] But it did request a "10 minute wash-up period at the end of each shift . . . in recognition of the so-called 'portal pay' principle [and] . . . if employees are required to change uniforms, walk to and from their work on their own time, then an allowance should be made permitting them to 'clean up' on the company's time."[21]

Such exchanges about "lost time" intensified. One union negotiator, C. Hammon, took issue with the new aggressive supervision, pointing out that "if the company were seriously concerned with lost time from work they should consider the large amount of [the workers' own] time lost by employees [standing in line and] picking up their paychecks each week." Toby Tobias, a company spokesman frustrated by the renewed struggle over work discipline, replied that "if they cannot abide by this agreement [five-minute overlap between shifts] we will have to go back from whistle to whistle, then place a penalty on violators." Power Custer suggested that the company "fire the violators," while R. S. Poole posted this threat on the company bulletin board: "If someone does not play fair with the [five minute overlap] rule they can expect disciplinary action of time off or possibly permanent discharge."[22]

The new struggle over job control was caused only in part by longer hours. Both the company and the union concluded that the elimination of the production bonus in 1941 was also to blame. Without a production incentive, workers seemed less motivated and careful. Union representatives conceded that a number of employees were "'shirking' or otherwise failing to carry their share of the load . . . [and] that maximum accomplishments could only be obtained by providing incentives to increase earnings"; with a modified production bonus, "there would be strong pressure on the part of the employees themselves to eliminate other employees who were 'shirking.'"[23]

The company underlined the problem, pointing out that

accomplishments since the discontinuance of the incentive bonus plan have not been as satisfactory by a substantial amount as they were under the bonus plan. In the Company's opinion this is primarily due to a lack of interest of people "keeping on top" of their jobs all the time as they formerly did. [When the bonus was in effect, workers stayed] near their machines at all times ready to take care of stoppages, anticipating breakdowns, and helping people on other machines who were having trouble. In most cases the present attitude is one of being away from machines while they are running, making no preparation in advance of breakdowns, and giving no aid to people on other machines.[24]

From management's point of view, some workers seemed to want production to foul up so that overtime would be necessary. The leisurely pace seemed geared to generating overtime rather than producing cereal.

The company floundered around, trying to deal with the fact that production was down. When the union opposed "the possibility of having a bonus plan similar to the one in effect years ago," the company explained that, without returning to the old bonus, it "would insist on finding some method of gaining the same accomplishments." The union representatives conceded the point.[25]

Initially, management tried to work through the union to extract promises from workers to do better. The union agreed to insert into the contract a pledge "to maintain quality and quantity of performance" despite "the company's not having an incentive bonus plan in operation." Furthermore, it urged workers to "help others to try to maintain full production" and not to abuse the break and lunch periods. "A fair day's work for a fair day's pay" became a watchword (or cliché) in the plant and union hall. The phrase is still remembered by workers in Battle Creek, and it is often repeated when the question of efficiency, overtime, and the bonus is raised.[26]

When all these promises failed to improve the production rate substantially, management suggested a modified production bonus plan. Company negotiators proposed that no further raises be granted under the cost-of-living adjustment provided by the 1941 contract "until an improvement above the accomplishments of performance that were in effect in 1941 [when the production bonus ended] had been obtained." The company then proposed that a "production index" be determined for each department that would be used in conjunction with the U.S. Department of Labor Consumer Price Index for the Detroit Area to compute the cost-of-living raises—thereby making "the cost of living bonus . . . contingent upon an improvement in the production index."[27]

The union rejected this proposal but accepted the production index and bonus in theory, agreeing that "maximum accomplishments could only be obtained by providing an incentive to increase earnings." Guarding against the return of the "rabbits," the union proposed that instead of weekly "extra payments" for "extra accomplishments," the production bonus be paid yearly "if the performance of particular *departments* warranted such payments" (emphasis added).[28] The company responded with a plan that called for quarterly as well as annual reviews of the production index but required a 2.5 percent improvement in the production index for every 5 percent increase in the cost-of-living bonus. To sweeten the deal, it offered workers a share of productivity increases due to "improved methods and equipment." The production index would henceforth include a proportion of the increases in productivity due to new machines as well as improvements due to worker performance, such as "less waste" and "avoiding delays and interruptions" on the line.[29]

The union then countered with a remarkable proposal "based on freezing the cost of living bonus at the present level"—in effect giving up the cost-of-living provision of the 1941 contract in favor of "an incentive bonus above present incomes [when] the production index is exceeded." It was offering to trade its cost-of-living bonus in exchange for full payment for all increases in productivity. The company rejected this proposal outright, suggesting instead that the cost-of-living bonus be left unchanged and that an incentive plan be set up that permitted workers "to share one-half of the net gains that might accrue at the end of each calendar year" above the 1941 production standard. The union then agreed to share increases in productivity "equally between employees and company," and the "Production Incentive Plan" went into effect on 1 August 1947.[30]

Immediately, the plan proved unworkable. Since the bonus was determined by the performance of a department rather than paid to individual workers, it did not work nearly as well as the old production bonus. Overtime remained a problem because it showed up in the weekly paycheck; the incentive bonus was distant and unsure, determined by several forces outside the individual worker's control. The workforce remained intensely interested in whether Kellogg's would have to resort to overtime to keep up with its orders. The company tried to salvage the incentive bonus by setting up a committee along the model of an old Safety Committee "which would concern themselves with two-way exchange of information and ideas to help accomplish a gain in the production index plan." But the committee unexpectedly took a new tack, focusing on "improvement of the production index by means of analysis of wasteful practices" in addition to "the individual waste of man hours."[31]

This committee also failed, and by December 1948 the company was still searching for a workable incentive plan, spending what managers called a "considerable amount of time" trying to deal with workers' inattention to the job and "shirking." Power Custer and other managers be-

CHAPTER FIVE

came impatient with the lack of results and, threatening to discharge workers for carelessness and inattention, began to hand out "yellow slips" (threats to fire workers) in order to control spoilage and product contamination. This caused some harsh exchanges in which the union accused Custer of "unreasonable and inhuman" tactics.[32]

But the new committee's suggestions were not forgotten. The idea of improving production by controlling waste and spoilage provided a new direction to a desperate management. During 1949, the company built on the idea, developing a more positive quality-control program that it named the "Waste Saving Bonus Plan." Rather than offering a bonus based on the amount of production, the new plan based money incentives on quality. Incentives were built up by departments and paid out quarterly to workers at a proportional rate, based on hourly base pay. The Waste Saving Bonus was in operation less than eight years. After the first two years, management realized that the cost far exceeded the benefits. The primary reason was that workers were able to claim a large and unregulated portion of improvements due to new machinery and quality controls, while at the same time continuing to collect large overtime payments. And trying to motivate individual workers by paying a bonus to an entire department remained a problem.

In 1957, the old problems came to a head. Complaining about a "speedup" (a word covering a variety of worker complaints, including the length and enforcement of breaks and lunch times, the "portal to portal" issue, as well as the actual line speed) and demanding overtime for Saturday work and an eleven cent an hour raise, the union went on strike. The strike lasted forty days and was resolved when management agreed to a seven cent raise and the union gave up the Waste Saving Bonus.[33]

The phasing out of six-hours and the various production bonuses resurrected issues of work discipline. Kellogg workers accustomed to the expanded freedom of shorter hours felt the renewed discipline of longer hours keenly. Having given up on shorter hours as an incentive and having failed to find a replacement for the production bonus, the company felt compelled to reestablish control at work, resorting to fines, threats, and firings. The old struggle over the imposition of work discipline that E. P. Thompson had described returned to Battle Creek.

Chapter Six

Human Relations Management: Reaffirming Work as Life's Center

In a mature Capitalist society all time must be consumed, marketed, put to use; it is offensive for the labor force merely to "pass the time."—*E. P. Thompson*

Failing to find a workable production bonus, discovering that money incentives were either ineffective or, in the case of overtime, counterproductive, and facing an entrenched group of six-hour workers unmoved by the promise of more money, Kellogg management was ready to try something different by the mid-1950s. Led by researchers from nearby Ohio State University and the University of Michigan, the Human Relations School of business management was becoming increasingly influential across the nation and seemed tailor-made for Kellogg's problems.[1]

Human Relations represented a fundamental change in management philosophy. During the early years of Kellogg's experiment, Scientific Management was at the height of its influence. Frederick Taylor's followers paid little attention to workers' attitudes, assuming that work was important to workers primarily for reasons external to the job, and that workers' happiness or "fulfillment" on the job was beside the point. Certainly, work conditions needed to be improved and fatigue dealt with. But the real goal of industry was to produce more in less time, just as labor's reason for being was higher wages and shorter hours. Work's perfection was less work for more money, for industry and worker alike. The scientific manager's watchword, "Efficiency," was defined by increased productivity, which was, after all, a ratio of things produced to length of time worked. As long as hours were shortened so that workers were not laid off, the term "labor-saving device" still made good sense.

Accepting the rule of efficiency, and seeking to "demonstrate" the production benefits of better working conditions and reductions in fatigue, researchers began to encounter confounding experimental results in the 1930s. The new findings showed that the old "external motivators" (hours and wages) were failing. The paradoxical results of the experiments at Western Electric's Hawthorn plant and the Relay Assembly Test Room led researchers like Fritz Roethlisberger and Elton Mayo to change their focus from conditions at work and the traditional motivators to the worker's state of mind on the job—to his or her *attitude* about work. As the historian Edwin A. Locke observed, "The Human Relations school paid virtually no attention to the importance of money, claiming that it . . . was swamped by the effects of social factors."[2]

Increasingly, researchers claimed that the most "significant variables" determining a person's behavior at work were "human factors"—things like beliefs, perceptions, values, feelings of success and appreciation, and group relations. Moreover, managers could not only measure such things as "worker morale" and "job satisfaction"; they could change them by adopting a proper "leadership style" and improving their own work attitudes.

In the mid-1940s Human Relations caught fire as managers throughout the country began to put its theories into practice. Replacing Scientific Management's assumptions about the overriding importance of "efficiency" and "labor-saving" with its own remarkable vision of perfect work, and leaving Brown and Kellogg's Liberation Capitalism far behind, industrial managers and psychologists began to imagine and then pursue work without toil, chock-full of joy, meaning, significance, satisfaction, and "intrinsic motivation."[3] Modern business thus began what was surely one of the most fantastic projects conceived in the modern age—the search for work that is its own reward.

FROM WORK AS MEANS TO WORK AS END IN ITSELF

The best-known and arguably most influential researcher and writer of this school was Douglas McGregor, whose *The Human Side of Enterprise* summed up Human Relations management theory and research over two decades. "Behind every managerial decision or action are assumptions about human behavior," McGregor began. Historically, business had accepted a collection of presuppositions that he labeled "Theory X." The first and most important of these assumptions, from which the others flowed as corollaries, was: "The average human being has an inherent dislike of work and will avoid it when he can." With "deep roots" extending back to the punishment of Adam and Eve, this view naturally entailed the notion that "most people must be coerced, controlled, directed, threatened with punishment to get them to put forth adequate effort" at work.[4]

These two assumptions led invariably "to the interesting conclusion that [work's] rewards can be used to satisfy [the worker's] needs *only when he leaves the job*" (McGregor's emphasis). Thus "it is not surprising . . . that for many wage earners *work is perceived as a form of punishment* which is the price to be paid for various kinds of satisfactions away from the job" (40–41).

McGregor argued that "Theory X," or the "carrot and stick" approach to industrial management, had stopped working. "After man has reached an adequate subsistence level," traditional forms of work discipline based on punishment on the job and incentives enjoyed away from work are not only ineffective; they naturally result in the decline of the importance of work and business, for "one would hardly expect [workers] to undergo more punishment than is necessary" (40). The appetite for more money would eventually give way to the desire for more leisure.

Instead of accepting this tragic end of economic progress, McGregor offered a "more productive" set of assumptions: "Theory Y." Like Theory X, it had a first postulate from which its other principles flowed: the "*expenditure of physical and mental effort in work is as natural as play and rest.* The average human being does not inherently dislike work. Depending upon controllable conditions, work may be a source of satisfaction—and will be voluntarily performed" (47, McGregor's emphasis).

The secret to making work as attractive and as much fun as play was first to realize that "man is a wanting animal." Scientific managers and utopian writers of the previous generation (and even some misguided contemporaries such as B. F. Skinner) had predicted that "freedom" would grow as necessity became increasingly "obsolete." But modern psychologists had "discovered" the real truth: that "as soon as one of his needs is satisfied, another appears in its place. This process is unending. It continues from birth till death" (36). Appropriating the language of psychologists like Abraham Maslow, McGregor speculated that human needs are "organized in a series of levels—a hierarchy of importance." First on the ladder were physiologic needs: the traditional hungers for bread, shelter, rest and survival. Moreover, "man lives for bread alone when there is no bread. . . . [H]is needs for love, for status, for recognition are inoperative when his stomach has been empty for a while" (36–37).

Once the physiologic needs are met, people become indifferent about them—"a satisfied need is not a motivator of behavior!" Instead, "needs at the next higher level dominate man's behavior." After the physiologic needs come the needs for safety and protection, then the social needs for belonging, association, acceptance, friendship, community, and love. McGregor pointed to the work of Elton Mayo, professor of industrial research at Harvard, who claimed to have discovered the "motive power" of the "need to belong," and who was among the first industrial psychologists to suggest the possibility of transplanting the essence of "community" from traditional neighborhoods, or working class "sub-cultures," into the modern "work group" (36–37).[5]

Near the top of the hierarchy, revealed only after long, diligent labor, "are the needs of greatest significance to management and man himself . . . the egoistic needs [for] self-esteem, self-respect, self-confidence, autonomy, achievement, competence, . . . reputation, status, recognition, and appreciation." Unlike all the rest, the "egoistic needs . . . are rarely satisfied; man seeks indefinitely for more satisfaction of these needs once they have become important to him" (38).

Finally, "a capstone, as it were, on the hierarchy" are the "needs for self-fulfillment . . . the needs for realizing one's own potentialities, for continued self-development, for being creative in the broadest sense." Like "egoistic needs," the need for "self-fulfillment" and development is infinite—no amount of satisfaction would ever be "enough," no point would ever be reached where "need" would no longer "dominate man's behavior" (36, 41).

People had always known about the importance of these "higher needs." But business and industry had mistakenly assumed that such matters received attention mainly outside the workplace. Companies such as Kellogg's that offered recreation programs and facilities to their employees perpetuated the mistake that free time rather than the job was the place for expressing the "higher needs" for community, acceptance, and so on. Following suit, economists had traditionally assumed that the economic and the nonpecuniary realms were sharply divided, that the one concerned "practical" economic needs, while the other concerned the "freer" activities of culture, mind, and spirit.[6]

McGregor's inspiration, and the genius of Human Relations, was to appropriate the economist's extraeconomic, nonpecuniary realm. Annexing the "Realm of Culture" to the job, Human Relations attempted to overcome what McGregor considered the outdated dichotomy between the economy and life "outside" the rational field of the marketplace.[7] From this incorporation, McGregor and his generation of Human Relations experts and industrial psychologists expected the final triumph of economic reason. As the job replaced time off as the locale for "human satisfaction," the free market's "matrix of logic" would steadily push back the wilderness of irrationality, myth, and emotion, and the engineer and scientist would lead society to an orderly world where desire and obligation, means and ends, conflict and community, consumption and production, and work and leisure would merge. In a world blessed by reason regent, men and women would rush to work as to a festival.

Not since Saints Augustine and Anselm had imagined perfect freedom as the union of human will with Divine purpose had such a blessed vision of the human condition been conceived.

But McGregor and his followers faced a formidable obstacle. Everyone except industrial psychologists still talked about work and leisure (life, free time, play) as opposites. Those still under the sway of Theory X continued to use contrasting words and syntax for the two "artificially separated" realms, opposing reward/opportunity/consumption with control/coercion/production. Because such language had a long history, built into accepted definitions and common discourse, the unfortunate antithesis persisted. In order to overcome the dichotomy, ordinary language had to be subtended by a broader, underlying syntax. Together with other industrial psychologists, McGregor found just the right words to do this in Abraham Maslow's hierarchy of needs.

Philosophers through the ages had talked about ascending through a hierarchy of freer, less work-like and needful activities. Generations of industrial workers had understood Liberty as freedom *from* bosses, industry, and economic necessity *for* "better" things outside work. Now, the human relations experts proposed that all human striving was really motivated by ever-renewed, eternal need. To be human was to be needful. Dismissing the "illusion" of freedom and the idea that some exuberant "bubbling out" of energy somehow took men and women beyond the human condition, they proposed perpetual need as a "more scientific" basis of human behavior.

The language of eternal need was consonant with the collapsing of leisure into work. As McGregor put it, "Man continuously puts forth effort—work, if you please—to satisfy his needs." Since the higher social, cultural, and "ego" activities were motivated by need, just as much as eating was motivated by hunger, "work" rather than "leisure" was the obvious way to speak of "satisfying" such needs. The language of perpetual need was also syntactically consistent with perpetual work: there was no rational place *outside* work and the industrial order because there was no motive beyond satisfaction of needs. Workers' traditional dream of the "progressive shortening of the hours of labor" and slogans like "Work to live, don't live to work," and certainly Victor Turner's liminal condition, had no place in the structure of language that resulted from Theory Y. Apart from rest and recuperation for more and better work, time away from work and consumption (the Human Relations writers seldom used the word "leisure") was a cipher in the modern world of need ascending, a relic of the confused, illogical past.

According to McGregor, Theory Y itself met a new and pressing need. Because industry and management had made it easy for workers to satisfy "lower-level needs, management has deprived itself of the ability to use the control devices . . . rewards, promises, incentives, or threats and other coercive devices. . . . [D]irection and control are of limited value in motivating people whose important needs are social and egoistic." A complete overhaul of industrial work discipline was "needed" to save work and industry. A new, effective work discipline, McGregor asserted, could be founded only on the workers' internalization of controls, on enlarged "self-control" and "self-discipline" made possible by the common, rational agreement that work in the industrial state could become more "satisfying" than any other aspect of life. Just as in "child rearing, it is recognized that parental strategies of control must be progressively modified to adapt to the changed capabilities and characteristics of the human individual . . . so industrial management recognizes" that it was essential that the needs of industry and the needs of the workers be "integrated" as "mutually supportive," and arranged rationally for the maximum satisfaction on both sides.[8]

McGregor argued that once people experienced the "satisfaction" of work perfected by the Human Relations experts, the older forms of discipline would slough away, and men and women would "work with a will," really wanting to do what they had always been enticed or forced to do. The older forms of punishment and reward would still have a circumscribed role to play, until the slow learners in the economy saw the light. Wages would also continue to be important, but primarily because things like pay parity affected the psychology of the working group.

Emerging out of Human Relations, and employing much of the same language, the second wave of modern industrial management research and theory—what scholars have labeled the "Work-Itself School"—went beyond Maslow's hierarchy. Led by Frederick Herzberg, a psychology professor at Western Reserve University in Cleveland, those who subscribed to Work-Itself built on the language of need but gave work and business an even heavier charge: *meaning.*

In one of his later books, *Work and the Nature of Man,* Herzberg summed up earlier developments: "Perhaps the greatest contribution that the behavioral scientists have made during the last half-century of research . . . has been to broaden the concept of the needs and nature of man from a solely economic organism to one that encompasses some of the more human aspects—the emotional and social needs" (9). His task, however, was "to offer a definition of man's total needs . . . that is consistent with the world of work" (x). Thus Herzberg confessed his debt to Human Relations and committed himself to its project of harnessing eternal need to modern work.

While business and industry could learn much from the psychology of need, Herzberg observed that "managers and other workers, while seeking practical help with business problems, are also eager to learn from psychologists what their own jobs and lives are about." Industry's need to find new motives to keep workers at work paled in comparison with the great social and psychological need to understand the puzzle of human existence. Going one step beyond McGregor's highest needs of ego and self-fulfillment, Herzberg claimed that "the primary functions of any organization . . . should be to implement the needs for man to enjoy a meaningful existence" (viii, x).

Religion and superstition had pretended to play this role historically, producing myths that organized life willy-nilly and seemed to satisfy the ultimate need for meaning, after a fashion. But for Herzberg, it was important to remember that by fulfilling the desire for answers to the questions of the purpose of existence, institutions gain and hold control of the people. . . . A premise of this essay is that every society has to establish myths in order to sustain its institutional forms. . . . The dominant societal power, whether it be religious, political or economic, propounds and directs self-serving myths because of its awareness that the stronger the belief in myths the easier it is to shape human behavior. . . . Institutions will perish without myths. (10–11, 13, 14)

The time had at last arrived when reason, embodied in science and applied by "professionals," could dislodge "self-serving myths" and replace institutions that misused "meaning" to perpetuate their power. Because "the permeation of life by the industrial spirit justifies the idea that business is the dominant institution in present-day society," the psychologist and business manager had a precious opportunity selflessly to guide mankind to true meaning. The long history of science's triumph over myth and superstition led to this point. With technology and business ascendant, benevolent management and industry could use their power as society's "dominant institutions" to establish and arrange meaning scientifically, according to "rational psychological principles" (ibid.).

Presented with such an opportunity, Herzberg observed, "It is wise to go back and ask once more, What is the nature of man? Not the nature of man as imposed by any particular economic or social institution, but the nature of man as it is in reality, regardless of the needs of the controlling forces." Whereas "the history of civilization is, in part, a history of man's attempt to provide himself with comforting mysteries . . . every mystery that man has developed to give meaning to life has been fair game for rational analysis by man's brain" (43).

Over the years, the Pyrrhonism of science's systematic doubt had refined and purified myth and unfounded meaning to the point where "there is only one illusion that has resisted destruction. That is man's potentiality—where he can go, what he can become. This is the article of faith that gives purpose to man's existence" (54) and provides the foundation for an authentic science of the need for meaning.

"Personality theorists" like Jung, Adler, and Maslow had come close to establishing such a science, with their "concepts of self-actualization, or self-realization." But it was left for Herzberg to show that "man's compelling urge to realize his own potentiality" was possible only through "continuous psychological growth" (56). He defined "psychological growth" in general terms as "the process of continuation . . . ; the essence of growth is to become more than one was before" (58). Characteristics of growth included "*knowing more, . . . more relationships in knowledge . . .* growth in *creativity . . .* utilization of potentiality, growth of *individuation.*" Linking "psychological growth" directly to modern jobs, he observed that "man does not work for profit or in order to avoid pain; but in a positive sense, he works to enjoy the excitement and meaning that achievement provides for his own psychological growth and thereby his happiness" (174).[9]

Like McGregor and the other Human Relations writers, Herzberg argued that whereas the older "Animal-Adam," or physiologic work motives were being satisfied and thus were failing, the newly revealed "Human-Abraham" nature could redeem industrial advance and "psychological-progress" (76). Basic "hygiene" needs still had to be satisfied at work. Like McGregor, Herzberg recognized that unfair pay scales could make the worker miserable. But the real challenge was "the re-education of workers and management in terms of a motivation orientation" (172). The industrial psychologist and enlightened manager had a heavy responsibility: to teach people in their charge to aspire to perpetual "psychological growth" in the workplace and, escaping the chains of illusion and superstition, satisfy their enduring need for meaning.

Herzberg concluded that the health and well-being of the nation were at stake in the reinvention of work:

Mental health . . . relates to man's actualizing his Abraham nature. This actualization depends upon what man accomplishes, and the major area in which he acts as a determining individual is on the job. Therefore, industry becomes the prime resource for psychological income that is necessary for mental health, just as industry provides an influential environment that contributes to the alleviation of the psychological deficits of man that lead to mental illness. Eventually, the improper utilization of people in industry will have a deleterious effect on the mental health of society." (190)

Herzberg ended *Work and the Nature of Man* with a rhetorical flourish, identifying "human needs for meaning" and "psychological growth" at work with "man's spiritual needs." He feared that "there is little time

CHAPTER SIX

[left] to develop another Renaissance that might give purpose, direction, hope, aspiration and a future to humans" (192). Thus the nation had to move immediately, and heeding Father Abraham, begin mass production of human meaning through the reinvention of industrial work. That which religion and superstition had done badly for millennia must now be performed efficiently and soon. Led by the principles of the Work-Itself School, industry could meet the challenge and turn out abundant meaning, "psychological growth," and life-purpose for the worker, just as it had produced enough and more soda-pop and baseball cards for the consumer.

Curiously, religious imagery was common among adherents of the Human Relations and Work-Itself schools of management. Such rhetoric may have reached a high-water mark with the 1957 publication of Abram T. Collier's "Faith in a Creative Society" in the *Harvard Business Review*.[10]

Collier began on a plaintive note, stating that the abundant provision of "goods and services, comforts and leisure . . . does not produce affection, understanding, or contentment." Higher wages were no longer effective as a motive at work because abundance and consumerism were failing to deliver on a fundamental level of human need satisfaction. For years, "businessmen in the democracies" and Marxists relied on economic growth and power alone, assuming that these were "enough" for most people. Recently, "the pendulum's swing has led many to see [business] as a search for psychological satisfaction." For Collier, however, the pendulum had not swung nearly far enough. Going even beyond Herzberg's "meaning," he suggested that modern business "is primarily an attempt to fulfill the spiritual significance of the individual and of society."

Collier reasoned that the widespread consumer malaise and the formless, modern ennui were the results of "the human condition," the "restless anxiety, a sense of need, an unlocated cavity in our lives. . . . Somehow, our modern democratic industrial society does not seem to be filling our deepest need." He continued: "When . . . personal discontent pervades our material abundance, it is perhaps not improper to suggest that as practicing executives we cannot avoid asking ourselves some broad and difficult questions: What am I really working for? Where do I really seek to go? . . . Just because our lives are spent in a factory or an office does not mean that we are . . . removed from these eternal questions. . . . [I]t is important for us . . . to find a sense of purpose in our work."

Seeking to answer the question "What will satisfy our unsatisfied yearnings?" Collier, following Herzberg, suggested that "creativity" was "the prime aspiration of man," and that "liberty, reason, and faith" were the "preconditions of creativity." But he reasoned that it was *faith* in a "creative society" and "*faith* in work" that would provide the "spiritual values" and sustenance for the soul that "underlie material achievements."

"Men in business . . . do not want to risk the charge of selling piety in the sky," but "they are coming to realize . . . that work had significance and purpose only to the extent that it is a fulfillment of their own, and other's, inner lives." Whereas McGregor connected modern work to man's "higher needs" for self-actualization and Herzberg harnessed work to the fundamental human thirst for meaning, Collier and others who used such religious imagery took the ultimate step, offering work as satisfaction for St. Augustine's old *cor inquietum,* the restlessness in every human heart. At its zenith, Work-Itself management anointed the modern "practicing executive" as the new high priest of work, who offered absolution for modern despair and a balm for the wound that is the human soul through the true "Faith in Work."[11]

Such discussions about infinite need and human meaning were not as new as McGregor, Herzberg, and Collier thought. Advertisers and economists had concluded long before the advent of Human Relations management that human needs were insatiable. During the 1920s, business and industry responded directly to the threat of "economic maturity," a perceived condition of abundance in which workers would continue to work less because they had enough to satisfy them, by agreeing with economists like Constance Southworth that the "capacity of the common man to want things" was infinite and could be stimulated by advertising and other forms of social pressure. By the end of the decade, Herbert Hoover's famous Committee on Recent Economic Changes was predicting a bright economic future because "the ultimate luxury" was becoming the "everyday necessity"—a delightful development primarily due to the enlightened efforts of advertisers who took a scientific approach to marketing.

When the Human Relations school appeared, economic growth had long been founded on perpetual consumerism and ever-expanding necessity. During the 1920s, the business community gave the idea a name, the "New Economic Gospel of Consumption," and devoutly preached it in the years between the world wars. Moreover, like Human Relations management, consumerism had been thrown up as a bulwark against work's decline. Businessmen like Henry Ford had stated specifically that they were in direct competition with expanding leisure, and that they planned to offer Americans a more attractive alternative to work for: eternally expanding luxuries/necessities.[12]

For all of its innovations and successes, the New Economic Gospel of Consumption was limited by the assumption of McGregor's Theory X. The Gospel remained focused on the external rewards of work: wages and consumption that were enjoyed outside the workplace. For a while, the Gospel protected against the danger that workers would continue buying back more and more of their own lives from industry, as they had been doing for generations. But the emphasis on consumption simply amplified workers' interest in work's external rewards, and as their real wages increased, so did their desire to have time enough to enjoy the new things they could buy—or so the industrial managers feared after the war.

Some have described the period just after the war as "waiting for the second shoe to drop"—that is, waiting for the Great Depression to start again. Just as economists and businessmen feared chronic "overproduction" just after World War I, industrial managers and psychologists after World War II feared the weakening of "external motives" to work. Like the prophets of consumerism during the 1920s, the Human Relations pioneers fought to save work by taking a new tack.

In a stroke of genius, managers and psychologists detached the language of eternal need from work's rewards and reapplied it to work itself. Instead of touting the doubtful joys of everlasting consumerism, these new saviors of work promised to provide jobs that were more to be desired for themselves than for their results. Traditional worker rhetoric relegated work to a subordinate role, as a means to other ends. Human Relations experts reversed this language, annexing the cultural/community concerns and activities that workers had traditionally expressed during "free time" and preempting the traditional worker critique of modern, alienated work. They promised to make work a "rewarding" and "satisfying" experience in itself, and thereby redeem it. Since the start of the industrial era, workers had sought to fulfill their aspirations for community, meaning, culture, mystery, wonder, and spiritual refreshment outside their jobs. Now, instead of a means to better things, modern work would emerge as an end in itself.

Management at Kellogg's followed these trends closely. Focusing attention on employees' attitudes and its own "leadership style," it tried to sell everyone at the plant the idea that work was the center of life.

Initially, Kellogg management encouraged all supervisory personnel to read John Neuner and Benjamin Haynes' *Office Management: Principles and Practices* and keep a copy on hand. This was a run-of-the-mill Human Relations text, one of many turned out during the period to summarize the new management principles.[13]

Power Custer, now vice president in change of industrial relations, was excited by the changes in management he saw around him. But rather than "inviting an outsider to discuss 'Leadership' who would not be familiar with our group," he thought it better for Kellogg's to conduct its own "Supervisory Management Development" conference in 1957 on "'Growth' in Personal Leadership." During the conference, Kellogg's initiated a contest for supervisory personnel, offering a prize for the best essays on "Leadership in the Kellogg Manner" and "How to Motivate Workers." The conference and contest resulted in the publication in 1957 and 1958 of 101 written responses from executives, supervisors, managers, directors, and foremen and forewomen, collected in two pamphlets. Dealing largely with worker motivation, the pamphlets "Leadership in the Kellogg Manner" (1957) and "Code for Good Leadership" (1958) reiterated principles of Human Relations management in the words and phrases of the locality.[14] Throughout both pamphlets, managers and foremen frequently referred to "Human Relations," "effectiveness in dealing with human beings," and "job satisfaction," and cited the latest research of organizations like the National Office Management Association. One concluded that "knowledge of human relations has become one of the most important traits a leader must possess to cope with labor unions of today."[15] Kellogg's managers now set out to apply the new principles to Kellogg's production problems and the entrenched six-hour workers.

Power Custer introduced most of the major themes of the pamphlets: the primary importance of attitude toward the job, the importance of "growth" and the "higher" human needs as motives to work, and the need for a personal faith in work, as well as the job community of worker and manager and the manager's roles as teacher, salesman, coach, and team-leader. With the other writers, he stressed the importance of language and how things are said.[16]

By far the strongest theme, and the most common word, was "Attitude." Senior executive R. S. Poole observed that "to obtain the results of a fair day's work requires an acknowledgment of the fact that people's attitudes toward their work can be changed. This is more than a hope, it is an undeniable fact which continually inspires us in our effort" ("LKM," 17). Another senior executive, D. M. Harrison, concurred that the conference had shown that "MOTIVATED AND INSPIRED . . . people can actually be changed. . . . This is a never ending task and likewise is a free-flowing well of rewarding experiences with people whose attitudes you have changed" (ibid., capitals in the original).

The speakers and writers consistently defined the new, improved attitude as the worker's "voluntary recognition" of the overriding importance of his or her job. Custer observed that the manager was a *"full-time* teacher" charged with the responsibility to "install [*sic*] responsibility in [workers'] attitudes toward their jobs by making them see their jobs are important to themselves and to the Company." He and others attributed most personnel problems to the "bothersome worker" who did not have the "proper attitude" or did not "realize the real importance of their jobs." ("LKM," introduction).

The primacy of work was everything. The factory was a kind of "school house" ("LKM," 7a). Its major teaching, "be happy in your work," was sound instruction for life; for anyone who was unhappy at work was bound to be miserable during his or her time off ("CGL," 12a). Since work was obviously the center of life, it had to be satisfying in order for the subordinate parts of life to be worthwhile. As one manager put it, "A leader should develop the talents of his people to their highest level, so they may lead more constructive and efficient lives" ("CGL," 23aa).[17]

The job was central because it could satisfy essential human needs that subordinate parts of life could not. "Need" language was second only to "attitude" in the rhetoric of the two pamphlets. For Custer, "leadership [was] fundamentally the ability to influence the actions of others. It means a keen knowledge of the basic needs to which men respond." Contestants provided lists of such "basic motives . . . to which a leader can appeal that make men act.": ambition, confidence, pride, self-respect, welfare ("LKM," 7aa and passim). Another reminded colleagues that their "volume of production depends . . . greatly on . . . your ability to deal with people. If the employees' needs can be fulfilled, and their respect for you as a manager can be obtained, success will be yours" ("LKM," 11).

The fundamental human need to belong to a group also needed to be tapped. "One of the greatest incentives for doing a good job is the hope and expectation of receiving approval from others. Without this approval from others, the employee soon loses his push and often obtains that 'I don't care' attitude. . . . [K]now your employees. . . . This gives them a feeling of well-being and importance" and "establishes an atmosphere in which their basic need to belong can be fulfilled" ("LKM," 5aa). Another noted that "we must feel a sense of partnership with our fellow workmen because we can win only as a team" ("LKM," 15). Others wrote of the importance of "satisfaction," "recognition," "approval," "security," "a feeling of belonging," "close personal contact," "essential relationships for real cooperation," "a friendly personal touch, . . . sensitivity to feelings, . . . listening," "constructive cooperation," and "friendly behavior" ("LKM," passim).

Several contestants stressed civil virtues such as good manners and politeness, enjoining the "leader" to be "considerate and courteous," to "avoid derogatory comments," and to say "please and thank-you." One observed, "A leader would be doing an injustice if he was to criticize a worker in the presence of others. It would be degrading"—and damaging to the work community ("LKM," 13).

Still others advised the would-be leader to "give them [workers] a sense of being your good friend . . . that you are really doing something for them," and to "talk to his people, find out what the worker does in his spare time, ask about the family . . . [because] it creates harmony, friendliness, understanding, and above all willingness to work" ("LKM," 20). One contestant concluded, "The first quality of leadership for you to develop is a capacity for 'Rapport.' That's a good word—look it up for yourself and you'll remember it longer. 'Rapport' means a sympathetic relationship with the group—harmony" ("LKM," 14).

Not only could the job be made the place for community; it could also satisfy the fundamental human yearning for personal growth and advance—what one writer called the "Hunger for growth." In the introduction to the first pamphlet, Custer wrote that "we should know how our people progress in their daily work. . . . [W]e must establish a goal that is beyond our reach . . . [and be] constantly seeking new knowledge. . . . [A good leader] tries hard to find ways of making work a 'good challenge'. . . . Avoids encouragement of an attitude of 'aiming low,' or 'less than best' " ("LKM," 4). In the introduction to the second pamphlet, another senior executive wrote, "First I believe for a code of good leadership that we must establish a goal that is beyond your reach" ("CGL," 103).

Reflecting the general mood, one contestant concluded that the most important thing was "always have a job on hand for when one is completed. . . . Keep the worker activated as much as possible. . . . A leader knows there is always a job to be done" ("LKM," 20). Others advised "let[ting] people have as much responsibility as possible," helping "the other person grow," and reaching out "for the highest level of accomplishment" ("CGL," 101). "Perfection is neither expected [n]or attainable. . . . [I]t is the 'reaching out' that counts" (ibid.). Thus the good leader is "constantly seeking" because the "self can be improved constantly" ("LKM," 8). Still another senior executive concluded that "growth and change are of greater importance [than development]. Those persons who are in positions of responsibility recognize this if they are constantly in the process of self-development and developing others. Socrates was aware of this when he taught his students to 'Know thyself' " ("LKM," 10, 114, emphasis in original). Kellogg's managers echoed Herzberg's emphasis on psychological growth as individuation: "People like to show individuality. Demanding [that a worker] do a job [exactly] your way will kill initiative" ("LKM," 11); "to 'be yourself' is important, but it does not limit a person. . . . [T]he self can be improved constantly" ("LKM," 13).

A few writers identified "growth" at Kellogg's with the nation's progress and glory and the betterment of the human race, concluding that "hard work and dedication to work made this county great" ("LKM," 5aa), and "the individual that recognizes the [value of] our competitive capitolistic [sic] system will definitely be successful" ("LKM," 8aa). One observed that "LEADERSHIP IN THE KELLOGG MANNER is [teaching workers to understand] that we live in a free, democratic nation and that it is only through our acceptance of our responsibilities to have the right attitude about work, to God, and to our local, state, and national governments that we can and will preserve those freedoms for our children and the company. . . . The successful Kellogg leader by his words and actions causes people to realize that the company is continually moving toward a new and better era" ("LKM," 9aa).

"Leadership in the Kellogg Manner" meant, to use Custer's memorable malapropism, "installing" such expectations and attitudes in Kellogg's workers. The goal was clear; how to make it happen was the challenge of "leadership."

The most common "installing" technique suggested throughout the pamphlets was "leadership by example." The true believer was irresistible. Managers counseled each other that if they worked hard enough and believed strongly enough, people seemed always to follow. A "leader must feel a sense of personal pride and responsibility to the job that he has accepted . . . so [that] all Kellogg employees should be proud to work for such an outstanding company" ("LKM," 3a).

"Enthusiasm" was part of leadership by example, as was "displaying sincere interest and exuberance in the job" ("LKM," 6a). One writer advised: "Develop job enthusiasm among your workers. First start by seeing that you have job enthusiasm yourself" because "[t]he enthusiasm of a leader for a cause or objective must be great enough to kindle a similar flame of enthusiasm in the heart of each follower" ("LKM," 104). Another agreed: "Enthusiasm is probably the best weapon for getting the job done. Everyone should be helped to see the importance of his job, and the supervisor who is enthusiastic has a better chance of passing this attitude along to his people" ("LKM," 113). By the same token, managers enjoined each other not to "display a negative attitude" ("LKM," 13), since "indifference rather than the lack of ability" is the chief source of problems" ("LKM," 14).

The two most common metaphors for leadership in the two pamphlets were "teaching" and "selling." One writer observed that a good leader "should be able to sell the employee on the importance of doing his job correctly, safely, and efficiently." Poole wrote, "We should never fail to try to sell an individual on the importance of his job." One entry was notable for its figurative language: "our product we are developing is not tangible and the consumers are not buying with money to derive satisfaction. Instead, our product is leadership and the consumers, Kellogg people, are actually 'buying' with their acceptance of our ideas to derive better attitudes and work performance. It takes many raw materials to produce a material product. Our raw materials, tolerance, sincerity, tact, honesty, etc., are leadership principles that we must use at all times if we are to consistently produce a high quality product" ("LKM," 36).

Others emphasized teaching: "One of the most demanding functions of a leader is that of an educator. The process of education is never ending. He is continually educating himself in personnel development . . .

and in turn he educates his employees in the performance of his duties." ("LKM," 8a). "As a leader he is also a *full-time* teacher. A teacher should constantly strive to improve himself and his technique so he can establish and *maintain* the proper climate for learning on the part of others" ("LKM," 106, emphasis in original).

Still others emphasized the role of faith, belief, and religion. "Once people . . . believe in . . . your own devotion to the job you can begin to be a leader" ("LKM," 7a). "Have faith in your people . . . in our God . . . in our country . . . in our job . . . and faith in ourselves" ("LKM," 113). The "Golden Rule"—"Do unto others"—embodied all that a leader should know and do: "First and foremost, follow the golden rule. . . . [A] little prayer will probably give us a better start" ("LKM," 3). Custer was, by all accounts, a pious man, ready to apply the virtues of self-sacrifice, devotion to duty, faith, and belief to producing cereal as cheaply as possible, and to place an "emphasis on a religious attitude" to "install" proper work attitudes.

Enthusiasm, teaching, selling, and sharing the faith were expressly designed to lead the workers to the "voluntary recognition" of the importance of the job. When the worker "bought" what was being sold, "learned" what was being taught, "followed" where he or she was led, or "was converted" to the true faith, that worker then "owned" the right attitude, and was thenceforth led from within—as one manager put it, "The man is able to control himself" ("LKM," 10). This internalization of control and discipline was the strongest rhetorical theme in the two pamphlets, becoming the very definition of a "good attitude."

Echoing McGregor's Theory Y, one manager described leadership as "the ability to get others willingly to do what you want them to do—one outstanding characteristic of a good leader is the way that he can get to the workers, and get them to cooperate voluntarily by making them want to work" (1). Another agreed that managers needed to "create the feeling among your employees of wanting to do a good job as well as working for the paycheck each week" ("LKM," 13). Custer stressed the importance of "self-control . . . self-improvement . . . " and "strong sincere desire" to work. Another concluded that leadership "includes getting others to willingly accomplish what you want them to do even when you are not present, even when they must use their own initiative to cope with unexpected situations . . . doing the job to the best of their ability, even improvising if necessary to improve on the job when appropriate" ("LKM," introduction).

The contestants also suggest another, subtler technique. Writing about the importance of team play and the sense of belonging, several (including Custer) advised the "leaders" to avoid "I or mine" whenever possible, and to use "we or ours" ("LKM," 108). Others agreed: "Use less of the word 'I' and more of the word 'we' when talking Company policy." Speak of "our people . . . not your people" ("LKM," 7).

The concern about which pronoun would help "install" community at the plant was part of a larger, more general concern with language. Managers recognized the power of language to change attitudes and thus the reality of work at Kellogg's. Custer advised "leaders" to use "respectful words to describe Kellogg people or their work," and to "cultivate a pleasant tone of voice and manner of speaking, realizing that how one speaks is often as important as what is said in getting the job done" ("LKM," 1). Several saw in modern business a new "emphasis on communication . . . much of industry today is still attempting to become proficient and master a successful system of communication" ("LKM," 1aa). One contestant suggested that the manager use workers' "language and not company language" whenever possible, and to translate instruction and orders into the common parlance ("LKM," 8). Although one of the writers poked fun at his colleagues' "antics in semantics," the large majority took language, tone of voice, dialect, and appearance seriously, and expected improved "communications" to assist the leader in teaching, selling, leading, and inspiring the workers to "own the right work attitudes" ("LKM," 4aa).

The majority of Kellogg managers repudiated the old, authoritarian management techniques of Theory X. Custer, once known for handing out yellow slips, observed that in "modern days a driver cannot get best results"—that the up-to-date manager is "a good coach rather than a hard driver." Other representative responses include: "A boss drives—a leader leads." "A boss will depend on authority—a leader depends on good will." "A boss says 'I'—a leader says 'we'" ("LKM," 115).

A few holdouts were cautious about Theory Y. They reminded their eager colleagues that beneath all the feel-good words was a "bottom line," that Kellogg's was in business to make money, and that, however it was packaged, authority meant control. One contestant reminded his associates that "your primary job here is to see that others convert materials into finished products at minimum cost. In doing this, [you must] make the best possible use of man power, machines. . . . [You must] be effective" ("LKM," 9a). Another noted that "the measure of success of an

CHAPTER SIX

industrial manager . . . is obvious—PRODUCTION" ("LKM," 5aa). Still another cautioned that "a Kellogg leader should be aware that he is primarily a business man. He is charged with the responsibility to see that some segment of this business prospers and he has the authority to direct the work of others toward this end" ("LKM," 106). In fact most converts to Theory Y admitted that there was a "bottom line" and that control and direction were still essential. They differed only in their evaluation of the best way to exercise control.

The recognition that there was a underlying reason for all the community building and teamwork, and that the human relationships nurtured on the plant floor were subordinate to the greater good of Kellogg's profits, led to a further word of caution. A few managers had misgivings about the sincerity of their colleagues, cautioning that the methods of Human Relations had to be firmly believed in and lived throughout one's life. Several warned against manipulating the workers by pretending to value community, teamwork, and friendship in order to get them to work harder. The "Golden Rule" was mocked and cheapened if it was used only in the service of profit. For this minority, sincerity was the heart of the new management techniques:

> One of the greatest leadership papers ever written was St. Paul's letter to the people at Corinth. The principles he advocated are as appropriate today as they were then. He spoke of love as the most important ingredient in life but how often have we heard love mentioned when we discuss the principles of leadership? He said this about love. "Love is patient and kind; love is not jealous or boastful; it is not arrogant or rude. Love does not insist on its own way; it is not irritable or resentful; it does not rejoice in wrong, but rejoices in the right. Love bears all things, believes all things, hopes all things, endures all things." Perhaps we believe such broad terms as character and love are not appropriate in today's language, but we can technique and gimmick ourselves to death. The best techniques, systems or methods are doomed if we don't have the leadership "absolutes" as our way of life. If we don't believe in such things as love and faith in leadership objectives, then we are as Paul said, nothing but a "noisy gong or a clanging cymbal". In today's terms, with sophisticated definitions and fine lines, these "absolutes" of leadership must be re-emphasized. ("LKM," 2aa)

But the majority was untroubled by questions of "absolutes" and means and ends; few had qualms about misusing the Golden Rule. Most saw Human Relations management as what would now be called a "win-win" game, creating a situation that met the needs of men and women for community, growth, and personal expression while the company enjoyed the benefits of a fulfilled workforce with the right attitude. Like Human Relations and Work Itself management, "Leadership in the Kellogg Manner" claimed to harmonize workers' capacities and needs at work with the needs of the company. Harnessing capital's need to expand the bottom line to infinite human needs made a powerful team, reaffirming work by returning the job to its rightful place as life's center.

The status anxieties of the managerial class also played a role. Surly workers who struggled against work rules and plotted for more overtime, together with determined workers who continued to mount the six-hour challenge, persuaded Kellogg managers that the traditional supports of work discipline were crumbling. If the problems represented by the six-hour workers festered, and if work and its rewards continued to decline in importance (as Human Relations theory predicted), then traditional patterns of status, prestige, and community control based on the job would be eroded. If time, attention, and energy were redirected to family, community, and self-directed leisure, business and the business manager would be the big losers. Outside the job and marketplace, control and organization were established on less formal, traditional patterns and often superintended by some of the "weakest" people in the community, economically and politically speaking. Where would the successful businessman and ambitious industrial manager be in a world centered outside the job? It was high time to reassert the importance of work and the workplace.

Kellogg's fond hope was that persuading employees to believe in the "intrinsic worth of work" would largely eliminate the threat to work and the motivation problem; productivity, work quality, "slacking," and absenteeism (the "dependent variables") would naturally improve, and the six-hour workers would be converted. If workers believed strongly enough in their work, discipline and control issues would no longer plague the manager, who would then be secure in his work status and job prestige.

This new strategy differs strongly from the company's efforts during the 1940s and early 1950s to motivate workers by a variety of money bonuses. Comparing Human Relations management with Kellogg's original six-hour experiment produces an even sharper contrast. Even though each management strategy was a reaction to and partial rejection of the one before, together they make up a historical sequence of management efforts to solve the problem of worker motivation caused by the weakening of work discipline.

During the depression Brown and Kellogg had tried to use work reduction to improve work, motivate workers, and build cooperation and agreement within the plant. They believed that workers naturally wanted free time to pursue better and freer activities. When W. K. was at the helm, management employed this shorter-hours strategy to get workers to agree to increase productivity, an experiment that enjoyed some success for nearly a decade. After abandoning shorter hours and uncoupling financial incentives from work reduction (and higher hourly wages from shorter hours), Kellogg management again faced the problems of motivation and discipline. It turned to Humans Relations, acting on the faith that productivity would naturally increase when work became the most rewarding aspect of life.

Whereas Kellogg and Brown had tried to deflect the problem of control at the job site by increasing the workers' freedom from work, management in the 1950s tried to accomplish the same thing by bringing workers' "attitudes," "perceptions," and "values" about work more in line with the "needs of modern business." Whereas Kellogg's had used work reduction as an incentive in the 1930s, the company came to use the "loss of work" or "denial of overtime" as severe disciplines in the late 1950s. Whereas the company once tried to "perfect work" by reducing the hours of labor, it later found that "a leader knows there is always a job to be done." Whereas Kellogg's had tried once to improve the quality of life by providing leisure services and recreational facilities, ultimately management converted to the belief that when workers had the right attitude about working, the subordinate parts of life would automatically improve. Whereas Brown and Kellogg had found it obvious that work was a means to other, more important ends (to a living wage and to "higher" activities), Kellogg management at last accepted work as an absolute, unquestioned value, an end in itself for which management was the salesman and industry the servant.

Since work was the center of life, it was foolish for workers to think that less of it could be a good thing or (apart from fatigue, sickness, or old age) part of human improvement. After the 1950s, management employed just such an ideological argument to press for the elimination of the six-hour day, adding to the more practical justifications (such as fixed labor costs) that had existed since the early 1940s.

Whereas support for work reduction had positioned Kellogg's in the avant-garde of twentieth-century welfare capitalism in the 1930s, its attempt to alter worker attitudes in the 1950s was typical of a widespread twentieth-century management response to problems of motivation and control in an abundant and expanding economy. According to the new teaching, basic industrial conflicts would be avoided when workers and management agreed about the importance of the job. The shared belief in the centrality of work, not spiraling wages and plummeting work hours, would be the basis of a permanent labor–management rapprochement. When everyone believed strongly enough in work and their jobs, when all realized that "hard work and dedication to work made this country great," society would see the end of labor unrest and class conflict and would at long last bid farewell to the working classes and their troublesome "culture."

Chapter Seven

Kellogg Workers Embrace
the New Work Rhetoric

During the 1950s, the coalition of senior workers and management strengthened in Battle Creek. Founded in the late 1930s on a practical tradeoff—higher total wages for fewer workers—the coalition grew around the absolute importance of "full-time" work. Attempting to defend their "wage-only" strategy locally, eight-hour workers made their own rhetorical contribution to Human Relations management, helping to shore up work discipline at the plant and maintain the power and status relationships in the community that had traditionally been established by work.[1]

Union leaders joined in using management's rhetoric, reaffirming the centrality of the "full-time" job (represented by the joint company–union slogan, "the principle of a fair day's work for a fair day's pay," written into contracts after the 1940s, usually in section 604). Even though the slogan became something of a joke over the years, workers still remember how seriously everyone once took it.[2]

Unlike managers, who had concluded that "external rewards" had lost most of their effectiveness, the union pressed as hard as ever for higher wages and "tangible" fringe benefits. By helping to propagandize work, using management's language about the job, and giving assurances of the workers' belief in hard work as an abstract good, the union accommodated management, solidified the coalition, and strengthened its bargaining position. From 1950 on, the union busied itself trading words for wages.

Giving up shorter hours allowed it to concentrate its forces and move more effectively on the wage issue. One worker observed that "6 hr shift elimination was for years a bargaining chip for the Grain Miller's Union. They used it to pry [money] concessions out of the company."[3]

The eight-hour workers began to speak of "full-time" work as imposed by outside necessity, a given, over which the individual had no control. Coincidentally, most workers abandoned the open skepticism about work they had expressed before the war. Instead they emphasized the seriousness of their jobs, contrasting the importance of work with the trivial character of the time away from it. During the 1950s, they joined management in supporting work as an ideal and reaffirming it as life's center and organizing principle.

ROMANTICIZING THE JOB

As the rapprochement between labor and management strengthened, the senior eight-hour workers replaced their criticism of work with mild though detailed suggestions about improvements in schedules and work rules. Forsaking the old view of steadily diminishing work hours as the ultimate job improvement, the union spoke about "job enhancement" in terms of small, incremental improvements, and of "satisfaction" as depending primarily on the "right attitude." Sidetracking the once-dominant issue of control at work, the union turned to the task of making the job seem more rewarding and "satisfying" by stressing cooperation with management to "get the job done."

As the cultural value of work ascended and that of leisure declined, true believers scrambled for more work, forgetting about who held the reins of control at the plant. For years, the scheduling of "extra work" and overtime was in the hands of foremen and "foreladies" who divided the time among their favorites. Ralph Parrish, a retired Kellogg worker, described the situation in a letter:

> Some foremen . . . seemed to have favorites. . . . A friend who I
> worked with later described his early experiences as follows: After he
> had worked a few months, a co-worker approached him and asked if
> he liked to play poker. He said the boss liked to get better acquainted
> with his help, so about once a week he invites some of the men over
> for a social evening. They usually play a little poker and he serves
> some sandwiches and a glass of beer or coffee to those who want it.
> 'We always try to see that H . . . wins enough to cover the cost of the
> refreshments.' Other employees liked to hunt and if they had good
> luck they would bring in a pheasant, some rabbits, or some venison for

H. . . . Similar deals for those who raised a nice garden and had more vegetables or fruit. . . . Some of the employees felt that those who participated were allowed to work more days than those who did not.[4]

Another man wrote that "the boss had pets and relatives who got the extra work." Still another commented that "seniority meant nothing to some of the older workers. In plain language, when someone was needed to work, that person who was a stool pigeon or a friend of the foreman got the extra days of work." Work allocation remained controversial through the mid-1950s until the issue was finally settled formally in favor of senior workers by amendment to the union contract. Section 901, paragraph *d* reads: "Senior qualified people will be given priority for all extra days." "Extra work" replaced "extra time versus extra money" in the conversations of eight-hour men.[5]

Some workers joined the more loquacious managers, such as Power Custer, in romanticizing their jobs and raising work to heroic proportions. Those with skilled jobs, working in such places as the Mechanical Department or Print shop, were prone to identify strongly with their craft and often used management's language to speak of "self-expression" on the job and to stress its "rewarding" aspects. Like management, they made strong claims about "hard work" and "the right attitude about work" as the factors that distinguished a good job from drudgery and a virtuous worker from a "bum."

A Work-Based Language of Morals

Critics called them "greedy" or "work-hogs," but male workers deployed a new moral language in which work became a moral solvent, justifying behavior that otherwise failed to meet community standards. "It's my job" or "I have to work" regularly took precedence over family or community responsibilities. Such language certainly had a broader circulation by the 1950s—probably a national one. It had been coined earlier, perhaps during World War II, when "It's my job" came to answer a variety of horrors. Movies in the fifties and later regularly featured John Wayne–like characters who would excuse some unspeakable act by saying "It's what I'm paid to do." Once a cliché, the convention has slipped into parody.

Kellogg workers used the same syntax locally when they justified voting for eight-hours and working overtime on the grounds that the nature, requirements, or structure of their jobs compelled them to ignore those without good jobs in the city, and so relieved them of moral culpability. "I have to work" was enough to refute the claims of family and community. "Hard work" and the "right attitude" about working also excused gross economic inequalities and became the high moral ground from which those with good jobs condemned others. Senior workers, secure in their jobs, agreed more than ever with what managers and owners had been preaching for years—that the reason some people were in bad shape was because they were lazy and unwilling to "work hard."

So pervasive was this rhetoric that even six-hour workers were drawn in. Charles Blanchard, remembering when he was single and worked the shorter shift, observed, "I didn't work as much as I should have. I took a little more off than I should have." Taken to its logical extreme, this language allowed one male worker to write, guilelessly, that he supported six-hours before he went to work at Kellogg's because "I thought I might get a job, but went to eight-hours as soon as I could to get more money."[6]

Work Myths

As part of the general reconstruction of work discipline, work myths grew up after the war. Great feats of work had been part of local legend since the frontier days, when mythic characters like Paul Bunyan performed Herculean deeds and local heroes arose as champions of work contests. But the modern myths concerned long hours and dogged persistence rather than great achievements. The men often told stories about working second and third jobs, taking obvious delight in describing eighteen- to twenty-hour work days, months of working straight through without a day off, and years with no vacation or holidays.

Asked whether he worked five or six days a week on the six-hour shift, one man concentrated on a short period of his life when he had to work double shifts for two months. He described in elaborate detail, with examples, the challenge he faced during that period: his fatigue, the fact that his children were strangers, that he never saw his home in the daylight. But he had no stories to tell about all the years that he worked six hours on a regular basis and, in a most evident way, steered the conversation away from questions about the two extra hours of leisure time he had for more than eight years. In fact, the author frequently detected embarrassment or something like a guilty unwillingness to talk about shorter hours among the men. The author often had the distinct feeling that male workers became uncomfortable, even hostile, as soon as six-hours came up in conversation and that they were relieved when the topic changed.

Myths about second jobs grew. One of the most common responses to the author's questions about how the men used the "extra leisure" was "a second job." If true, this would strengthen the author's claim that work was valued more highly and leisure debased after the 1940s. But such claims were almost certainly misleading, having more to do with workers' perceptions than with reality. As much as one would like to take these claims at face value, it is necessary to look deeper.

The author's survey shows that only about 35 percent of Kellogg's male workers ever had a second job. Since most jobs were badly paid, intermittent, highly seasonal, lasted under three years, or all of these, only 10 to 15 percent of Kellogg's males had second jobs at any given time. Although this number is significantly higher than the Battle Creek, regional, and national averages, such figures by no means account for the strong claims that practically all male workers had another job as long as they worked six hours.

Similar assertions were made about Goodyear in 1956.[7] Second jobs became the media "take" on the shorter-hours story during the fifties, as reporters copied each other's explanation that workers wanted to work six hours so that they could work another job as well. The wildest reports in the press asserted that 33 percent of the workers on the short shift had second jobs in Akron, but even these stories failed to account for the other two-thirds. "Explaining" commitment to six-hours solely in terms of second jobs has always left out the large majority of workers. Such explanations reveal more about the people who made the claims than about the fate of shorter hours. The "second job" was a rhetorical device, providing an excuse for the men who were not working "full-time." This "covering rhetoric," even more than the "facts" about second jobs, is a strong indication of the degree to which leisure was denied and work elevated in Battle Creek.

The general revision of the local rhetoric even extended to the plaintive cry of a shy man deformed in his relations with other people by a life centered exclusively on work and business. W. K. Kellogg's well-known remark "I never learned to play" was turned on its head by management and eight-hour workers to suggest that single-minded concentration on work was the key to his success and a model for others.

Consistent with these changes was the desertion of an important minority of women, who rejected six-hours for more wages in the late 1950s and 1960s. Men's and women's jobs had always been divided at the company: most women worked in their own packing departments, and the women had always been paid less. During the late 1940s and early 1950s, when the majority of both men and women were on six-hour shifts, the women made efforts to have their *hourly* pay scale upgraded to bring their wages more in line with the men's.

During the campaign to discredit six-hours, Kellogg management identified six-hour departments as "girls' departments" and assigned disabled, sick, or older employees there as well. Eight-hour departments became "men's departments." Wage discrepancies were justified on the basis of "less money for less work." Thus management shifted the issue of comparable pay from hourly to weekly pay, branding the six-hour shift as the cause of gender pay differences.

In the mid-1970s, some of the Kellogg women joined forces with local women's rights groups. Condemning six-hours as a sexist ploy to subjugate women, they called on management to "allow" the women to have "full-time" jobs and to abolish all hours-based "gender distinctions" between departments. Accepting management's rhetorical forms and symbols, they argued that women were just as needful and as physically fit as the men, and had just as much to gain from their work—meaning fulfillment, status, power, and similar benefits. They suggested that the company circumvent the department-by-department voting procedure and mandate eight-hours company-wide, or face possible sex-discrimination suits. The company posted notices in the plant, claiming that federal law required that women's and men's work be equal in number of hours so that wages would be more "comparable."[8]

As a result of a lawsuit brought by some of the women, the company agreed to "open up" the eight-hour departments to women. Thus Kellogg management successfully deflected the issue that most Kellogg women were still interested in—comparable *hourly* pay—but failed in its bid to use the issue to force all the women to work eight hours. Indeed, this episode was soon forgotten, and the majority of women continued, unabashed, to fight for equal hourly wages (as they did in a forty-day strike in 1957), hold onto shorter hours as a job benefit, and champion work sharing to help the unemployed.

A NEW LANGUAGE OF ABSOLUTE NEED

Unlike most of the women, the eight-hour converts faced the problem of justifying higher wages to the community and particularly to laid-off workers. During the 1950s, Kellogg's eight-hour workers were among the best paid blue-collar workers in the city. The difference between their pay and that of the average Battle Creek worker was a matter of public notice and comment.[9] To justify even higher wages in negotiations, eight-hour workers and the union began to emphasize "need" or "necessity" more than ever, resorting to an increasingly pure rhetoric. Together with "a full-time job," "need" and "necessity" were spoken of and defended as absolutes, unqualified by any standard of need and unrelated to the pay of other workers.

Like many in the early twentieth-century Labor movement, Kellogg workers during the depression and the 1940s spoke of necessity declining as wages increased, of the possibility of getting "enough" or "too much" and of being "able to work shorter hours." They also spoke of "needs" or "necessity" in relation to nonpecuniary values, saying things like "I need the extra money, but I need the time at home more." After the 1950s, most of the eight-hour workers dismissed these traditional rhetorical forms in favor of unqualified need, insisting that they never had "enough" to work less than "full-time"; the phrase "extra money," so widely used in the 1930s, virtually disappeared. Art White, a retired Kellogg worker, concluded, "You never have enough, do you? . . . Nobody has enough. Gosh! . . . Enough of anything. Money."[10]

Comparing the rhetoric of the Kellogg workers over the years, one is struck immediately by something very close to a reversal. In contrast to the "rhetoric of freedom" of the 1930s and 1940s, most male workers who were employed after 1950 spoke either of being driven to work "full-time" by a necessity that they could not resist or of being unable to "afford" shorter hours. Regardless of circumstances, such as the nation's economic health, the individual's personal fortunes, the fact that Kellogg's paid the highest hourly wages in Battle Creek, marriage, or family condition, by far the most common explanation workers gave for abandoning six-hours for eight was "necessity" (invoked in words and phrases such as "need," "can't afford six-hours," "have to work," "no choice," "didn't make enough money to live on," "nobody could make a living working a 6 hr shift").[11] The majority no longer talked about freedom and control when asked about the "extra time." They no longer spoke of increased free time as a job benefit or as something of value that they were willing to "pay" for.

Examples of the new language abound. The men spoke often of "having" to get a second job when they were working "only six hours," and of "needing to work 14 to 16 hours a day" as a consequence—a "need" that vanished when the two hours were added to the "regular" job.[12] Responding to the author's questions about why the six-hour shift was eliminated for the men, the men frequently considered a one- or two-word response sufficient: "money," "more money."[13] One of the clearest reversals in terms involved "overtime." Originally understood as a penalty to encourage the company to hire more workers, it finally was absorbed by the language of need, becoming part of the wage issue—a way for protected workers to earn more money and for the company to maintain "flexibility" and avoid hiring more people.

The 1950s and 1960s are often described in hyperbolic terms. Surprisingly, the men who worked during the Great Depression tended to speak matter-of-factly about those days, saying things like "it was a job" and "we didn't have much money . . . but we got by and entertained ourselves." Speaking about "having to work eight hours" after the 1940s, workers were much more prone to use strong, exaggerated figures of speech. Questions about being able to "afford the extra time" were commonly answered in terms of high drama: the challenge to "keep the wolf from the door," "feed the family," and "put bread on the table." John L. Lewis's remark about "eating less" if the miners wanted to "loaf more" had resonance in Battle Creek, where the two extra hours became the figurative difference between life and death.

Most workers gave the appearance of taking their figures of speech quite literally. If the author dared to ask, "You don't really mean that you would have starved to death if you kept on working six hours?" the typical response was defensive, as if the author had accused the speaker of lying rather than of making his point strongly. James McQuiston (director of the Standards Department in 1933 and retired assistant to the vice president in charge of production) lectured the author about "the facts of life economically" that compelled people to work eight hours, calling six-hours "unrealistic," "nonsense," "a pipe dream."[14]

Of the group of workers contacted by the author, only three of the males who were employed after 1950 continued to talk in terms of "extra time" versus "extra money," a way of speaking common during the 1930s, and still prevalent among the women, which couched the hours issue in terms of choice. One man wrote, "I enjoyed working six hour shifts. But in all honesty my family and I enjoyed more the extra money I made by working an 8 hours shift." Another said, "Of course we gave up some income [working six hours] but it was worth it." Some of the national press coverage of shorter hours during the 1950s and 1960s also stressed choice, reporting that "what the workers want is more money, not more leisure." But over the years the rhetoric of absolute need nearly obscured this vocabulary among Kellogg men.[15]

Several workers spoke of necessity in terms of advancing "automation" or "technology." According to this new reasoning, instead of limiting the work humans have to do, automation "required" longer hours, or made the "short-shift obsolete." Others spoke of the "needs of modern management," observing that as management advanced, eight-hours, overtime, and as few workers as possible became the "scientific thing to do."

But hints of uncertainty remained. A few workers were puzzled that six-hours was "well liked to begin with" and that some kind of change had apparently occurred. Some simply refused to talk about how workers living in worse economic conditions than they could "afford" the "extra time." But others struggled with the fact that male workers during the depression and after the war had apparently been "able to afford to work only six-hours," and had voted for shorter hours instead of higher wages and "tangible" benefits. One explained his own conversion in terms of "*learning* that six-hours was not enough (he underlined the word)," and several said that "modern life is different—it just costs more." But the most common response was to dismiss the question as silly or become impatient with the questioner.[16]

Alex Senyszyn, a retired eight-hour man, somewhat wistfully admitted that there were males who could afford the extra time. "There was some dedicated . . . sportsmen, fishermen. Now, they cared less. They were like the so-called hillbillies down South; they don't care. They just want a few dollars for necessities and, hey, they'd rather be hunting and fishing all day long. . . . There are some people around here like that. . . . They just wanted to get by, that's all. . . . I wish I could have the same attitude. I mean, believe it or not, that's a good attitude. They actually had the free time. They turned down the overtime."[17]

While the "language of need" was complex, it was not as sophisticated as management's psychologically based language of "need-ascending." Nevertheless, the two shared several important rhetorical forms, primarily the permanence of "need" and the denial of a "serious" reality outside work-to-satisfy-need. Moreover, both worker and manager employed a work-based language of morals, based on the more fundamental language of need. Without phrases such as "can't afford six-hours," "have to work full-time to survive," constructions such as "It's my job" or "I have to go to work" would not have become moral imperatives.

RETREATING FROM LEISURE

Like management, senior male workers were concerned about the loss of status and control. Several men told about the friction that resulted when the men spent too much time around the house: "The wives didn't like the men underfoot all day." "The wife always found something for me to do if I hung around." "We got into a lot of fights." Many of the men confessed that they were at loose ends when they were working six hours: "I did this and that" and "nothing special" were common recollections. Few of the men who supported eight-hours had definite ideas about how to use their free time. Consequently, some felt dominated or put upon, being cast into unaccustomed roles as care-givers or servants and "taking orders from women."

Those who identified strongly with "men's full-time work" often felt uncomfortable in more relaxed, informal social settings outside their jobs, being "embarrassed" or "hauled around"; "visiting all those relatives?!" "sitting around listening to them running their mouths," and "hiding out-back until they [friends or relatives] left."

One of the most common complaints was about the amount of talking that went on. For the eight-hour men, the discourse that occurred outside work and work-based male institutions seemed excessive, new, pointless, and threatening. Frequently they reacted with satire: "Those women would go on like chickens, talking about nothing." Few saw such discourse as a force promoting community and identity outside the workplace.

During one interview, an eight-hour man remembered an old *Saturday*

Evening Post article that somebody brought into the plant in the 1950s and "showed to everybody." He left the room and returned with a yellowed clipping of "Holiday for Howie," a wonderful story about a man whose employer decided to institute a four-day work week. The article was handed around his department and became the topic of conversation at the plant for a week or so.[18]

The *Post* story, written by Nancy Pope Mayorga, describes the struggles and trials of "Big American Howie," who was "bred from Northern European stock" to be "vigorous, . . . restless, energetic, ambitious," and who finds himself face to face with a new expanse of leisure. At first Howie tells his wife, Dolores, "Now I will be really living! When a guy can push a button and make a hundred pairs of shoes and two hundred pairs of pants—and look at Univac—it's ridiculous for people to be working five days a week. Killing themselves. . . . Brace yourself. What I envision is two work days a week."

The first long weekend was "great. On Friday he washed the car, changed the oil, . . . crossed-switched the tires" and dreamed great dreams for his new leisure—travel, education, time with the wife. But soon Howie begins to slip. He starts to watch TV, drink too much beer, and get into arguments with his wife, who is definitely the one in control at home. He asks her, "Well, Doll, you don't like it? You don't want me around the house maybe."

To fight the creeping boredom, a co-worker advises him to sign up for some night classes, take up golf or a hobby. But Howie continues downhill, "staying in bed late" and drinking even more. Slowly it dawns on him that "he [and his co-workers] hadn't learned to handle time. All he could do was try to kill it . . . signing up for a night course he didn't want to take." The author of the story comments, "All the while, crazily, more time being made. . . . For what? . . . [P]laying cards . . . an extra cocktail before dinner. And science adding years to a man's life. For what? So that at eighty he can learn to dance? . . . Speed and time to be filled. . . . Is that all our civilization has contributed?"

Face to face with boredom and the meaninglessness of existence, Howie "felt like crying." Instead, "lifting his eyes from the earth," he has a vision—of "Time, gliding, receding, and suddenly, easily—for the flash of an instant it opened out to him into Eternity." In this epiphany, Howie learns the "secret! To find time in Eternity . . . that life is not just fragments of diabolical or pointless nonsense . . . but one significant whole."

In a jolting transition, the climax of the story follows:

And there would be comfort in the remembering [of the vision], and sanity. But already the little spark . . . had winked out, leaving him . . . a sense of wonder. He got up thoughtfully and drove home.

The next morning he left the house early, went straight to Acme and signed up for two days at the drill presses. He came home that night with a broad grin.

Dolores worries that he might work himself to death at this second job, but Howie reminds her, "I was being slowly killed, *amor*. . . . Time is not for me." Realizing that it was work that made her man a real man, and that leisure was turning him into a bum, his wife gushes, "Oh, Howie!" The story concludes with Howie full of new dreams for all the money he is earning: "a new car, with all the gadgets! color TV! . . . We'll be really living! Smile, Doll!"[19]

The man who saved this story recalled that it struck a responsive chord among his friends at work. He concluded, "That's just the way it was working six hours . . . like in the story the men just didn't know what to do. . . . It was bad for them. Read the story if you want to know what it was like."

The extra time outside work was simply not as secure for the men as the job. Issues of status, identity, control, and human relations were a good deal more confused. To the men, women appeared to have an advantage—they had been outside industrial work much longer and seemed more comfortable around the home and community. They also appeared to do better in the human exchanges that took place outside the competitive and highly structured workplace and marketplace.

Instead of struggling with the fluid (or liminal) state and the threat of change represented by the extra two hours, most of the men retreated from those who had been "outside" for so long and appeared to have the upper hand, falling back to their jobs, where male status and identity were more reliable. "I have to work" was more than a moral claim, it became the cry of retreat for a generation of Kellogg men.

FEMINIZING LEISURE

While glorifying "the job" and speaking of "full-time" work as a necessity by definition, eight-hour workers (with management) trivialized leisure, speaking of time off work as "lost," "wasted," "silly." They tried hard to find excuses for the few men who still supported six-hours after 1960: they were sick or old, had to farm or work a second job, were in school, or worked in places like the Bran Shed that required hard physical labor. One man (no. 136) took pains to inform the author, "I was *put* on 6 hour shift because I injured myself on 8 hour shift," reiterating at the end of his letter, "I was *placed* in a 6 hour job because of a physical injury." (The italicized words are underlined in the original.) Those for whom no excuse could be found were an enigma—true deviants from the work-only norm, labeled "sissies," "lazy," or "weird."[20]

The men even tried to find excuses for the women: they were not "the primary bread winner," "had to do the housework" or "take care of the kids." While the women continued to make the traditional, positive claims about the extra time, the dominant rhetoric condemned the six-hour women who had no good excuse as "silly girls." James McQuiston explained to the author that the reason six-hours lasted into the 1980s was that "the women liked it. . . . [T]hey go shopping for six hours. . . . And they didn't want to let loose of that. . . . They hung on to that like a puppy to a root."[21]

As a part of the rhetorical shift, shorter hours was thoroughly feminized: "six-hours was for the women." Management of course, promoted this distinction throughout the 1950s, but the men needed little persuasion; most were true believers. A typical response was: "primarily 8 hour shifts were considered male jobs & 6 hour shifts were female jobs. After the women's movement, women tried and were successful in getting into some of the male dominated jobs."[22] Other representative phrases include: "6-hours is not normal for a man," for a "family man . . . it's stupid," "this [six-hours] was for married ladies," "women aren't up to full time work," "the women didn't understand work and how important a job is, they thought they can do it part-time," "six-hours is part-time, and for the women."[23] McQuiston explained patiently to the author that men "couldn't afford the luxury of six-hours. . . . [A] man being the head of the household . . . had to provide for his family. . . . You can't do that in six hours. So little by little the men went off and the women . . . never had it so good."[24]

The content of the time outside work was also feminized; hobbies, home projects, artistic interests, were dismissed as "silly" as they were measured against the expanding importance of work. By the time the author visited Battle Creek, bird watching, church work, women's clubs, garden clubs, and even the word "leisure" had become the butt of jokes and ribald comments. For example, one worker concluded that "The six hr. shift was the reason for much hanky-panky going on in both sexes!"[25]

Some of the men questioned the author's sanity. One wrote to ask, "Can't you find something more worthwhile to waste your time with?" James McQuiston solemnly advised the author that "there's not a whale of a lot of social significance in the 6 hour day. . . . [I]t was a trivial thing, only for the women. It was just not important. You should do research about something else—you say you study leisure? Does your college pay you to do this?"[26]

NATIONAL LABOR DEVELOPMENTS

After World War II, the national labor unions continued to build a coalition with the Democratic Party, extending the "quasi corporatism" of wartime into the cold war and taking a definite turn to the political right. Nelson Lichtenstein describes these and other events as the spread of "interclass accommodation," or "labor–capital accord." Meanwhile, the labor union in Battle Creek was building its own practical and rhetorical accord with Kellogg's on local job-related issues, solidifying and strengthening the minority arrangement worked out during the 1941 strike. The two developments were interrelated and bore directly on the six-hour experiment.[27]

Just as William Green and the AFL had encouraged work sharing at Kellogg's through their push for national thirty-hour legislation in the thirties, so the AFL and American Federation of Grain Millers (AFGM) supported the local union's retreat from shorter hours by their rhetoric, policies, and political positions after World War II.

David Roediger and Philip Foner attribute labor's withdrawal from the shorter-hours battle to antilabor legislation such as Taft-Hartley, the spread of mass culture, and the rightward turn of labor itself. But the historian Ronald Edsforth argues persuasively that an even more fundamental ideological shift occurred: that it was not the expulsion of Communists so much as the drift of people like Walter Reuther toward Roosevelt's work-creation policies that defined labor after the war.[28]

I have argued that during the 1920s and 1930s, work sharing and shorter hours had a broad-based constituency that stretched from Hoover's conservative, voluntarist business projects through compromise attempts like Governor John Winant's proposal, through the AFL's thirty-hour bill, and beyond to Townsend's radical retirement proposals. It was not until after the war that shorter hours came to be identified mainly with labor's left wing, when the more radical members used shorter hours to oppose Reuther in the United Auto Workers (UAW).[29] I have also maintained that Roosevelt's administration was largely a reaction to the AFL's thirty-hour legislative proposal, and that the watershed political event of this century came when FDR, after holding labor and work sharing at bay for two years, embraced government-supported work creation as the alternative. This alternative became the defining policy of the second New Deal and has endured as FDR's liberal heritage.

"JOBS, JOBS, JOBS" has become political dogma, stretching across the political spectrum, while "the progressive shortening of the hours of labor" has lost its political voice. The Fair Labor Standards Act (which was labor's thirty-hour bill until Roosevelt co-opted it, extracted its work-sharing teeth, and refashioned it as part of his work-creation policy) effectively linked wages to hours as an either/or choice, reversing labor's traditional philosophy.[30]

Edsforth shows that after the war labor leaders like Reuther began to desert the shorter-hours, work-sharing cause to embrace Roosevelt's crusade for work creation. Speaking of Keynesian solutions, deficit spending, liberal Treasury policies, and "mass consumption" as the ways to create more job opportunities, and of higher wages as the solution to chronic problems of unemployment caused by automation, labor ignored nationally legislated work redistribution and failed to pursue work sharing in negotiations. Instead, labor heeded the advice of Leon Keyserling (chairman of Truman's Council of Economic Advisors), Chester Bowles, and Eleanor Roosevelt, and agreed that the way to prosper was to press for higher wages in a constantly expanding economy—in short, to support FDR's vision of government supported capitalism.[31]

Typical of the new rhetoric was Keyserling's speech at a conference of the Industrial Union Department (IUD) of the American Federation of Labor–Congress of Industrial Organizations in 1957. The nation's economic growth had been slowing down, he warned: "Technological productivity has not decreased . . . but production has lagged and the labor force is decreasing because we do not have enough purchasing power to create the demand needed to match our ability to produce. . . . We need a program to build up to full productivity . . . to realize America's potential." Keyserling, following the rhetorical drift of economists of his day, hinted several times that shorter hours was a "drain on total production" and would "lower the standard of living." Reuther frequently made the same point in blunt language: workers had to choose between more money or shorter hours, and for him the best, or only, choice was more money.[32]

Edsforth and Asher cite Reuther's explanation, delivered in 1949, for his abandonment of the fight for thirty-hours:

> The 30 hour week is a popular demand. . . . But what is our problem when we talk about workers' needs? Is our problem that we have got too many things in terms of clothing and housing, radios, automobiles, educational opportunities? Do we have too much of these things now and the fight is to quit making these things and have more leisure? . . . If you have a 30 hour week, you get a reduction in overall production of 25 percent . . . [you would] take out of productive effort 570 million man hours per week. . . . Our fight is we still don't have enough material goods . . . things that go into making up a high standard of living. . . . When we get to the point that we have got everything we need, we can talk about a shorter work week, but we are a long way from that place as far as my understanding is concerned.[33]

Soon afterward, the national press was covering Reuther's and labor's retreat. *Business Week* explained the "Shorter Work Week: A CIO Paradox" in 1954:

> The backbone of the UAW strength is a large group of "old-timers" . . . with long seniority in the industry. When layoffs impend, their interests are opposed to those of newer members who have less seniority. Shortening the work week would make them share the loss of earning time equally with the younger hands. Holding the work week at 40 hours, but cutting the number of employed, would leave them where they are, since layoffs are made on a strict seniority basis. Unless unemployment gets really bad and even the "old-timers" are threatened, Reuther will steer union policy to favor the interests of this group.[34]

U.S. News and World Report detected "a feeling among union officials that workers are not anxious to get a 30-hour week," and quoted George Brooks, research director of the Pulp, Sulfite and Paper Mill Workers, as saying: "Workers are eager to increase their income, not work fewer hours."[35] The *Nation's Business* quoted Reuther: "Greater leisure, for the time being can wait"; it attributed George Meany's "doubts about reducing working hours" to the "Soviet threat." Even John L. Lewis, who fought much of his life to limit hours in the coal mines, agreed: "The question of the six-hour day is one of cost. . . . When you reduce the day from eight to six hours it means a 25 per cent increase, at least, in costs. We have to consider the facts of life. If you want to stop eating so much and loaf more, we can get you the six-hour day."[36]

Such language echoed exchanges that took place during the 1941 strike at Kellogg's. The local rhetoric that branded shorter hours as "too expensive" and not a "real benefit" and even as "loafing" was voiced only by a small minority in Battle Creek before the war. After the war, such ways of speaking spread widely and came to dominate the national debate. Organized labor's old language was encapsulated by the maxim "Whether you work by the piece or by the day, decreasing the hours increases the pay." This linkage of wages and hours with a conjunction (both/and) was almost totally replaced by a disjunction that forced a tradeoff wages *or* hours.

Workers had probably recognized this disjunction much sooner; the Kellogg workers who observed, "Only an idiot would think you get as much working six-hours as eight," and "That's a silly ? [sic] Naturally 10 hrs a week more would get you more money," were speaking in timeworn idioms.[37] Yet workers had persisted in the struggle for work reduction for over a century. The national union leaders' claims about "need," their tacit assurance that workers would never admit they had "got everything we need" or would never choose to "eat less," and their hints that leisure hours were wasted, "take[n] out of productive effort," or used for "loafing," were new developments.

A direct challenge to labor's longstanding support of the "progressive shortening of the hours of labor" as well as to the traditional grassroots support of the cause, the spread of these new ways of speaking was a principal reason for national labor's abandonment of shorter hours. According to the new rhetoric, shorter hours was no longer a step forward; nothing really mattered but the bottom, cash line.

One reliable gauge of labor's shift was the *American Federationist*'s neglect of shorter hours. During the 1930s the topic received constant attention, reflecting labor's vigorous campaign for thirty hours. But after 1945 and through the 1950s, the issue virtually disappeared from the *Federationist*'s pages. Even the *IUD Bulletin*, work-reduction articles are hard to find, obscured by many articles touting economic growth as a cure-all. In the industrial unions, the emphasis had clearly shifted to endorsing government programs that stimulated economic growth and promoted "job creation." The IUD's position was spelled out in its first official Labor Day message, delivered in 1956: "National policy must be geared to an expanding economy, to full employment and to rapidly rising living standards." No mention was made of work reduction or job redistribution.[38]

For at least a decade after the war, Reuther, Meany, and the craft unions tended to react to local pressure rather than providing leadership on the shorter-hours front. The few times that the AFL addressed the issue were in response to demands from local unions.[39] Illustrative of this reactive position was an incident that occurred during the 1956 presidential campaign. In a frenzy of speech-making in Colorado Springs, Richard Nixon recalled Hoover's 1928 pledge of a "chicken in every pot" and, upping the ante, pledged that with the Republicans running things, everyone would soon have two cars in every garage and three television sets scattered around the house, but would only have to work four days a week. The hyperbole won the speech extensive coverage across the nation.[40]

Reuther immediately telegraphed Dwight Eisenhower and other Republican leaders and, making his own media splash, called Nixon's bluff, demanding that the administration show "unequivocal commitments of concrete government support for a shorter week," and that "the next session of Congress . . . propose and actively support amendments to the Fair Labor Standards Act . . . progressively reducing the workweek without reductions in weekly wages, beginning immediately, so that the four-day, thirty-two hour workweek will be reached in a reasonable period of time." Eisenhower quickly distanced himself from Nixon's gaffe, retreating to platitudes about a distant world to come where there would be plenty of money, leisure, and happiness for all.[41] All of this was high political farce, and no one, least of all Reuther, took it seriously. But the fact that shorter hours had been reduced from a central national issue to such nonsense speaks for itself.

Another revealing event occurred the same year in Akron, Ohio. The Goodyear plant in that city had gone to a six-hour day during the 1930s. Workers voted to go back to six-hours after working eight during the war, and withstood management pressure afterward. But in April 1956 the Rubber Workers' Union moved against the wishes of the majority of Goodyear workers and pressured the local to conform to an eight-hour industry standard, offering empty promises to return to the issue after establishing wage "uniformity" throughout the industry.[42]

Edsforth is correct in concluding that a "rank-and-file constituency for a renewed shorter hours movement" was "stifled 'from above' by labor leaders with different priorities." Segments of the labor movement continued the historical battle for shorter hours for a while after the war, mainly at the local level.[43] But the scarcity of local studies means that a satisfactory explanation of workers' desertion of shorter hours has not yet been given. Since it is at the local level that shorter-hour's sentiment persisted, it is in the patient, gray detail of local accounts rather than in archives of national unions that the complete story will be found.

Shorter hours emerged as the issue of the working classes in the nineteenth century and endured as a grassroots phenomenon well into this century. Hence, the withering of the movement, even though more apparent at the national level, must be traced back to the decay at the local roots. Similarly, the few glimmers of hope for renewal are now found in the "greening" of communities and in the revival of a genuine local desire for time outside the industrial state and marketplace—the time essential for the regeneration of local culture.

National developments did, however, have a direct bearing on the way Kellogg workers talked about unemployment. The union and Kellogg workers were much more inclined to give up responsibility for work sharing at the local level when national leaders assured them that so long as the government "stimulated economic growth," plenty of "good jobs" would be created. During the 1950s the local union accepted what had by then become labor's new conventional wisdom—that automation and technological unemployment were national political problems rather than the direct responsibility of local labor. Thus assured, eight-hour workers turned from sharing their own work to fight for bigger paychecks, better protection of their full-time jobs, and as much overtime as their seniority permitted, salving their consciences by voting for politicians who chanted "JOBS, JOBS, JOBS."

CHANGING DEVIANTS

Such national developments undermined support for six-hours in Battle Creek and strengthened the local forces that were eroding the shorter-hour movement. The eight-hour workers used both the new politics of

"JOBS, JOBS, JOBS" and the new rhetoric of unqualified necessity to answer six-hour critics who called them "money-hungry" and laid-off workers who accused them of being "work-hogs." By the end of the 1980s, the need-rhetoric brooked no examination, no comparisons, and no questions—not from management, other workers, the press, or, especially, scholars.

The definition of deviance had changed in Battle Creek. During the 1930s, the "work-hog" was the outsider; by the 1960s, it was the six-hour worker who was branded as different.[44] "Leisure" had become the rhetorical opposite of "serious" and "important" and "useful." The rhetorical links between "extra time" and "freedom," between "shorter hours" and "job benefit," had been broken.[45]

The new rhetorical forms emerged in Battle Creek from the local coalition of labor and management just in time to halt the drift of endless work to shorter hours, work effort to leisure. But the change in rhetoric was part of a larger strategy of retreat. Walter Lippmann called it the "escape from leisure," a shift back to existing cultural forms and away from the uncertainty and the challenge represented by shorter hours. Forces more fundamental than a mere evolution of language patterns were in operation. Unstructured time threatened traditional patterns of male authority and control. Simply put, women seemed to be more of a menace to the men during the "extra time." During this historical period, the traditional issue of control at work took a back seat to gender issues of control and power outside the job, as males joined with management to reaffirm work as life's authentic center.

Just as important as a threat was the "silliness" represented by unstructured time. Free time outside cultural forms based on work and the marketplace loomed for the men as a freedom too far, an unsafe place of perpetual change and uncertainty. And so the retreat to "full-time" work was sounded in Battle Creek.

Chapter Eight

The Six-Hour Mavericks

As senior workers continued to reap most of the benefits of the coalition with management, differences between the six- and eight-hour workers increased. Controlled by the eight-hour men by 1950, the union supported the company's plan to extend the department-by-department vote to the remaining six-hour units, over the objections of most women and workers without seniority. Six-hour supporters still insisted that any vote should be plant-wide, patterned after the two votes taken just after the war that returned a two-thirds majority against eight-hours. But the union adopted management's language and insisted that the department-by-department procedure was the "democratic" thing to do.[1]

Consequently, throughout the 1950s a series of votes were taken in the six-hour departments, following company procedure. Management permitted any worker to circulate a petition for his or her department to vote on an eight-hour schedule. Whenever a given percentage of the workers signed the petition (the percentage declined with time), management scheduled a vote, lobbied the workers to accept longer hours, publicized the arguments against shorter hours, and conducted the vote, all the while touting the democratic advantages of the system. Whenever a majority voted to keep six-hours, the procedure usually started again after a short delay.

This process caused conflicts and divisions among the workers. As the number of six-hour departments shrank, the petitions were increasingly unpopular, and six-hour supporters frequently challenged workers who were circulating them. Occasionally the petitions were jerked away and torn up, and fights occurred regularly.[2] One woman described the change: "Working six hours, people were more relaxed—as each department would change [to eight hours] many people would become angry thinking that the Co. was trying to eliminate their jobs. A lot of jobs were eliminated or doubled up."[3]

Senior workers stepped in and lobbied for the company. Using the new work rhetoric, they ridiculed the six-hour supporters and tried to sell the company's "more money for longer hours" line. Gradually the strategy worked, as department after department voted to end the six-hour shift through the 1950s. By mid-decade the balance had shifted, and the six-hour workers became a diminishing minority.[4]

In 1960, after a comfortable majority were working eight hours, management changed its position and began to press for a plant-wide vote. The six-hour workers reversed tactics as well, insisting on keeping the department-by-department vote and championing "minority rights." They had enough clout in the union to hold the company at bay on the issue until the mid-1980s, when the union finally accepted the "necessity" of a joint vote by all the remaining six-hour workers.[5]

During this process, those who wanted to work six hours transferred to the remaining short-shift departments, which became hotbeds of shorter-hours sentiment through the 1960s, 1970s, and 1980s.[6] Closing ranks, the six-hour workers formed a mutually supportive, combative, and self-identified group. Although their numbers were thinned, the remnant was purer in allegiance. Under attack from union and management, and fighting what seemed more and more to be a losing battle, they perfected their rhetoric, paring down their reasons for supporting six-hours to clear, short phrases, and sharpening their criticisms of those who had deserted the cause to keen, often-repeated barbs.[7]

After 1960, the majority of six-hour workers were women. The percentage of women grew as more men deserted, until over three-quarters of the six-hour workers were women. A few six-hour men remained into the 1980s—true deviants working either in the "girls' departments" or in the remaining six-hour "men's departments" such as the Bran Shed and Tank Farm. One woman observed that those without seniority supported the extra shift "for obvious reasons." Another worker remembered that "the union was fearful of [this] very active minority, mostly female, who posed threats to union officials."[8]

FIGHTING WORDS

Holding onto "their" six-hour shift until 1984, the six-hour workers came into direct conflict with the plant's higher wages–fewer workers coalition, challenging the new work rhetoric that solidified the alliance of senior males and management after the 1940s. By their dissent, they brought the new language of work as the center of life, total need, and trivialized "leisure" into bold relief, setting the new rhetoric against the background of their traditional shorter-hours language. With their traditional words of resistance, the mavericks contended in active discourse with eight-hour workers and management, keeping the six-hours issue alive for over forty years, even though at last the new work language and work culture emerged from the discourse as victors.

Certainly, many of the six-hour workers acquiesced in the new work rhetoric, accepting the characterization of six-hours as "girls' work," mainly for "housewives." Such people said they liked their six-hour shift for personal reasons and voted to hold onto it, but they repeated the senior men's observations that shorter hours were only for "females" who "really did not have to work," or "shoulder the responsibility" of "supporting a family." These workers also tended to employ the work-based moralistic language of the eight-hour men and to accept the accusation that the extra two hours away from the job was of little use or even "stupid" compared with work. The few males in this group echoed the dominant excuse language: they "had" to work less because they were sick, disabled, or old, or they farmed, had a physically hard job, or had a second job.[9]

But a core group of six-hour workers persisted in using the older language. Like their sister-workers of the thirties, and the majority of workers in the mid-forties, they held on to a vision of increased control and expanded freedom outside work, rejecting the Human Relations managers' claims that work should be the center of life. This group was diverse, with wide-ranging opinions about work and leisure. Moreover, their discourse was characterized by an aggregation of languages and issues; it was not pure, by any means, being highly influenced by the dominant cultures around them. But it had a clear center. In their diversity, the mavericks were unified by the traditional defense of their "extra time" and by their attacks on the new work rhetoric.[10]

A degree of dependence on work was inevitable, they admitted; after all, their job at Kellogg's paid the bills and vouchsafed their independence and control outside the plant. But absolute dependence on any job for their identity and for their needs as humans was nonsense: what the company was preaching in its Human Relations sermons was, in the words of one worker, "voluntary slavery." To these mavericks, the "freedom to work yourself to death like a dog" was irrational; industrial "progress" was absurd if it only meant "work forevermore." The mavericks also rejected management's "intrinsic worth" argument. They continued to criticize work at Kellogg's as a chore, worth little in and of itself, and to look for superior, freer activities and associations outside work. Just as workers had been doing throughout the industrial world for nearly two hundred years, they persisted in speaking of work and their jobs primarily as a means to an end. They joked about management's efforts to tell them how rewarding it was to work at Kellogg's, and they made fun of the men who struck heroic-worker postures. They held on to what they believed was simple common sense, maintaining that they were freer and more in control of their lives outside the plant than at work.[11]

The word they used most often to describe their jobs was "boring"; their most common conclusion was "the less of it the better." When they had to work long hours, some described feelings of frustration, despair, and even panic: "watching my life tick away with the clock"; "I couldn't bear to work eight hours, standing there on my aching feet"; "I couldn't wait for the shift to end"; "the clock just didn't seem to move, sometimes I thought I would scream."[12]

Joy Blanchard observed that the "only problem you have [with retirement], if you are raised in the generation of the work ethic, is you really feel guilty when you stay at home." But when the author asked her if she thought her time at work was as "rewarding" as the time she spent at home, she exclaimed, "I sure didn't! I hated to go to work, and I was delighted when I got out, and as I say, you left your mind at home. It was awful." She was most eloquent in defense of the life she lived outside the job, repeating that the various jobs she worked were never the most significant parts of her life. In comparison with the rest of her life, work was "way down the list." She explicitly rejected the claims of others—managers, "media," and "feminists"—that work was more meaningful than her "freer" pursuits outside work, such as "being with [her] boys" when they were growing up, reading, volunteering at the public library, enjoying nature, and spending time with her husband. Speaking for many of the Kellogg women, and echoing what industrial workers had been saying for nearly two hundred years, Ms. Blanchard concluded: "I had better things to do with my life than work for Kellogg's."[13]

The notion that a person could rise through hard work, devotion, the "right attitude," and persistence to a "good" (intrinsically rewarding) job met with considerable skepticism. The mavericks tended to make fun of true believers who devoted themselves to their jobs, staying all day and night at the plant. One described them as "drudges and grinds," and expressed pity for their families. Grace Lindsey saw the larger historical context clearly. "When they would keep voting on eight hours ever so often . . . I used to say you're going backward, you ought to ask for four days. I used to say that to the union people. You're going backward when you're asking for more work. But we never got anywhere with that."[14]

Some bought into the dream of "good jobs" for their children, but they continued to doubt that "work as its own reward" was a possibility for the majority of workers in Battle Creek: a few "good jobs" might still be found, but judging from their experiences only a very small, newly privileged group would have them. Advances in Human Relations management and technology notwithstanding, the overwhelming majority of jobs still seemed to be what they always had been, necessary but bothersome parts of life.

With the workers of the thirties, the mavericks held onto an older vision of work perfection—shorter hours. The six-hour workers commonly described working the six-hour shifts as "like a family." Those shifts seemed "unhurried," "relaxed," with "no pressure." Other representative phrases include "over before you knew it," "I could do the shift in a snap." "Everybody enjoyed their work—they enjoyed it, they loved it." When the job no longer took most of a person's energy and day, it became what it truly should be—subservient, no longer obscuring what it provided. Once work was tamed and put in its place, it could be done with relish and even enthusiasm. In language reminiscent of Lewis Brown's relay metaphor, mavericks spoke of short working hours and "hard work" as a natural pair—"hard work" meant intense working, not long hours. Not expecting too much from the job and doing it with dispatch and efficiency, a person could get on with the business of living. As one worker eloquently put it, "Why did I like working six hours? I did as much work as the ones on eight-hours who pretended to work and stretched it out and talked about it a lot—but I *got off* early and went home and did things" (emphasis added).[15]

The mavericks also resisted the new language of absolute necessity, continuing to talk about a choice between "extra money" and "extra time." Using a construction that had been dominant before the war, one woman wrote, "I loved the 6 hrs [because it gave me an] opportunity to devote my time elsewhere . . . [but] I didn't miss at all the extra money some got working longer." Golda Sharpsteen recalled that the six-hour women were unhappy when the plant did away with that shift because "the extra money [they made from working eight hours instead of six] didn't mean much to them." Explaining why he "followed the six-hour shift" from processing to the Bran Shed, Wayne Gleason, a farmer, said, "I was getting along real good, so there was no use in me working any more time than I had to. . . . There was more money involved in the eight-hour day but it didn't make any difference to me." By contrast, after the 1950s most of the eight-hour workers stopped talking about choice, substituting "have to work full-time" and "finding extra work" for the old time versus money formula; they had even begun speaking of steadily expanding overtime as "necessary."[16] The mavericks frequently made fun of the men's claims about "need," saying things like "only the needy and the greedy" voted for eight-hours. Several ridiculed heroic work postures, piercing the eight-hour workers hyperbole with taunts about imaginary "wolves" and "starvation."[17]

Wayne Gleason was fond of retelling the story of a friend who "gave in to the pressure" and transferred to an eight-hour department. But the "extra money" he earned was a pittance, and one day his friend gloomily assessed his choice. "He said that the only thing he got out of working eight hours was a second-hand, worn-out car that was always in the shop." Gleason, with evident delight, told of another friend who made the switch and, the week after, had to face his divorced wife in court. "She took it away from him, he had to use all the extra money he made working eight hours to pay alimony." Gleason concluded, "Everybody thought they were going to get rich when they got that eight-hour deal and it really didn't make a big difference. . . . Some went out and bought automobiles right quick and they didn't gain much on that because the car took the extra money they had."[18]

One worker told the story of the death of six-hours in his own way. "It did away with one shift—a lot of people lost good positions. [The company] did not hire for a long time [after 1984]. . . . My opinion about shorter hours is, with modern machines you could accomplish much more in a short time—it would spread the employment out. The management does not look at it that way [because] the fringe benefits per employee really count up. Six hours was what got me to Kellogg's. I really like the six hr. shift, I bid out of a couple dept. for the reason the Bran Shed was the last 6 hr dept. for men. I was a 6 hr man."[19]

A "Kellogg couple" analyzed the "need" others were talking about in terms of their improvident choices. The wife observed that people "weren't as geared up" when they were working six hours. "Now they think that if they haven't got a big boat to take or whatever . . . and some of them are really right down to the wire, if they don't get a certain amount of money they're in trouble." The husband agreed: "It used to be that we didn't buy things unless we had money saved for it. . . . Now a days they have credit cards that they can get umpteen amounts of things and 'I'll pay tomorrow.' Well, sometimes tomorrow catches up, you know." In such cases, the mavericks viewed "necessity," "need," and "have to work" as the words of voluntary slaves who, mortgaging their lives, sold themselves into bondage. Such people had given up their freedom on their own. No longer able to control the time of their own lives, they pretended that they were in the grip of an impersonal "necessity."[20]

Such stories illustrate two vital points. Evaluating "need" in terms of what people were really spending their "extra money" for, the mavericks offered a critique of consumerism, shoddy goods, and thoughtless, wasteful spending. Second, their criticism asked, "Is it worth it?" The question implies an economic calculation that differed from the majority's cash-only reckoning, a kind of time-based cost–benefit analysis. The mavericks tended to measure the financial benefits of working in terms of work's nonpecuniary costs, such as the cost of losing one's marriage, one's place in the community, or one's opportunity to "live a little." For them, the choice between leisure and "luxuries" involved a complex of pecuniary and nonpecuniary considerations that could not be simplified into an absolute "need" for cash.

Certainly, the primary reason most of the mavericks gave for being at work at all was "need," "necessity," "have to." Nevertheless, they continued to speak of their need for more money in terms of other needs and values, such as work sharing, and they persevered in labor's traditional call for higher wages *and* shorter hours. Further, the mavericks continued to insist that six-hours was "realistic" and that it was possible for them to make "enough" on the short shift to live reasonably; they still spoke of being free to choose to work less than eight hours. They rarely said that their economic "need" was so great that it could "force" them to give up the "extra time" and additional control over their lives. They spoke often of the need for money and the need for time off together, and of balancing the two needs by controlling their work hours.

Both the eight-hour men and the six-hour mavericks laid claim to "necessity." Some of the men accused the married women of not really having to work and of taking away a man's job. After all, a man "had to support a family" and therefore faced real "necessity." But the women were solid in defense of their own "need" to work. The way that the two groups proposed to settle the stalemate is revealing. The men proposed that the women give up their jobs so that men could work "full-time" (reducing the number of workers on the payroll). The six-hour mavericks offered to share their work rather than claiming that their need was absolute or took precedence over another's need to work. They continued to accuse the eight-hour men of taking more than "their fair share" of the available work; for them, the "need" the men spoke about when they were already "making more than enough" was deceptive—unqualified "need" was a ruse used to justify their greed to others with real, even desperate, need.[21] Fighting against the prevailing rhetoric, the mavericks continued to speak of their "need" to work as relative; calculated in terms of wise or foolish choices, in comparison with the needs of others and the need to do their "own work," and in relation to their preference for doing things outside their jobs and housework.

The most obvious difference between the mavericks and other Kellogg employees was the way they talked about unemployment and work sharing. Even though their language was more traditional, after 1960 it became distinctive because of the ascendancy of the opposing work-based language of morals. Instead of accepting the need to work full time as a moral solvent that absolved personal choice and blurred social injustice, the mavericks persisted in taking personal responsibility for their work behavior and expecting it from others. Unlike most of the men at the plant and organized labor in general, the mavericks were not content to accept abstract economic theory in the place of individual responsibility, and they resisted the rationalization that unemployment was simply a national problem to be solved by national economic growth. For them, dealing with unemployment entailed more than voting for liberal politicians who promised to create more "good jobs."[22]

Like W. K. Kellogg and the workers of the 1930s, the mavericks tended to see unemployment, at least in part, as a local problem, to be met locally by a fair redistribution of the available good jobs. The unemployed and those without decent jobs had faces. The mavericks spoke repeatedly about relatives or neighbors who needed work and would "love to get on at Kellogg's," but seldom about "the national unemployment problem." They repeatedly took personal exception to the "work-hogs" who were leaving no work for those truly in need. One remembered that her nephew tried for a long time to get a job at the plant, but "Kellogg's was laying off people while some of the men were working really fantastic amounts of overtime—that's just not fair."[23]

One woman wrote, "I felt when they voted for the women to go on 8 hours after I returned, it only caused a whole shift to be unemployed. It was only the older, hungry money [sic] people who wanted 8 hours, not caring about younger employees." One woman remembered that once she had thought that six-hours would be the "next step, after eight-hours" for all workers, but that the "only thing is, too many people were greedy." Helen Colles remarked that "they weren't satisfied. They always wanted more money. . . . They get more money but for the long run, I don't know if you gain much. . . . People are never satisfied."[24]

Another woman wrote that only "those who were greedy or needy" wanted eight-hours. It "would make fewer jobs and automation was already taking lots of jobs. Young people were looking forward to getting jobs at Kellogg's and would have less opportunity if there were no 6 hours. One other thing about having fewer employees is that it weakens the union. Automation has really taken jobs." Another commented, "Anybody who realized the elimination of 6 hr shift would mean fewer jobs" voted for six-hours. Another remarked, "I think the 6 hr. shift was the greatest that ever happened in the work force. It gave more people employment especially women."[25]

Several of the workers commented on the shrinking payroll, attributing the change to the elimination of the six hour shifts. One woman wrote, "Now [1990] Kellogg's is working employees double shifts & week ends besides being on 8 hours, so more jobs are not available that would be otherwise. . . . It saddens me as Kellogg's used to be an employer of so very many people." Another noted, "A lot more people were employed on the 6 hour shifts. There used to be about 5,000 employees when I first started work [1953] and now about 2,000. . . . [S]omething's wrong down there." A male worker wrote, "At one time Kellogg had 4,000 workers, now about 2,000—in five more years [probably] 1,200, so things do change." One told the author that when she "started there was better than 4,300 and some, and when I quit there was a little over 2,000. . . . [N]ow [management] is thinking of quantity"—instead of people and their need to work.[26] Cecelia Bissell recalled that "Mr. Kellogg said in the beginning, 'Let's employ more and let them work less hours and they'll do a better job for you,' and I believe it. Well, I'm old-fashioned."[27]

A few of the mavericks, as well some of the eight-hour workers, talked about the senior male–management coalition, which was as evident to them as it is to the historian. Art White remembered that "the company figured there was too much benefits. So they started out by separating. They said to the mechanical people, you work 8 hours. We're gonna pay you time and a half Saturday. Whooeee. So that sort of split things up. . . . There was this guy . . . that came into the toilet, had a booming voice, 'By god, look at this,' holds out his check. Made a hundred and . . . who cares what he said he made because he worked Saturday. And the rest of the guys sitting behind the toilet doors thinking, 'My god, how did he do that? He's as dumb as I am' . . . so it . . . it gnawed at you."[28]

One woman condemned the more money–fewer workers deal because it eliminated so many jobs: "Employers and stockholders' greed [was] not [the] only thing, employees are greedy too. . . . [They give] little thought about sharing the work . . . to provide more jobs. Unions going for benefits and wages only . . . locked employers into a system that required keeping the number of employees down. . . . So we build a bureaucracy whose jobs depend on people staying poor." Another woman observed, "W. K. Kellogg was for six hours so to cut down on unemployment. When he died and it was taken over by [the] board of directors they wanted to cut down on benefits to so many people. They started putting in automatic machines and computers and laying off people . . . and the union went along with this because of the money." Another blamed "the union's demands for higher pay and fringe benefits and the company desire . . . to automate and cut its workforce to affect these demands."[29]

"It just seemed to be like money was the main thing," Cecelia Bissell said. "We'll pay you more money and you'll do what we say and that's it. And I thought, no, that's not the way to go. Maybe it's money wise. [But] you have to live with yourself. . . . I had the best time of any when I worked [six hours]. I still remember it like it was yesterday. . . . The fun we had and we still got the work out and we did good work. . . . I'm on my way to a Kellogg luncheon with girls I used to work with, and we talk about it once a month—how it used to be."[30]

In sharp contrast, most of the male workers talked about the reduction of the payroll in terms of "necessity": "The company had to cut the payroll to be competitive," "six-hours was not efficient," "it was impossible for the company to keep so many people on, they had to cut back the number of workers." "Hell, [six-hours] just won't hold water," Mc-Quiston concluded.[31]

Joy Blanchard used some of the most revealing and lucid moral language to be heard in the city. After discussing the history of Kellogg's for over an hour and gracefully submitting to television cameras in her living room, she escorted the author to the door, making small talk about families. Standing by her front door, she spoke about her children's lives and her worries for them, worries that "are always there for parents no matter how old [the children] are." She was concerned that one of her two sons, even though he had a "good job—it pays well," worked all the time, "night and day. He has no time to live, to visit and spend with his family, and to do the other things he really loves to do." But her daughter was "still struggling, looking for a good job," and was out of work more than she would like to be.

Blanchard read a moral into the story of her children, equally gifted and willing to "work hard." "Something is not right" in the economy, she observed, when work causes serious problems of "overwork for so many" and unemployment and marginal employment for even more. "People should remember what Kellogg's did, there is a lesson to be learned."[32]

Another worker made a similar observation. "I think . . . 6 hr. was the answer, also if more factories had adopted 6 hr. there wouldn't be such a drastic difference in pay checks."[33] Velma Plumb asked the person interviewing her if she had ever heard of Arnold Toynbee. When the interviewer admitted that she had not, Ms. Plumb responded, "Anyone going to college should have heard of Arnold Toynbee. . . . I recall reading something he said. 'We will either share the work, or take care of people who don't have work.' He said it in so many words."[34]

It is impossible to judge how widespread such ideas were in Battle Creek and even harder to determine their origin. But the historian cannot but marvel that workers' conversations in the early 1990s still echo economists and historians from the first part of the century. The "welfare economists'" abstract notion that the free operation of the market frequently results in immoral outcomes, and the more concrete claims of John Ryan and Stuart Chase that a shorter workday is an efficient way to redistribute work and a fair, voluntary, and effective way to redistribute income, survive in the ordinary conversation of the people who live in Battle Creek.

The mavericks employed an older moral language of personal responsibility and remained skeptical of the prevailing claims made in the name of the "free market." The wonderful proposition at the heart of laissez-faire capitalism, that the greatest good for all is obtained in a marketplace where everyone is seeking only his or her own advantage, was critically examined in Battle Creek. The mavericks argued forcefully that it was not right simply to get as much as possible for oneself and let others take care of themselves. They continued to see personal choice as an integral part of moral economic behavior, and they founded their defense of six-hours on concrete, moral grounds, using words like "work-hog," "greedy," "sharing," and "fair."

Their language of morals was more complex than that of the majority because it did not include the "hard work" test. Certainly the mavericks valued work as part of responsible living, agreeing that the foundation of moral action is taking responsibility for oneself, financial and otherwise. But "hard work" had not become the fetish it was for the majority—it was not a moral solvent, absolving a person from other moral claims of the family and community. Responsibly included, but transcended, "hard work" in the modern economic arena. For the mavericks, words such as "enough," and a sentence such as "Excessive working is bad for a person and those around him," still made good moral sense.

Moreover, unlike the eight-hour workers, the mavericks did not establish "hard work" as the moral high ground from which to condemn others less fortunate. Luck, economic class, and social position had as much to do with financial well being as "hard work." Commenting on the men's claims, one woman concluded, "They should try being a woman sometimes and work like a dog for little at the plant and nothing at home—then they would know what 'hard work' is."[35] In the mavericks' view, most people worked hard enough when they were given a fair chance; laziness was not the issue. Accordingly, some criticized the "hard work" moral test as unfair, especially as used by the "work-hogs" and managers who controlled access to work. As one worker put it, "Those that shout the loudest about hard work, pretend to work most of the time and stretch it out as long as possible, and do less real work than anybody." He cited a current television commercial for a national investment firm that made the claim, "We make money the old-fashioned way. We earn it." "Horseshit," he exclaimed. "They do less real work than anybody and shout the loudest about it."[36]

For the mavericks, the fourth shift was a moral issue. It became a symbol of their willingness to respond to laid-off and unemployed workers in personal terms and to speak of their own "need" in relation to the "needs" of others.[37] They also took issue with the majority's claims that six-hours was "unrealistic" and" impractical." Like Brown and W. K., they stressed the "efficiency" of shorter hours, arguing that as much was produced in six hours as in eight because there were fewer breaks and people were willing to work harder. "I feel they got more production in 24 hrs on the six hour shifts. . . . [People] worked harder with no 'burnout' [and there were] shorter 'break times.'" "People worked harder on 6 hours and did not get so tired—the average employee did not do any more on eight hours than on six—[they] took more breaks [on the eight hour shifts]. . . . [S]ix hr. [was]Δa happier place to work." "Various jobs never became boring and it seemed as tho the shift was over very rapidly. . . . Every one seemed to look forward to going to work. I believe there was less abuse of quick breaks and lunch relief and greater job attention." "Refreshed employ[ees arrived] every 6 hrs. [so there was] no slacking off at the end of the shift. Work areas cleaned up 4 times a day instead of 3." "[A] new crew every six hours is bound to be better than three crews at eight hours. . . . You're not tired. . . . [Y]ou're kinda pepped up." "Now they stretch the work out—make it last as long as possible. They do it because they want overtime—if you can make the work last, you can get more work."[38]

Several blamed the coalition for pressing hard for the kind of benefits that penalized the company for having a large payroll. "Company paid benefits, is what killed the 6 hours." "Fringe benefits began to creep in and began to expand to the point that they were a cost factor that began to alarm the company. As union contract demands were negotiated and benefits expanded, it created a common term called 'the cost of having a person on the payroll.' Items such as: Health insurance, Life insurance, unemployment insurance (state & federal), free work clothes, laundry, subsidized food service, even providing soap and a employees' credit union, all became a fixed charge per person. Reducing the number of employees thus became [a] constant desire of the company and of course the 6 hour shift was the area the company could make gains." A Kellogg couple agreed that "you got a union in and each year the union wants more, [and] more benefits. Now I'm not against unions, but I do say some of them run themselves up. . . . And I think that's one reason why they had to jump up [to eight-hours] . . . to combine certain things if they wanted more money for [benefits], they had to combine more jobs." Still another talked about the "cost effectiveness" of longer hours, arguing that eight-hours came back because the "company had to pay benefits for a whole shift of people."[39]

One remarked that "it didn't have to be that way—benefits used to be tied to hourly wages and pro-rated—but the union pressed for flat benefit rates, like health insurance, that cost the same for all workers no matter how long they worked or how much they make—so it is no wonder that management is trying to get rid of as many workers as possible.[40]

DEFENDING LEISURE

The men trivialized and feminized leisure. The mavericks countered with a traditional but fading vision. They presented leisure as a reasonable alternative to work as the center of life, holding on to the old notion that work was important primarily as a means to other, more important ends. They continued to support increasing leisure as a legitimate, practical reward for submitting to work discipline and for enduring the rigors of industrialization. For them, expanding leisure was still a reasonable freedom needed to compensate them for modern jobs that were *less* intrinsically rewarding.

Defending leisure against work's mounting cultural hegemony, the mavericks took issue with accusations that time outside work was good for nothing but idleness and the foolishness of women. They opposed the rising tide of words and stories that made fun of time away from work, and they distinguished what they did in their free time from what they saw the majority of the men doing. Several accused the full-time men of "doing nothing but watching TV" or "laying around" after work. The men, of course, tended to invoke necessity: they had "little energy for doing things" when they left work. Whatever the excuse, the mavericks claimed it was the full-time men who led the way to passive, isolated, and worthless leisure. "Most of the men just stop trying when they got off work." "It was a chore to get him [the husband] to do anything at home or go anywhere—they [the men in general] thought it was enough to go to work."[41]

Of course such leisure was silly, even debilitating. But it was decidedly not what the mavericks had in mind when they defended their extra time. As one woman put it, "The benefits of the six hour work day depends upon the quality of the use of time made available by the shorter hours." While "crafts," "recreation," "hobbies," "pastimes," "games," even "leisure" were being discredited in the local discourse, the mavericks continued to speak of free time in more traditional ways, as "a chance to go places and do things." Leisure was for vigorous activity and important purposes; it was not easy or merely a time to be idle. It was the very reverse: "When you get off work, that's the most important part of the day, when you can get your own work done, and live a little."[42]

The mavericks tended to talk about the new, enervated leisure with regret. Some spoke of having lost important parts of their lives because of the advent of worthless leisure and the dominance of mass culture. "We used to talk more, tell stories and do things together. Even though we were poor and couldn't do a lot [of activities that required money] those years [during the Great Depression], we had more fun together—going on trips and walks, down to the lake. It seems like we just did more . . . now people stay home and watch television. They only go out to the malls and to shop." The women spoke most often of family activities being shortchanged. But some also mentioned doing fewer things with friends and in the community. For example, one remembered that "we used to visit more, spend the night or a couple of days—take more time for reunions and so forth—now it's work all the time."[43]

Few blamed the mass media and consumerism exclusively. They talked as often about the change in how people felt about work and leisure. As Joy Blanchard said, most workers "found nothing better to do" than watch television, shop, or gossip, so "they just as well go back to work."[44]

THE PROMISE OF LEISURE, PART ONE:
PRESERVING CULTURE

The mavericks held out for their vision of positive leisure. Speaking about their time outside their industrial jobs, they used much of the same language as the women in Best's 1932 study, speaking primarily of "being free to," "able to," "have a chance to." As in the thirties, a "language of freedom" was the dominant idiom. "The women were just crazy about [the six-hour shift]," Cecelia Bissell remarked. It "gave us time, like I said, for our families, . . . it gave you time for your homework, [but it also] gave you time for outside activities."[45]

As in the thirties, the mavericks' syntax reveals a complex, comparative use of "freedom" that allows the following sentence: "When I get off my job at Kellogg's, I have the chance to do my work at home; when I get through ordinary housework I find some time to do a little gardening, after which I might be free to read to the children." This language of "freedom ascending" is the obverse of the language of "need ascending" used later by management, the eight-hour workers, and Maslow.[46]

Like the workers in the earlier period, the mavericks spoke mainly of their "extra time" as freer than their jobs, and they emphasized the increased personal control they experienced when they "got off work." They also spoke of "getting the housework out of the way" and of having "some time of my own" after the job at the plant. Other representative words, phrases, and language patterns that closely resemble the 1930s usage include descriptions of leisure as time "outside" both work and housework, their claims to ownership of the extra time (expressed by the general use of personal pronouns, such as "extra time to myself"), and their discussions about using leisure to preserve traditional cultural forms and explore new social arrangements and activities.[47]

Representative examples of the maverick's language include: "Loved [working six hours. . . . It gave you much more time to do more outside the job, . . . more time for family affairs . . . time to enjoy my home and family." "[Six-hours] gave me more free time to do other things and I was seldom too tired to . . . play." "I worked the noon to six [shift]—I could get children off to school—keep house in good shape, prepare food for dinner, go to work, come home, have dinner with the family and still have time and energy to enjoy family & hobbies." "I loved the 6 hrs. [It gave me the] opportunity to devote my time elsewhere & still gave me ample income for a lot of extras." "[It] made a vast difference in attitudes regarding their work." A six-hour man wrote, "Loved working 6 hr—more free time. Preferred 6 p.m. to midnight—days free for hunting, fishing, family. Wife and I worked different shifts so [we] could supervise our children." "[It gave me] time for . . . fun." "Of course we gave up some income but it was worth it." "Everyone talked more leisure time." "[Six-hours] gave me time to enjoy my home and family." "Some people were so sad about losing 6 hours, they quit."[48]

The mavericks emphasized the importance of leisure as the savior of culture and tradition, even more than the women in the 1930s. Perhaps because they were witness to the accelerating decline of community and family caused by mass culture, they were even more anxious to find an antidote. Many of the complex, traditional activities and products that defined culture for the six-hour workers in 1932, such as food preparation, gardening, making clothes, home decorations, music, even conversation, were increasingly bought and passively consumed by the 1980s. In the midst of this collapse of both "the discussional" and the public places for discourse, the mavericks turned to their extra time, finding there an opportunity to keep important parts of their lives going that were in danger of disappearing altogether.

Taken in the right way, the mavericks believed that mass culture, packaged foods, and modern technology could be a blessing. They embraced modern life when it meant more freedom from drudgery and housework. Labor-saving devices at home and the modern supermarket were just fine if they were not misused. But when they took away challenge and encouraged passivity, they were dangerous. Like the women of the thirties, the mavericks distinguished between free activities and their work at home on the basis of choice. "When I have to fix meals every day, that's not much fun. But when you can buy bread, but still you bake for yourself once and a while, that is." Just as in the thirties, leisure provided a limited opportunity to conserve and transform common, traditional household crafts and skills that were superannuated by the culture of consumerism.[49]

Two women mentioned preparing food for holidays as an example of conserving and transforming leisure. Whereas they used whatever labor-savers were available to free them from the daily grind, when the holidays came, they were "glad" to spend hours in the kitchen, preparing traditional foods and getting things ready for the festivities—especially if others joined in. They used these special occasions to teach children about traditions and encourage conversation. One woman talked about rituals of setting the table: how she loved putting in the extra table leaves, using the fine china and tablecloth. She told how important it was for her to see her children playing under the table during the meal, where she had played as a child.[50]

Some women criticized the men for corrupting the time that family and friends had together and for not taking active roles in the celebrations and rituals. Football on television was specifically mentioned as a point of considerable contention. One woman suggested that holiday celebrations are declining also because people have become more passive and are trying to buy celebration. "People's ideas of fun have changed—now it's the less you have to do the better. I remember so much more going on during holidays. We had more to talk about and to do together, the food and decorations and all. Now people just gossip."[51]

A revealing interchange between husband and wife occurred during one of the author's trips to Battle Creek. Art White, using language the author had come to expect, began the interview by denying that he ever had any extra time in his life, and insisted that when he worked six hours he had to work other jobs as well: "You couldn't exist without [a second job]. You couldn't even sub-exist." But as the interview progressed, and his wife, Donnelly, joined in, the discussion turned from the pat rhetorical forms to details.

ART WHITE: I purposely bid into a six hour department so that Donnelly and I could get up, go to breakfast like we are doing this morning . . . , go to work, work diligently for six hours, then come home and go to supper.

AUTHOR: Now, wait a minute. You gave me the impression that the only thing that you did when you had the six-hour day was work. Now you are talking about something else. Are you spending more time with your wife here?

ART WHITE: Of course, of course. [After the children moved away] there was just Donnelly and I. What you gonna do? Get a divorce?

DONNELLY WHITE: I like Art. I like to be with him a lot. . . .

AUTHOR: Did you think that [six-hours] was good for your marriage?

DONNELLY: Yes!

AUTHOR: The time . . . breakfast?

DONNELLY: Oh yes, yes.

ART: She is a very good person to be with.

DONNELLY: Yes.

ART: You do, Donnelly? It didn't hurt?

DONNELLY: No, some people say . . . that too much time around your partner is bad for you, but some people thrive on it.[52]

One woman resisted the identification of "housework," however grueling, with the kinds of industrial, rationalized work she had to do at the plant. She expressed resentment at those who equated the two and who said "the women preferred six-hours because they had housework to do." Those who confused the two kinds of work had never experienced housework, in her view—its complexity, its demands, its difficulty, or its rewards. Several of the mavericks challenged the company and the unions for trivializing their housework and home duties as well as their "leisure," and countered with their own attacks against the new myths and romance of "the Job."[53]

Like the women of the thirties, they were perfectly capable of distinguishing drudgery from household activities they chose to do and enjoyed. As in the thirties, commonplace crafts and skills that once had been part of regular home duties were transformed when they were chosen for themselves, set aside in a special time and place such as a holiday, when people were, as Johan Huizinga observed, "apart together."[54]

Other home- and community-based traditional activities, such as storytelling, "doing things together as a family," "church work," "helping out in the community," visiting, active sports, skating, and softball were also threatened by mass culture and the trivializing of leisure. Like the workers of the thirties, the mavericks spoke of their hope that "extra time" would help to keep such activities alive, remembering that when "people were not working all the time, we seemed to have more time and do more things together."[55]

When Amy Saltzman's excellent Downshifting was published in 1991, the author decided to ask some of the Kellogg workers about the metaphor that she used to focus her book, the "empty front porch."[56] Each Kellogg worker confirmed Saltzman's claim, agreeing that the front porch was once an important public space in neighborhoods all over Battle Creek, at least during the summer and fall. Before the coming of television, it was an informal place where community business and discourse regularly took place. Before the 1950s, families would sit and talk daily in the evenings after dinner, neighbors would drop by, and kids would get together to play, watched by the adults. But they also agreed that the front porch is "empty now . . . practically nobody sits outside now, if they aren't working late, they are watching TV"— "and the kids are by themselves and run wild."[57]

Several of the mavericks recalled trying to preserve what their neighborhoods used to be. After talking about the empty front porch, each added that she still was trying; one was active in the garden club, another in her church, still another as a volunteer working with a seniors' club. But the key ingredient missing was time: "Nobody has time today—everybody is working overtime." One speculated that if the six-hour day had continued, "maybe things would be different, maybe we would spend more time together and maybe still be sitting on the front porch."[58]

Describing what they did in their "free time," several mavericks mentioned "helping out" in the community, doing volunteer work at the library and in the schools. They contrasted their volunteerism with what they saw as a rising tide of apathy and unconcern among the majority who had given up their community responsibilities, mouthing platitudes about "hard work."[59]

It is revealing to trace the path of several of the interviews conducted by the author and his students. A typical conversation would start with the question, "What did you think about working six hours, and what did you do when you were off work?" After praising the short shift, several mavericks responded that they made "good use of the extra time," doing creative household projects and crafts and helping out in the community. They would then give examples, "I was very active in my children's schools and the PTA," and conclude with criticism of those who "thought they were too busy" to do volunteer work, adding that the reason communities and families were falling apart was that most people claimed they had more important things they "had" to do.

Farming was one of the most common responses to questions about what people were doing when they worked the six-hour shift. As in the thirties, the farming that the mavericks described was a complex mixture of concerns, some financial, others cultural. One man admitted that his efforts were more "hobby than farming." He had inherited a marginal but beautiful farm east of town and had in his youth tried to "make a go of it." "Farming changed," large farms crowded out the small operations, and he had to sell off parts of the farm over the years. But he held on to the home place and a few acres and to the parts of farm life he loved. He got a job at Kellogg's during the war, working the short shift. The extra time permitted him to keep a few cattle and sheep and raise enough corn to feed them. He also continued to take care of the old orchard and enlarged his garden so that he was able to sell some fruits and vegetables each year. But his main source of income was Kellogg's. As he put it, "I borrowed from the credit union in the spring to cover my farming, and if I got

CHAPTER EIGHT

enough in the fall to pay it back, I was happy. If I could break even on the farming, that was all I wanted."[60]

A few persisted, trying to work six hours at Kellogg's and keep a modern, complex farm operation going. But most were cutting back, preserving selected aspects of farming during their leisure just as the women were preserving certain home crafts and traditions. Like the women, the "farmers" often gave away what they produced to neighbors and friends, for the same reasons: the produce was "special," distinguishable from store-bought and therefore perceived to be much better. "You can't buy tomatoes at the store, I don't know what they sell that looks like a tomato, but it's not a tomato" is a representative claim about the advantages of things produced outside the marketplace—produced carefully, for the sake of the doing.[61]

One man kept bees and raised some timber "on the side." He said that he regretted that traditional farm skills were disappearing with the family farm and that children would have to grow up not knowing the responsibility and satisfaction that come from caring for plants and animals. He told how he loved to "fool" with bees, even though his wife complained about the expense of the hives and "supers." His children complained as well about being made to help out, but he argued that the experience taught responsibility and work discipline. He also hoped that by making the extraction and canning of honey into a family activity, he could share his love for traditional farm activities: "What are they going to do otherwise on Saturday? Working in the garden will give them something to be interested in when they grow up. If they can see how rewarding and satisfying [farming] is, I have given them something valuable, something worthwhile."[62]

"Kellogg's used to have one of the best ball teams in Battle Creek," one couple recalled. " . . . [B]ack then [1930s–1940s], Kellogg's and Post's and Clark's and IPI . . . all had good ball teams. . . . [T]hey were just like the American League and the National League. . . . [O]ut there where the [city] park is now, he [W. K.] had a swimming pool and a wading pool for the youngsters. . . . Back then they could be content with things like playing ball. We weren't as geared up."[63] Several other older workers commented on the loss of semi-pro and amateur baseball and softball in Battle Creek. One man remembered, "Everybody used to play and the women, at least softball—the whole town turned out for the games—it was where everybody got together in the summer. That was just magic—like baseball ought to be played—you knew most of the players and talked to them on the street. So much went on in the afternoons at the ball field, all sorts of things besides the game. You had characters in the stands, yelling and telling stories. Kids would be all over playing. I could tell you stories from now till dark. But now it's all professional and impersonal and just for the money, nobody has time for local sports—all that money has ruined things."[64]

The Blanchards talked about bowling. Mr. Blanchard recalled that "bowling was quite the thing" in the 1940s, and that because he lived near the youth building in town, he spent much of his free time there playing a variety of games with friends. "There was a group of us, three or four of us." Mert Barber spoke of changes in the Kellogg Sportsmen's Club. When he worked for the company, fishing was a popular local activity. The club sponsored ice-fishing contests with prizes donated by local sporting goods shops—all "very informal. . . . Now it's a whole different thing. If you go fishing you have to have a ten-thousand-dollar cruiser. [It's a] different kind of fishing—we fished with night crawlers for northerners and perch and bluegill—the trout fishers were a bunch of ordinary guys. Now it's real fancy and expensive."[65]

While none of the mavericks expected the return of amateur sports played as they used to be, several described the disappearance of games like softball and ping-pong to illustrate a larger point: that something was lost when leisure and participant sports were degraded and culture commercialized. Amateur sport stood as a reminder of enjoyable community activities that involved large numbers of people in active participation. As such, it survived in stories as emblematic of something better than passive and mass amusements; it was a memory to pin their hopes on and to show the way to something better.

THE PROMISE OF LEISURE, PART TWO:
CREATING CULTURE

The mavericks spoke somewhat less often than the workers of the thirties about the changes in social roles taking place during the "extra time." Whereas there was considerable discussion about who was responsible for "home duties" in 1932, when unemployed husbands were at home, the mavericks did not press quite as hard on this or other controversial matters.

A few Kellogg Couples did, however, comment on child care. Joy Blanchard, for example, insisted that one of the most significant results of six-

CHAPTER EIGHT

hours was that her husband, Charles, took an active role in raising their children, becoming a "room parent" at their school when a male at primary school was a novelty.

When the author showed her a draft of this book that neglected this story, she wrote insisting on its significance. "We were ahead of the times," she stressed, leading the way in liberating women from bondage at home and freeing men for home activities such as child care. She saw expanding leisure as a great support for the modern family—a resource that husband and wife could use to strengthen and develop the family. With several others, she regretted the loss of the time spent with the family and concluded that the scarcity of time at home was a primary reason for crime, teenage pregnancy, and the decline of families and communities.[66]

Several of the mavericks recognized that the extra time was a cultural resource, available for the extension of existing culture and creation of the new. Like the women Best interviewed in 1932, they spoke of their gardening as part of a community effort, involving neighborhood beautification projects and garden clubs.[67]

A few of the mavericks linked education with leisure. They talked about their education in terms of the dreams they once had of finding a job related to what they studied in school. What they had been led to expect—that their schooling would have something to do with their future work—had not come true. The interests and skills they had picked up in high school or college, in music, writing, art, nature, even history, would have gone for nothing unless they had kept them alive outside their work. One spoke of the piano lessons she took through school, her dreams of playing as a "professional," and the reality of life and work. She then described playing as a volunteer "at school and the church," the role her music played in her family, occasions when her family would sing together while she played, and how her "playing for fun" taught her children to love music.[68]

Another had been an amateur naturalist all her life. She dreamed of "becoming a biologist" when she was in school, but "there were not that many jobs for biologists." Telling a story that was often repeated by the mavericks, she described leaving school for the "real world" and adjusting to the disappointment with the world of work by turning to her "free time." As an adult, she continued to study nature as she had as a young woman. "Birding" was her passion, getting her up in the early mornings to roam the parks and fields of the county. She argued that "you really don't need to be a professional to be a naturalist, even though the pros usually look down on the amateur." She claimed that her observations and collections were as valid as those of any naturalist who was paid by the state, but she was willing to do these things for free, for their own sake. This made her nature-study special: "I think I might even enjoy nature more than the pros—for me it has nothing to do with work or a job, it's totally when and where I want to do it. I don't have to answer to the people who give me money or worry about reputation and position." She also envisioned her role in the community as a special teacher, taking children and adults outside to show them the wonders of nature, "so they can learn to enjoy nature throughout their lives—nature is something that everybody can do and should learn to love. This is what I try to teach, doing it for the love of it—you know that's what 'amateur' means, don't you?—'for the love of it'?"[69]

One woman spoke about learning to play tennis in middle age. She was active most of her life, working and caring for children. She had also been athletic in school, playing softball. But her tennis was different; for her it was a "life time sport, something that is good for me and which I enjoy." Another kept a diary most of her life, writing almost daily. She protested that "it's not much." Still, it was evident from her conversation that the daily writing was an important part of the life of the mind, as important to her as the "serious writing" of those who publish books and articles. She said that she had loved to write all her life, and that she was "good at it," winning a prize in school for composition. Instead of just giving up when she graduated, she persisted. Even though "some of my folks think it's silly," she found in her daily writing a practical opportunity to express herself and to experience one of the most sublime of human activities. She also hoped that she would inspire others to write by her example, and dreamed that people would eventually read her works when she was gone.[70]

One woman made a lifetime hobby of family and local history. She was full of information and stories about Battle Creek and eager to share them with a stranger. She was the first to describe the senior male–management coalition and the higher benefits–wages for fewer workers deal at Kellogg's; she understands that six hours ended because "people changed their minds about work and leisure." During our interview, she brought out some family albums and gave a detailed account of parts of her family's past and the history of her Battle Creek neighborhood. She took pride in being the family historian, remarking that she was "the one they called" about names and events from the past. She understood perfectly that by keeping their past, she was providing coherence and identity to the group of people she cared most about. But she also said that she did it for "fun. . . . It's what I love to do. Bring out the albums when everyone comes back home. You should see the children. They love to look at their own pictures, but their eyes light up when they see pictures of their dad as a baby and their grandma. . . . They love the stories too that go with the pictures."[71]

Listening to her, the author began to question his own motives and wonder whether it was right take her stories and use them for his own purposes. Who was the real historian in the room, and which history, the author's or the amateur's, contained the other? The author imagined that she would be telling about the "historian" from Iowa City in the years to come, and that the truth she told might be the real history, the more authentic account to come from that interview.

Several of the mavericks experimented during their leisure, finding an unexpected place to use their modern education. They were well aware that "hobbies," "crafts," and "pastimes" are devalued in the language and avoided in schools. Nevertheless, they persisted, arguing for the legitimate role of lifetime sports and the democratic uses of the liberal arts. Like the women of the thirties, they created new culture in their time outside the dominant institutions of work and the state. Fragile and scorned by the dominant culture, activities such as lifetime sports survived with the six-hour day.

The mavericks talked less about the promise of modern, technological kinds of leisure activities than the women of the thirties. When they discussed their extra time, they rarely talked about movies, radio, television, driving, and the like except in a critical fashion. Perhaps because they were embattled, holding out for shorter hours against the odds and watching their traditional cultures collapse before the onrush of mass culture, the mavericks were more defensive and "conservative," speaking more about their hope that leisure would preserve endangered culture and shying away from technological forms of leisure.

THE PROMISE OF LEISURE, PART THREE:
A PEACEABLE KINGDOM

A few of the women, a minority of the mavericks, expressed surprise that the men felt threatened by the changes in social roles that the extra leisure permitted. "Holiday for Howie," the story that appeared in the *Saturday*

Evening Post in the fifties, amused and perplexed this group, for they did not agree that the issue was "who was in charge" of the extra time. Rather, they saw the new time as an opportunity to find a place *outside* conflict, exchange, and exploitation for people to be together, freely and peaceably.[72]

After establishing that the place for leisure was *outside* need, work, and social roles, this group used two groups of words to describe their leisure: one building around the undefinable "play," the other around the more concrete "together." The women described their leisure as a "time apart" by talking about "play," "fun," "enjoyment," "laughter," and "having a good time." They also spoke in terms of "being together," "sharing or giving," "doing things" or "spending time together," "getting together," "taking part and participating," "mutuality," and keeping "company."[73]

Being apart together, "no one has to be in charge when you're having fun." A person who always tried to give orders in such conditions was a "spoil sport," and had not learned how the game was played. Someone often had to plan the games or trips, someone had to organize things, and round up others to take part—"otherwise nothing would ever happen." Of course, the time beyond jobs was the traditional domain of women, who had been outside the modern work marketplace longer than the men. But for these mavericks, "who was boss" during leisure was beside the point, for "you can't make a person have a good time." Once the shared, free activity began, people had to join in voluntarily. Moreover, the game had its own logic and structure; it always had rules. Competition and struggle might very well be part of the activity, but they were confined to the game. When the activity was over, so was the competition.

Mavericks offered several examples of "being apart together." One spoke of playing with children. She remembered that she and her husband always took time "just to play with the kids" when they were growing up; they were not trying to teach or control them so much as sharing the play with them. Often the family would play ball or tag or other games in the yard, and she "had as much fun as the children." She spoke critically of people who were always trying to accomplish some useful, extraneous purpose when they were doing things with children. "Why not just play and have fun with them sometimes?"[74] For her, the play with her husband and children took place, at least in part, in a world outside utility, function, and control—a world Eugen Fink describes as suffused by "the color of joy." The reason a person worked, kept house, and satisfied other needs was to get to this place.[75]

CHAPTER EIGHT

Another woman spoke about the evening meal. She described a time before television when the family took time to sit around the table after they had eaten. "We would talk for what seemed like hours, I don't know, three or four times a week. We had time just to talk, tell what happened during the day, discuss things—sometimes we argued [laughter], but mostly we enjoyed each other's company—that was enough." Another told of the family's being together after leaving the table, "just sitting together" reading the newspaper and finishing homework. Even though the activities were done separately, the family was together and often interacted—one person would read something from the paper, another would ask about homework. "We seemed like we were more peaceful and together, and not so rushed *all* the time with no time even to sit down together." The front porch described above in this chapter resembles the dining space these two described; both provided the free place for Huizinga's "time apart together."[76]

Several of the women spoke of jokes, teasing, and laughter to illustrate what they meant. Elaborate practical jokes and detailed funny stories were sometimes included in this "time apart." Such things depended on a protected place to work—telling funny stories and teasing required trust and mutuality, without which the joke would fail and the teasing backfire. One told of moments during the day that she "stole" to "be quiet and just to look at the world" around her. One man spoke of getting up an hour earlier than he had to, before the family got up, in order to enjoy the peace of the house and to read his book undisturbed.[77]

One woman told about unexpected visits from neighbors and phone calls when she "just talked and talked—people thought I talked too much maybe, but how can you know about anything unless you talk?" Even though her discourse was devalued as "gossip," she insisted that the spoken word was still a part of living in a human community, and she continued "to keep in touch and keep up with what was going on."[78]

Another described a "coffee klatch" that endured for some years in her neighborhood. Nearly every morning "some of the women got together to talk after they finished their work." They had already "done what they needed to do," and the reason they all got together was "for the company and the talk." One of the men spoke of taking thirty minutes or an hour after work to stop at one of the bars down the street from Kellogg's for the same purpose. "After work I was able to spend a little time with my friends over a beer. . . . Why? Just for the company."[79]

This language is in marked contrast to the language of the industrial psychologists who led Kellogg's managers to implement Human Relations principles at the plant. Whereas the psychologists and managers elaborated a language of "need ascending," speaking of need and of work to fulfill need as an a endless ladder, the Kellogg workers spoke of a terminus and an opening out—of "taking care of business" and "doing what needed doing," and then of turning to activities they did not have to do or need to do, for the "fun of it" or "just for the company." Perhaps Cornel West's term "existential democracy" conveys the idea best.[80]

In their language, particularly in the typical phrases "have fun together" and "for the company," the workers made claims about the community and their own lives in the community as complete in themselves, existing outside ordinary need and function, and certainly outside the economic realm and worlds of structured authority. The workers seldom spoke of "needing" to socialize or play with their children the same way they spoke of needing to work at their jobs, shop for groceries, or do their housework. They referred rather to a condition of fullness in which work to satisfy need was left behind.[81]

Giovanni Gentile's description of culture echoes the mavericks' syntax and is true to their experience of the extra time:

Work differs from culture in two vital qualities. Work . . . by its use of nature as a means to satisfy human needs, creates wealth, the value of things. Value depends wholly on such human necessities. . . . Economic value is therefore always relative, a means to an end. This end by its very nature is something apart from economic value, apart from the material object in which that value is incorporated. Economic value being thus always relative, so is the work which creates it. Culture on the other hand . . . [has] true and absolute value, because its end is not outside but inside itself. . . . Culture is an end in itself, not a means to an end, since it is not useful, [and] serves no ulterior purpose.[82]

The six-hour mavericks were among the last workers in the city to question whether the reward for hard work should be more work to do, forever. They were also among the last to affirm the traditional working-class vision that after "necessaries" had been gained, work should then become the road to better things *outside* the job, need, and the market. They were among the last to challenge the new "full-time-only" rhetoric of management (as well as the mass culture) with traditional, commonsense phrases like "Work to live, don't live to work." They spoke of "necessity" and "need to work" in relative terms, in relation to an eschatology—as part of a process ending in a free place outside need. Fighting against the prevailing work-based language of morals, they spoke of "enough," of the "need" for time away from the job and the "need" for more money together, and weighed their "need" to work against the needs of others in the community without a good job. They defended six-hours and their extra time, claiming the new leisure as time to save traditional activities, crafts, and skills; to preserve the family and the community; to explore new cultural forms; and, finally, to establish the free place outside need, conflict, and control for the doing and creating of democratic culture for its own sake, beyond utility and the marketplace.

Chapter Nine

The Death of Six-Hours

In an environment where work was idealized as the center and most satisfying part of life, "necessity" was unrelieved by "enough," and work was without end, the remaining six-hour workers had little chance. Under siege through the 1960s and 1970s, the group nevertheless held their position into the 1980s. Constituting a quarter of the work force (a percentage fairly constant from 1957), and firmly united, they were a strong minority voice in the local union and managed to hold on to the department-by-department vote so long as their interests did not directly interfere with the majority's high-wage/benefit strategy.[1]

In the late 1970s, however, Kellogg's began to speak of "necessity" in new ways and broader, more abstract contexts. Even though its sales were at record levels, the company discovered that it was "losing market share"—that is, selling less of the total amount of cereal sold nationwide. The company claimed that this "strong competitive pressure" within the cereal industry "forced" it to modernize its operations to make them more "efficient." It used this new "necessity" to pressure employees, the city, and the state.

MODERNIZATION, DOWNSIZING,
AND URBAN RENEWAL IN BATTLE CREEK

In January 1980, William E. LaMothe replaced Joe Lonning as chairman of the board of directors. With LaMothe at the helm, the company decided to expand and diversify as well as continue downsizing its payroll. Planning to build a $62 million "company headquarters" as part of this expansion, Kellogg's demanded concessions from the city, the state, and Kellogg workers as the price for keeping its main office in Battle Creek.[2]

The first demand was that the City of Battle Creek broaden its tax base by incorporating its wealthiest suburb, the Battle Creek Township: unless the merger occurred, and unless the inner city was revitalized, the company would "pull its main office out of Michigan. With it would go 700 jobs." LaMothe acknowledged that many residents would view the ultimatum as blackmail, but the public ballot taken 2 November 1982 approved the merger. After the city-wide merger vote, some opponents suggested printing up bumper stickers reading "Kellogg's: The Home of Battle Creek," but the town's labor unions, the Chamber of Commerce, the National Association for the Advancement of Colored People, and a majority of city officials backed the company.[3]

The company proceeded to present the city with at least five new conditions for "keeping its jobs" in Michigan. In addition to demanding that the city obtain a $16.8 million Urban Development Action Grant (UDAG) from the federal government to improve the downtown area, the company pressured the Battle Creek City Commission to grant it a 12-year, 50 percent property tax abatement (an all-time record in the city, saving the company $22.5 million) and guarantee that Stouffer's Hotel and other McCamly Square businesses would continue operations for at least five years. The commission agreed to everything. It authorized the city to lend $16.8 million up front to finance the new construction, and to issue city bonds based on the repayment of the loans to fund capital improvements in the downtown area. This package was approved by the UDAG, to "preserve jobs."

As part of the deal, the company pressured the state to give the city $1 million to develop a "linear park system" through the city and adjoining the proposed building. But when Governor James Blanchard decided to use the earmarked Kammer Trust funds to create "summer jobs for youth" instead, Kellogg's again threatened to take "its" jobs out of Michigan because of the weakening of state support. This sparked a fascinating debate in the state over how best to spend public money to provide more work, and who was most entitled to it.[4]

Again Kellogg's prevailed, and the "linear park system" was built with state funds through the downtown area, along the banks of Battle Creek and the Kalamazoo River, and beside Kellogg's new "company headquarters." But this "linear park" was designed not for recreation but to adorn Kellogg's new building, "revitalize" the inner city, "attract businesses," and ultimately, create more jobs.[5]

Few people use the linear park today: some unemployed or homeless men waste their lives, a few secretaries have their lunch there in warm weather. The fine park has proven to be mostly for show, an adornment to Kellogg's magnificent new edifice. It is certainly not an invitation to leisure or a better life beyond working. The new corporate workers obey the new time customs of corporate culture and spend very little time outside the walls of the new headquarters. The park is above all a monument to work and to keeping "Kellogg's jobs" in Battle Creek.

Just as Kellogg's new building dwarfs everything else in the downtown area, the grounds and gardens just behind it outshine the other public parks and open spaces in and around the town. But the new linear park and the Kellogg's grounds are the opposite of W. K. Kellogg's old parks and forest preserves. The parks he built at the old plant and at Gull Lake were a preparation for the coming of "mass leisure." Corporate answers to community front porches and family living rooms, they were "free places for the free use of free people." But the parks around Kellogg's new cathedral are more museums and monuments than places for active use and public discourse. Even in the summer, they have the feel of a Michigan winter: frozen reminders of the vital public spaces that W. K. provided and an older worker culture used and appreciated. The abandonment of public spaces downtown has left a vacuum, now often filled by those most displaced by the spread of the culture of work.

In making its new demands for "public" parks, tax abatements, and restructuring, and through its elimination of the six-hour shifts, the company elaborated and extended the work-based language of morals. Building on the "hard work" test of moral worth, the company elevated "jobs" as a moral solvent. Whereas eight-hour workers used "have to work" and "it's my job" to deny community and family responsibility, Kellogg's managers substituted the "jobs" the company "provided." Accused by some of corporate blackmail, the company calmly invoked "necessity" and "jobs," and Battle Creek's political mainstream immediately conceded.

By 1984 such "provision" of jobs was thoroughly politicized in Battle Creek. Management discovered that the work it needed to buy could be defined not only as a benefit to the workers at Kellogg's but as a kind of public resource as well, and it began to use its "jobs resource" to bargain with the state, the city, and the unions. Jacques Rancière described how nineteenth-century workers faced the "absurdity of having to go on begging, day after day, for this labor in which one's life is lost." The absurdity grew to even larger proportions in Battle Creek in the 1980s.[6]

Certainly, this kind of corporate language was widespread by then. American business culture had long used the prospect of creating more work for more people, or the threat of available work's decline, to excuse sins ranging from the destruction of the environment to the paying of sub-poverty wages. Since the 1940s, corporations all over the world had, in the name of "jobs," opposed minimum wages as well as environmental and safety regulations, and excused rapacious corporate behavior that had outraged previous generations of Populists and Progressives.

After FDR revolutionized American politics in 1935, establishing the principle of government responsibility for creating work to sustain "full employment," business followed in the forties and fifties, building a pow-erful political and rhetorical position on the foundation of more work for more people. Kellogg's managers simply adapted the new "jobs-based" language of morals (and the political rhetoric of "JOBS, JOBS, JOBS") to justify what they were demanding in Battle Creek. They found unusually fertile ground there in the discourse of local eight-hour workers, who, in their contest with six-hour workers, had already committed themselves to work as the foundation and mainstay of morality.

The most difficult part of Kellogg's modernization scheme was dis-lodging the six-hour workers, now numbering 530 people. In addition to diversification and expansion, part of LaMothe's strategy to meet the company's loss of market share was to trim Kellogg's payroll. In May 1984, Kellogg's board of directors threatened to relocate if six-hour workers did not vote for eight-hours, a threat they reiterated until the workers voted on 11 December. In any case, management added, the company planned to decrease the "number of employees . . . 25% [in] each [six-hour] Department," thereby reducing its total payroll by 160 workers immediately, with projections over five years of a total reduction of 500 workers (from a workforce of 2,500 to 2,000). Just as W. K. Kellogg introduced the six-hour day to create more jobs, LaMothe proposed abolishing six-hours in order to eliminate jobs; the parallel is unmistakable.[7]

The company initially offered workers improved pension benefits if they would give up the short shift, only to have its offer soundly rejected by a vote of the six-hour workers early in June. Rebuffed, the board of direc-tors again threatened to relocate most of the jobs at the plant to other cities and reduce Battle Creek to a "satellite" operation with fewer than 650 jobs unless all six hour departments voted for eight hours immediately.[8]

Responding to the protests of the six-hour workers, the union at-tempted to limit the number of jobs that would be lost. It persuaded the company to soften the blow by offering early retirement incentives and relying more on attrition than outright layoffs. It also managed to postpone immediate action and negotiate an "incentive package" for those who would accept eight-hours "voluntarily." The "incentive package" was a novel twist on the old "incentive bonus," once a mainstay of management's efforts to improve productivity. Redefining "incentive" as encouraging people to give up their jobs, the company offered $5,500 to workers who retired within a short "window-period." The package included an agreement not to terminate six-hour workers for three years, payment of health benefits for 180 days for workers laid off over the course of three years (employees were not fired during the transition, but many were laid off), and some improvements in the pension plan.[9]

Six-hour supporters were enraged by the way negotiations were carried on and the "incentive package" was worked out. After the negative vote in June, Kellogg's board of directors contacted the international union, threatening as usual to move jobs out of Battle Creek. The company and the international then conveyed the threat to Local No. 3, after which the local's executive board authorized its negotiating committee to "enter into discussions with the Kellogg Company for the purpose of alleviating the potential of the Battle Creek Plant becoming the size of Memphis (677 hourly workers)" before bringing the issue up with the membership.[10]

But word leaked out. One six-hour "representative" asked, "Why has the international been discussing the affairs of the local union behind our backs???" Another asked, "Why with such an important concern . . . does our local want this information kept SECRET???? IS THIS RIGHT !!!!! IS 6 HOURS GOING THE WAY AND IN THE MANNER THAT OUR PROFIT SHARING DID???" (capitals in the original). Just as the workers at Goodyear were abandoned by their national unions in their fight to keep six-hours in the 1950s, the Kellogg workers were stranded in an untenable position.[11]

In the face of the first real company threat to the eight-hour majority over the issue of six-hours, the local and national union leadership crumbled, came to an agreement with management behind the backs of the six-hour workers, and, arguing the company's case, urged six-hour workers to recognize the "necessity" of cutting the workforce and accepting the negotiated "incentive package." Because the jobs that were to be lost and the concessions that were to be made were confined to the six-hour departments, the union and the eight-hour majority agreed to major contract concessions.[12] A strike was never discussed; alternatives that put any burden on senior eight-hour workers such as seniority restructuring were never seriously considered.

Thus pressured by the company and the union, the workers "voted" to give up the six-hour day on 11 December 1984. The *Battle Creek Enquirer* quoted Joseph Sessions, AFGM local business agent, as saying, "The members did not like [to vote for eight-hours], but they voted for it for the pure fact of saving jobs at the Kellogg plant in Battle Creek."[13]

The workers remember the event in detail. One woman described the change: "Kellogg's gave 6 hr people a good deal for retirement if we would vote 8 hrs. If we didn't they would also move most of the jobs somewhere else. We were almost forced to vote in 8 hrs and over 200 people retired (mostly women)." Another wrote: "Kellogg's had tried several times to get a vote to go 8 hours plant wide for all. It would cut down on personnel and the benefits they had to pay out. The votes for 6 hours won out, but in 1984 & 1985 Kellogg's reconstructed [*sic*] and threatened to move out of state if the plant didn't go to 8 hours and the City of Battle Creek and Lakeview didn't merge. The threat won out." Another remembered: "The company was automating . . . the different departments and they were eliminating jobs. The company gave a bonus if one would take their retirement [early] . . . so automation eliminated jobs." Still another noted that "the company request[ed] to make all shifts uniform and reduce the workforce in line with automation and less employees and less fringe benefits." Another wrote, "Remember, fewer employees mean fewer benefits, insurance, pensions etc. . . . [The] company would rather pay more overtime than hire more people. There's a real socio-economic issue here. I hope you are on to it." One recalled, "probably would not have been hired, as it was, I loved 6 hrs, as it gave me much more opportunity to devote my time elsewhere & still gave me ample income for a lot of extras. . . . I retired before they did away with the 6 hrs and made the women all go on 8 hrs. But from my observation in talking to friends, still working . . . , there was a vast difference in attitudes regarding their work. They more or less lost interest and didn't look forward [to] going in to work, like we all did on 6 hrs. There was a much more relaxed attitude under six-hours, not the tension [that exists] on 8 hours."[14]

Ina Sides recalled, "I spent less time with my family, less time with my husband, less time on Sundays in church; [working eight-hours] minimized everything—you know? And I did start having a lot of illness. . . . I was told and I read that [W. K. Kellogg] really initiated the six-hour unit to keep the family together and that was the main point! So we just couldn't understand [all the pressure to give up six-hours]! Like I said, we didn't like it one bit."[15]

Several others retired rather than work eight hours. As one woman put it, "I couldn't take 2 more hours on cement. . . . The stress and constant rushing was doing me in but I was lucky and had just turned 55 so could retire with benefits but [with] a cut pension. . . . As an incentive, Kellogg's retired about 150 of us at 8 hour benefits." Joy Blanchard remarked, "But, boy, the minute they voted eight hours—why, I left." Another woman recalled, "I wouldn't have retired if we would have stayed 6 hrs." Another remembered, "Some people were so sad about losing 6 hours, they quit." Another estimated that "the change cut [union] membership by 25%," because of the exodus of six-hour women who retired.[16]

In return for its cooperation, the company worked out a "productivity agreement" with the union, reaffirming and strengthening the coalition between management and labor. The company agreed to a $300 million modernization program to automate the production line—eliminating even more jobs over time (by attrition and fewer new hirings), but raising the pay of the protected workers.[17]

Again an historical parallel presents itself. Whereas W. K. Kellogg understood progress as more machines, shorter hours, and an expanded payroll, Kellogg management and the union finally came to understand increased efficiency in terms of more machines and fewer employees. Today Kellogg's policy is "the fewer workers at the plant, the better," even though the few remaining workers are paid well above the industry and regional averages. And labor at Kellogg's, with the voice of the shorter-hour minority silenced, is in solidarity with this strategy.[18]

SIX-HOURS' FUNERAL

The fifty to sixty workers who attended the six-hour shift's funeral at Stan's Place in neighboring Springfield spoke of what had happened as "one of the biggest changeovers at the cereal plant in many years." They made an event of the last day, 8 February 1985, constructing a full-sized "cardboard coffin painted black to signify [six-hours'] death & our sadness." The women placed the coffin, complete with a cut-out skeleton, on the workroom floor, where it remained throughout the day. Most wore black armbands that last day to commemorate the "death," combining real sorrow with humor.[19]

They made a memorable occasion of the event that evening, with traditional death rituals—some of them extremely old. Transporting the casket and skeleton to the bar after the last work shift of the day in something resembling a funeral procession, they held a wake there, with the "body" lying in state on one of the bar tables. Three central actresses in the drama, Katie Norton, Lou Clevenger, and Carol Henderson, played various roles in the mock funeral. According to the *Enquirer,* Henderson "cavorted" in the casket and danced around with the paper skeleton, in a mock ritual that brings to mind vivid images of an ancient *danse macabre.*

"We had a funeral," Ina Sides remembered. "Some of the employees made a makeshift casket, they had me with my poem, and if I remember right, a couple of them [who] were carrying the makeshift casket had on black robes, and we were crying. . . . Well, not really crying, but—there are a lot of good actors in the world, ham actors. We were acting like we were really upset, and, oh, it was nice. You know, we got the point across."[20]

Eulogies were given. The women spoke again of their "devotion" to shorter hours, recalling that the "six-hour shift was embraced by generations of women." They recalled most of the main reasons they had fought for shorter hours: family, freedom, control, "values other than just more money," "fun," "exploring the world," "jobs for those that needed them." Military metaphors were used, comparing six-hours to a hero who had fallen in battle. Novel, expressive phrases appeared—Ina Sides's couplet, "Our bodies will never forget 'you' / For you were good to them, too!" gives some hint that the women's rhetoric was becoming richer, rising even to the poetic through the final days. They also got off a few parting shots at the vision of work as the center of life, "greedy work-hogs," and "all-powerful necessity."[21]

Those present at Stan's Place agreed that even though younger workers with less seniority had the most to lose, the older employees "hated to see the old shift end" most of all. Long after the threat of termination or layoff was over, the older women remained firmly committed to a vision of freedom and to a cause they had fought for against formidable opposition for years. Some had fought for over four decades.

During the "funeral," someone read Sides's poem. It ended with her "sorrowful" couplet:

And now get out the *vitamins*—give your doctor a call
Cause old 8 hrs. has got us "all". . . .[22]

AFTERMATH

Retired workers often remark that Kellogg's management has gone downhill since the death of W. K. and the end of six-hours. As one woman put it, "Back when Kellogg's was on the six-hour shift it was much more of a family and all worked for a better product and were concerned about their work. . . . [But] the concern has gone and it's not family anymore." Another remarked, "They claim they could make better benefits for employees. [I] don't think it has made that much difference. Just more pay for a week's work. But a lot of unhappy people. They say it's not the same place to work anymore." Another wrote that her husband still has contact with "younger fellow workers who let it be known that things are different now and not for the better. As with most companies, 'lean and mean' is the way to go. They have their methods of cutting costs that adversely affect workers. Downsizing the [labor] force cuts benefit costs for the company. It is often cheaper to pay overtime costs than to hire. . . . There is a point of diminishing returns for these management geniuses." Betty Smyth said, "I left in '85 and those still there say it isn't the same, it's like a snake pit working in it."[23]

One of the biggest changes is in the amount of the workers' time that the company demands—a change many associate with the deterioration of the work experience. Because there are so few workers on the payroll, overtime and holiday work are much more common and often required. Even though the pay is good, the "price" a worker has to pay to work there is significantly higher, according to the six-hour retirees. Workers' discourse now concerns "burnout," exhaustion, and the lack of time at home. As one put it, the vote for eight-hours "opened the door for 56-hour weeks." Cecelia Bissell said, "[T]he last ten years I worked there was nothing like it was before. They started getting these young men and all they could do was eliminating, eliminating, eliminating. . . . Everything was elimination, double up on the work, do this, do that. . . . '[L]et's get quantity and forget quality.' [Y]ou know you only got two hands, and there is just so much you can do. Eight hours is too long. . . . [Y]ou don't

CHAPTER NINE

have time for your kids. I think a lot of them got out of there because of that. So I decided when you get to that point where you hate to get up and go to work, time to get out." The six-hour women who still work at Kellogg's agree: "You can't find anybody who will admit she voted against six hours."[24]

Concern about chronic unemployment and marginal jobs remains. "Maybe they should go on the six-hour day again," Smilia Popovich advised. "[E]verywhere jobs are scarce. Kellogg's reduced unemployment and maybe it should be done again."[25] But discontent about long hours and sentiment in favor of work reduction are disorganized and confounded, just as language critical of work and supportive of time outside work is scattered and discounted by the dominant rhetoric of necessity and culture of work that thrive in the city.

Along with the vision of increased efficiency and productivity through the elimination of workers, other, more orthodox visions of progress under capitalism came to Battle Creek. With no workers questioning work's centrality by their shorter-hours example and with a production plant nearing full automation, "work as the center of life" became secure as an ideal, and management's attention shifted from personnel management to "product diversification" and corporate expansion.

Certainly, W. K. Kellogg wanted to sell as much cereal as possible and devoted a good deal of his life to the effort. But his efforts and vision were limited compared with those of today's prophets of diversification. Current management's more orthodox capitalist vision of progress centers on eternal economic growth and on continually finding new things for consumers to need, work for, and buy. The vision is founded on belief in an abstract, even mystical, "economic expansion," but it relies on tangible "New Products" (a phrase now spoken in special, almost reverent tones) that "create jobs" and result in new, serious, and important work activities that build the market, not detract from it. Today Kellogg's management is animated by visions of "Kellogg's Pop Tarts" and of unexplored galaxies of yet unimagined things to work for—things to be found at the frontiers of science, in gene splicing and genetic engineering. In the service of this faith, the corporation now embraces work without end.[26]

Although Ina Sides finished her poem with "old 8 hrs. has got us 'all'," the story of the Kellogg women's defeat is not one of simple failure. For over four decades they demonstrated that they were not in the grip of irresistible "economic necessity" by continuing to work less than "full-time," choosing shorter hours just as workers had done for over a century before World War II. Even though they lost their cause, they were not "simply overridden or manipulated" but left "their own clear marks" on the history of American labor.[27]

The mavericks held on to the old notion that paid work was important primarily as a means to other, more important purposes, and that shorter hours was still a legitimate, practical reward for submitting to modern work discipline. They were among the last workers in the city to question whether the reward for hard work and industrial progress should be more work to do, indefinitely, and to affirm the traditional working-class vision that after enough "necessaries" had been won, work should be the road to better things. They were among the last workers to challenge the new "full-time only" work rhetoric of management and the union with traditional, commonsense phrases such as "Work to live, don't live to work," and to speak of "necessity" in relative terms.

Holding on to "their" six-hour shift, they came into increasing conflict with the higher wage/fewer workers coalition of management and the union. They challenged, on a fundamental level, the new ideas and rhetoric that were emerging as work discipline's modern underpinnings. By their dissent, they brought the language about work as the center of life," unqualified necessity, and trivialized "leisure" into question. Their resistance showed that the new foundations of work discipline were not absolutes or unavoidable consequences of "modern life," as others claimed, but were in fact historically relative and of very recent construction.

During the nineteenth and early twentieth centuries, few workers assumed that the reward for hard work was more work to do forever, or that necessity would expand so much that additional free time would be impossible. Rather, work was the road to better things: first to enough wages to meet "basic needs" and then to "free activities" outside what the early socialist writers called the "sphere of necessity." In accord with what their good common sense told them, "Work to live, don't live to work," generations of workers struggled successfully for shorter hours and their "own time." This vision has been eclipsed by modern claims about absolute necessity and by the belief that progress is infinite economic growth through work's eternal renewal.

The Kellogg mavericks were among the last holdouts against this change—what André Gorz called "*métamorphoses du travail.*" Their story is a monument to the human struggle for control over one's life and for substantial freedom beyond need and necessity. The history of Kellogg's six-hour day, likewise, is proof that the choice between "extra time" and "extra money" involved questions of cultural change, beliefs, and even moral commitment, more than irresistible economic necessity or some predetermined human need to work "full-time."

Kellogg six-hour workers were heirs to labor's traditional belief that "the progressive shortening of the hours of labor" was a reasonable job benefit. Their story serves as a reminder that there are legitimate and realistic historical alternatives to infinite economic expansion and "work without end," and that there is a more down-to-earth hope for the future than a fantastic utopia where a majority of workers have "good, full-time" jobs.

The memory of shorter hours and the mavericks' fight remains fresh in Battle Creek, providing at least a glimmer of hope that the workers' historic cause and competing vision of freedom may yet be revived. The Kellogg mavericks were faithful to a vision that endured for over a century and a half: that increased leisure and higher wages *together* constitute authentic progress and that the work hours should, as William Heighton wrote in 1827 in one of labor history's earliest documents, be reduced from twelve to ten to eight to six and further, "until the development and progress of science have reduced human labour to its lowest terms"—until work and economic concerns become adjuncts to, rather than the centers of, modern life.

Notes

INTRODUCTION

1. *Moon-Journal,* 1 December 1930. The *Moon-Journal* was Battle Creek's evening paper; the *Battle Creek Enquirer* (hereafter the *Enquirer*) was the morning paper.

2. Bill Miller, "R.I.P.: Kellogg's 6-Hour Shift," *Enquirer* 9 February 1985. The inaccurate date may have been remembered because Kellogg's made the six-hour day "permanent" on 14 April 1931. Author's survey, no. 779. Workers remember the occasion as sad, because "everyone mourned the passing of six-hours." Interview with Paula Swan, former president of AFGM Local No. 3, 18 October 1991. (Unless otherwise indicated, all interviews were conducted by the author.) See Chapter Nine, "The Death of Six-Hours."

3. Undated newspaper clipping from the *Enquirer,* sent to the author by a retired Kellogg employee; interview with Ina Sides, at her home in Battle Creek, 28 July 1993.

4. See Chapter Two for a full historiographic review of the fight for shorter hours. For an introduction to the issue, see John D. Owen, "Workweeks and Leisure: An Analysis of Trends, 1948–75," *Monthly Labor Review* 99 (August 1976): 3–8; John D. Owen, *Working Hours: An Economic Analysis* (Lexington, Mass., 1979); John D. Owen, *Working Lives: The American Work Force since 1920* (Lexington, Mass., 1986), 23; Benjamin K. Hunnicutt, "The End of Shorter Hours," *Labor History* 25 (1984): 373–404; David Roediger and Philip Foner, *Our Own Time: A History of American Labor and the Working Day* (New York, 1989), xi (quoting Owen), 259; Gary Cross, "Worktime and Industrialization: An Introduction," and David R. Roediger, "The Limits of Corporate Reform: Fordism, Taylorism, and the Working Week in the United States, 1914–1929," both in Gary Cross, ed., *Worktime and Industrialization: An International History* (Philadelphia, 1988), 2, 16, 136; Benjamin Kline Hunnicutt, *Work Without End: Abandoning Shorter Hours for the Right to Work* (Philadelphia, 1988), 22; Juliet Schor, *The Overworked American: The Unexpected Decline of Leisure* (New York, 1991); Karl Hinrichs, William Roche, and Carmen Sirianni, *Working Time in Transition: The Political Economy of Working Hours in the Industrial Nations* (Philadelphia, 1991).

Others, writing more for general audiences, have also discussed the end of shorter hours. See Witold Rybczynski, *Waiting for the Weekend* (New York, 1991); Amy Saltzman, *Downshifting; Reinventing Success on a Slower Track* (New York, 1990); and Suzanne Gordon's excellent *Prisoners of Men's Dreams* (New York, 1991). See also Witold Rybczynski, "Waiting for the Weekend," *Atlantic Monthly* 268 (August 1991); 35–39; and Vicki Robin and Joe Dominguez, *Your Money or Your Life* (New York, 1992).

5. Journalists and reviewers who have addressed the "overwork" story include: Gerald Friedman, Review Article, *Annals of the American Academy of Political and Social Sciences* 505 (September 1989): 190; Alexander Keyssar, Review Article, *American Historical Review* 76 (April 1990): 612; Nelson Lichtenstein, "The Death of the Six-Hours Day," *New York Times Book Review* (29 January 1989): 15; Suzanne Gordon, Review Article, *Washington Post*, 29 August 1989. See also Jo-Ann Mort, review of *Our Own Time* by Roediger and Foner, *New York Times Book Review* (11 March 1990): 3.

The most common response to questions about the end of shorter hours is to ask another question: "How could people afford to work less?" The popular press's explanation of overwork is that Americans have been forced by economic conditions to work longer. Steadily increasing leisure, we are assured by most writers today, is romantic nonsense. Such questions and assumptions imply that some broadly conceived economic "reality," transcending ordinary social and cultural changes, determined the course of events. The author challenges these assumptions and argues that economic "realities" as they relate to work and leisure have a cultural origin.

6. Gutman is quoted in David Montgomery, "Gutman's Nineteenth-Century America," *Labor History* 19 (1978): 417.

7. Herbert Gutman, *Work, Culture and Society in Industrializing America* (New York, 1977), 79.

8. For a similar cultural argument see E. P. Thompson, *The Making of the English Working Class* (New York, 1966), 9–10. In *The Poverty of Theory and Other Essays* (New York, 1978), 88–89, Thompson reiterates his contention that history is created by men and women who are the "ever-baffled, ever-resurgent" subject of their own history. He cautions once again against making claims about universal constants, transcendent forces, irresistible economic necessity, transhistorical human nature, and the like and points to the importance of ordinary workers as the agents of historical change and continuity.

In recent years, historians following the lead of the French labor historians have been writing what Lynn Hunt and others call "the New Cultural History." Such writers have also challenged the economic, psychological, and social interpretations favored for decades by Marxists and Annales historians, turning instead to what Thompson called "cultural and moral mediations." See Lynn Hunt, ed., *The New Cultural History* (Berkeley, 1989), introduction; Lenard R. Berlanstein, "Working with Language: The Linguistic Turn in French Labor History," *Comparative Studies in Society and History* 33 (1991): 426–40. Berlanstein, for example, maintains that the prestige once enjoyed by the "new labor historians . . . belongs to revisionists who are learned in poststructuralist theory, cultural anthropology, and literary criticism." With Hunt, Berlanstein characterizes the "new cultural history" as embracing "community . . . sign and language," while avoiding generalizations about cause based on universal principles or covering laws, whether class or other formal economic determinants. See Lenard Berlanstein, ed., *Rethinking Labor History* (Urbana, 1993), 3–5.

Lynn Hunt describes a "major shift in emphasis" among fourth-generation Annales historians, who have recently maintained that "economic and social relations are not prior to or determining of cultural ones; they are themselves fields of cultural practice and cultural production—which cannot be explained deductively by reference to an extra-cultural dimension of experience." Such writers "deny the ontological priority of economic events" and insist that "culture and community, not economics or class," are history's "critical forces." See Hunt, *New Cultural History*, 62; see also William Sewell, Jr., *Work and Revolution in France from the Old Regime to 1848* (Cambridge, 1980), 11, on the primacy of culture over "real" economic forces. Gareth Stedman Jones and William Reddy make similar claims about culture's independence from the marketplace; see Jones, *Language of Class: Studies in English Working Class History* (Cambridge, 1983); and Reddy, *The Rise of Market Culture: The Textile Trade and French Society, 1750–1900* (Cambridge, 1984). See also Suzanne Desan, "Crowds, Community, and Ritual in the Work of E. P. Thompson and Natalie Davis," in Hunt, *New Cultural History*, 47–71; Roger Chartier, "Intellectual History or Sociocultural History? The French Trajectories," in Dominick LaCapra and Steven L. Kaplan, eds., *Modern European Intellectual History* (Ithaca, 1982), 30; Roger Chartier, *The Cultural Origins of the French Revolution*, trans. Lydia Cochrane (Durham, 1991).

9. Lynn Hunt, *Politics, Culture, and Class in the French Revolution,* (Berkeley, 1984), 25; Hunt, *New Cultural History*, 17, 19; Berlanstein, *Rethinking Labor History*, 6; Peter Schöttler, "Historians and Discourse Analysis," *History Workshop*, no. 27 (Spring 1989): 37–65; Sewell, *Work and Revolution*, 11. In this book I explore changes in local institutions and Battle Creek itself, such as the design and location of gardens, parks, and other public amenities.

10. Bryan D. Palmer, *Descent into Discourse: The Reification of Language and the Writing of Social History* (Philadelphia, 1990), offers a powerful critique of the linguistic turn in social history, making the case for the continuation of class analysis. I am convinced that questions of gender and class were important in shaping the discourse about working hours in Battle Creek, and look for ways

in which issues of power and control influenced the course of the six-hour discourse. See also Roger Keesing, "Anthropology as an Interpretive Quest," *Current Anthropology* 28 (1987): 161–62. Keesing writes that "cultures are webs of mystification as well as signification. We need to ask who *creates* and who *defines* cultural meanings, and to what end."

There is probably a case to be made that the words and signs used in the six-hour debate were subject to what Paul Ricoeur called the "profound dynamic" of the context of symbols. Within community discourse, words and signs live a life of their own in which their meanings are transmuted outside conscious human intent, and, "regardless of things exterior to language," take on different "associations" from the "structured field of signs"; see Paul Ricoeur, "Structure, Word, Event," in *The Conflict of Interpretations: Essays in Hermeneutics* (Evanston, Ill., 1974), 84, 86, 92–94. I rely on the historical categories of class and gender and leave semiotics alone.

11. Hunt, *New Cultural History*, 63; Jacques Rancière, *La nuit des prolétaires* (Paris, 1981; trans. Philadelphia, 1989), vii and introduction; Natalie Z. Davis, "City Women and Religious Change," in *Society and Culture in Early Modern France* (Stanford, Calif., 1975), 65–75. Davis and Rancière show how groups with little political or economic power exerted an influence in their community by controlling how time was spent outside the marketplace and traditional social roles.

Steven Ross, John Cumbler, and Roy Rosenzweig have also demonstrated the significance of free time for the creation of worker culture in the United States. Ross claims that "although work was a central focus of daily life, it did not produce a single working class experience" for workers in Cincinnati. Cumbler draws similar conclusions from his study of workers in Lynn and Fall River, Massachusetts, where experiences in lunchrooms, poolrooms, bowling alleys, clubs, and social centers were the basis for the formation of a "working class ideology." Roy Rosenzweig argues that workers' "basic values, beliefs, and traditions" were expressed outside their industrial jobs and the marketplace, during leisure time. See Steven J. Ross, "Workers on the Edge: Work, Leisure, and Politics in Industrializing Cincinnati: 1830–1890," (Ph.D. dissertation, Princeton University, 1980), iii–v, 317–404; John T. Cumbler, *Working-Class Community in Industrial America: Work, Leisure, and Struggle in Two Industrial Cities, 1880–1930* (Westport, Conn., 1979), 7–12, 28–38, 114–28; Roy Rosenzweig, *Eight Hours for What We Will: Workers and Leisure in an Industrial City, 1870–1920* (Cambridge, Mass., 1983), 222–28; quotation on 223. See also Benjamin K. Hunnicutt, "The Jewish Sabbath Movement in the Early Twentieth Century," *American Jewish History* 69 (December 1979): 196–225; David Roediger, "The Movement for the Shorter Working Day in the United States before 1866" (Ph.D. dissertation, Northwestern University, 1980), 5. Such writers view the leisure resulting from shorter working hours as the foundation of working-class local culture.

12. A revealing discussion of play and leisure runs through Victor Turner's writings. Turner suggested in several places that modern leisure is analogous to tribal societies' "antistructures"—phases of rituals and celebrations that allow participants to stand outside the static social order and objectify established roles, rites, and duties. Following the Belgian folklorist Arnold van Gennep, Turner called these times and places "liminal."

Turner developed his thesis by pointing out that such free states introduce "new forms of symbolic action" and are "particularly conducive to play . . . and to experimental behavior . . . undertaken to discover something not yet known. . . . In liminality new ways of acting, new combinations of symbols, are tried out, to be discarded or rejected." With Huizinga, Turner concluded that culture changes (or "emerges") through the medium of play during periods of "liminality." See the following works by Victor Turner: *Blazing the Trail: Way Marks in the Explorations of Symbols* (Tucson, Ariz., 1992), 52 (quotation); *The Ritual Process* (Chicago, 1969); *Process, Performance and Pilgrimage: A Study in Comparative Symbology* (New Delhi, 1979), 94–98; *From Ritual to Theater: The Human Seriousness of Play* (New York, 1982), 20–25. See also Scott Christopher Martin's superb "Leisure in Southwestern Pennsylvania, 1800–1850" (Ph.D. dissertation, University of Pittsburgh, 1990), 7–10; Johan Huizinga, *Leisure the Basis of Culture: A Study of the Play-element in Culture* (Boston, 1950), 1–27.

In tribal societies, antistructure is generally supportive of the existing order. In modern culture, however, leisure has emerged as an enlarged private "freedom to transcend social structural limitations." Modern leisure thus has the potential to establish "an independent domain of creative activity, not simply a distorted mirror-image, mask, or cloak for structural activities in the 'centers' or 'mainstreams' of 'productive social labor.'" See Turner, *From Ritual to Theater*, 33.

Being thus "outside," Turner believed that modern leisure, even more than tribal antistructure, may be the opening for new discourse, new ways of talking about existing social forms and roles, and consequently an avenue for cultural transformation: "Liminal phenomena are . . . often subversive, representing radical critiques of the cultural structures and proposing utopian alternative models. . . . Liminal and liminoid phenomena constitute metalanguages (including nonverbal ones) devised for the purpose of talking about the various languages of everyday, and in which mundane axioms become problematic, where cherished symbols are . . . reflected upon, rotated, and given new and unexpected valences." Turner, *Blazing the Trail*, 57.

Jürgen Habermas discusses modern leisure in strikingly similar terms, positing a fundamental historical change in human culture that he describes in various ways, but in no terms more compelling than "the collapse of the discussional."

Before the modern era, "culture" was often homemade, the product of "communities of discourse" that produced language and sign, understanding and meaning on their own and in active exchange with other groups. But these "communities of discourse" have collapsed, replaced in the modern age by a super-culture that is passively consumed by most of us and produced and performed by an increasingly small elite. Writing about the transformation of "a public that made culture an object of critical debate into one that consumes it," he concludes: "No longer cultivation [*Bildung*] but rather consumption opens access to culture goods." See John L. Hemingway, "Emancipated Leisure: Jürgen Habermas's Analysis of Leisure and Consumption," paper presented at the National Recreation and Parks Association Symposium on Leisure Research, October 1993, San Jose, Calif. Hemingway has brought to light some of Habermas's long-forgotten writings on work, leisure, and cultural collapse, including "Die Dialektik der Rationalisierung: Vom Pauperismus in Produktion und Konsum." *Merkur* 8 (1954): 701–24.

13. Robert M. MacIver, "The Great Emptiness," in Eric Larrabee and Rolf Meyersohn, eds., *Mass Leisure* (Glencoe, Ill., 1958), 118–21.

14. J Rancière, *Nuit des prolétaires*, vii and introduction; Eugen Fink, *Oase des Glucks Gedanken zu einer Ontologie des Spiels* (Freiburg, 1957), trans. Sister M. Delphine as "The Ontology of Play," in Ellen Gerber, ed., *Sport and the Body* (Philadelphia, 1979), 76 (quotation); originally published in English in *Philosophy Today* 4 (Summer 1960): 95–110; Joseph Pieper, *Leisure the Basis of Culture* (New York, 1952), 12; Turner, *Blazing the Trail,* 54.

In *Nuit des prolétaires,* Rancière describes workers' experiences outside industrial work, during "those nights snatched from the normal round of work and repose"—the conversations, philosophizing, and writings of a small group of workers who, in daring to write and speak, broke down the barriers between the literate and the working classes. Moving within the interstices of both class and work, they played a critical role in developing a working-class consciousness in pre-1848 France, coining idioms and phrases that circulated widely and helped fix a national language of class in France. Animated originally by the "absurdity of having to go on begging, day after day, for this labor in which one's life is lost," workers devoted a good deal of effort to criticizing industrial work and rejecting industrialists' attempts to propagandize and mythicize labor. See *Nuit des prolétaires* (Paris, 1981), vii and introduction.

15. Interviews with Joy Blanchard at her home in Battle Creek, 10 August 1989, 24 July 1993.

16. Turner, *Blazing the Trail,* 54; see also 49–51. For an explanation of "flow," see Mihaly Csikszentmihalyi, *Flow: The Psychology of Optimal Experience* (New York, 1991). Turner and Csikszentmihalyi were colleagues at the University of Chicago.

17. Richard Butsch, ed., *For Fun and Profit: The Transformation of Leisure into Consumption* (Philadelphia, 1990).

18. Turner, *Blazing the Trail,* 54.

CHAPTER ONE

1. "Kellogg Company Announces Six-Hour Day and Basic Pay Raise to Aid Employment: Takes World Leadership in Inauguration of New Industrial Work Policy," *Moon-Journal,* 24 November 1930. See also memo, E. H. McKay to Walter C. Hasselhorn, 7 September 1933, Local No. 3 of the American Federation of Grain Millers' Archives; Battle Creek, Michigan (hereafter cited as Local No. 3 Archives); Lewis Brown, notes for a "Foreman's Meeting, 19 December 1930," miscellaneous letters, lecture and speech notes, and clippings, Lewis Brown's papers. Lewis John Brown's papers are preserved by his son, William Brown of Phoenix, Arizona.

2. Kellogg quoted by Horace B. Powell, *The Original Has This Signature—W. K. Kellogg* (Englewood Cliffs, N.J., 1956), 188; Lewis Brown, notes for a "Talk to London [Ontario, Canada], 13 February 1931," bound notebook, Lewis Brown's papers.

3. "The Proof of the Pudding: Kellogg's 15 Month Experience with the 6-Hour Day," *Factory and Industrial Management* 91 (April 1932): 157–58; "Six-Hour Day Proves Success," *Kellogg News* (21 April 1931)—the *Kellogg News* is an in-house publication of Kellogg's in Battle Creek; Lewis J. Brown, "Operation of 6-Hour Day in Plants of the Kellogg Co.," *Monthly Labor Review* 32 (1931): 1414–21.

4. The term "Liberation Capitalism" is the author's invention.

5. *Moon-Journal,* 24 November 1930. The issue of total weekly wages was complicated by the seasonal nature of cereal sales (a saying was common at Kellogg's that during the winter people ate hot cereal, and during the summer, cold); a thirty-hour week alternated seasonally with thirty-six hours. Kellogg's focused on the fact that it would be "paying the highest rate per hour of any of the larger firms in our city—and much greater than the average throughout the country." A year later, Kellogg's again raised hourly wages by 12.5 percent, strengthening its claim of offering the highest hourly pay. The issue of hourly pay as distinct from total weekly earnings was still critical in the 1930s, reflecting the workers' view of shorter hours as a job benefit on a par with wages.

6. A survey team from the Women's Bureau of the U.S. Department of Labor (see Chapter Three) examined Kellogg's payroll books in mid-1932, comparing wages before the change to six hours and wages after the second hourly pay increase. They found that 77 percent of the workers received less weekly pay under six-hours. Over 40 percent received 10 to 20 percent less; nearly a third received

o to 10 percent less; and one in eleven over 20 percent less; 45 workers (23 percent) showed an increase in weekly wages. Ethel L. Best, *A Study of a Change from 8 to 6 Hours of Work,* Bulletin No. 105 of the Women's Bureau, U.S. Department of Labor (Washington, D.C., 1933); National Archives, U.S. Department of Labor, Women's Bureau, Raw Data, Box 153.

Business Week (22 April 1931): 16, found that even though some workers were being paid less than in 1930, still "more money [was] being distributed to Kellogg workers as a whole."

Beginning in 1933, labor accused business in general of cutting wages whenever it cut hours. Kellogg's was sensitive to labor's accusation, and in January 1933 James McQuiston, director of the Standards Department, wrote to Mary Anderson, head of the Women's Bureau, about the New Hampshire Plan that was making headlines across the country. Organized by New Hampshire governor John G. Winant, an influential group of businessmen and professional people made an effort to respond to labor's objection that workers were bearing the entire burden of unemployment. The New Hampshire Plan called for business and labor to share the costs of shorter hours equally, workers by taking a modest weekly pay cut (partially offset by increased hourly pay and by deflation), business by increasing hourly wages and expanding the payroll (the plan called for a fifty/fifty split between labor and management to cover the larger payrolls). Labor expressed more interest in this plan than in share-the-work schemes like the Teagle Campaign.

See letter, W. James McQuiston to Mary Anderson, Director of the Women's Bureau, 20 January 1933, National Archives, U.S. Department of Labor, Women's Bureau, Raw Data, Box 153. McQuiston asked Anderson "to mention that Mr. Kellogg and the Kellogg Company [were] the originators of this plan . . . [and include] a statement [in the bureau's report] that the plan has later been . . . called 'The New Hampshire Plan.'"

See also J. G. Winant, "New Hampshire Plan," *Review of Reviews* 86 (November 1932): 24; O. McKee, Jr., "New Hampshire Does Her Bit," *National Republic* 20 (October 1932): 6; *Enquirer,* 24 November, 6,7,8 December 1930; *Moon-Journal,* 1 December 1930; "Cereals: Six-Hour Day Helps Kellogg Co. Do More Work," *Newsweek* 9 (16 January 1937): 27.

7. Winant, "New Hampshire Plan"; *Moon-Journal,* 24 November 1930; Brown, "Operation of 6-Hour Day in Plants of the Kellogg Co." Unlike Ford's experiment with the five-day week in 1926, Kellogg's six-hour day was launched in an expanding market—demand for cereal was still firm. Moreover, a week after four-shift operations began, W. K. Kellogg announced that the company would end 1930 with the greatest volume of sales in its history. No one accused Kellogg of trying to limit production of cereal, as critics had accused Ford of cutting hours in response to soft demand in 1926. Through the depression, Kellogg's problem was to make enough cereal to meet demand.

8. Brown was greatly influenced by the scientific managers, remarking that he "always liked to talk about scientific management as since [the] beginning of my business experience [I] have been acquainted with men such as Emerson etc." Lewis Brown, "Notes on talk to Branch Manager members of the office force and Foremen," 9 January 1928, in bound notebook, Lewis Brown's papers.

9. *Business Week*, (22 April 1931); Brown, "Operation of 6-Hour Day." See also letter, Chas. Baldwin, Acting Commissioner of Labor Statistics, U.S. Department of Labor, to Lewis Brown, 26 May 1931, folder of correspondence and miscellaneous items, Lewis Brown's Papers; Chapin Hoskins, "Is the Six-Hour Day Feasible?" *Forbes* (July 1931): 16–18, 28.

10. For the "relay race," see Brown, "Operation of 6-Hour Day."

11. Henry Ford, "Why I Favor Five Days' Work with Six Days' Pay," interview by Samuel Crowther, *World's Work* 52 (1926): 613 (for quotation); see also "The 5-Day Week in the Ford Plants," *Monthly Labor Review* 23 (1926): 1163; for Ford's views during the depression, see Henry Ford and Samuel Crowther, "Unemployment or Leisure," *Saturday Evening Post* 203 (August 1930): 19.

12. Lewis Brown, "Three Kinds of Income, A Personal Letter to You," no date, but certainly written during his stay at Kellogg's; also Lewis Brown, "The Six-Hour Day," *Executive Service Bulletin* (August 1931), both in folder of correspondence and miscellaneous items, Lewis Brown's papers.

13. *Moon-Journal*, 24 November 1930, see also 1, 2, 3 December 1930; *Enquirer*, 24 November; 6, 7, 8, December 1930; Brown, "Operation of 6-Hour Day"; "Cereals: Six-Hour Day Helps Kellogg Co. Do More Work," 27.

14. *Moon-Journal*, 24 November 1930; "Decreasing Hours of Labor: A Growing Movement Here and Abroad," *The Index* (April 1932), folder of correspondence and miscellaneous items, Lewis Brown's papers.

15. *Business Week*, 10 December 1930. "Nation's Eyes Focused on Kellogg's Six-hour Day," *Kellogg News* (28 April 1931). Lewis Brown kept a scrapbook of more than 255 newspaper and magazine articles about his 15 April 1931 announcement in New York City that the six-hour day was to be permanent at Kellogg's. Most newspapers ran the story on the front page, usually the Associated Press or United Press version. Notable exceptions include B. C. Forbes's syndicated column and original stories carried by the *New York Times, New York Evening Post, New York World Telegram, New York Investment News, Akron Times Press, Provo Evening Herald, Nashville Tennessean, Philadelphia Record, Battle Creek Enquirer, Moon-Journal, Milwaukee Journal, Madison Courier, Topeka Daily Capital, New Bedford Times, St. Louis Globe Democrat, Waterbury* [Conn.] *Republican,* and *Business Week* (22 April 1931). Scrapbook of newspaper clippings pertaining to the six-hour day, Lewis Brown's papers (hereafter Scrapbook).

Merryle Stanley Rukeyser, a columnist for Universal Service, Inc., praised six-hours in "Prosperity Seen Dependent on Aid for Unemployment," *The American*

(New York City), *The Herald* (Washington, D.C.), *The News* (Baltimore), and other papers. Scrapbook.

16. "Kellogg Strikes at Unemployment," *Factory and Industrial Management* 80 (December 1930): 1148 a, b.

17. *Kellogg News,* 3 March 1931; letter, F. R. Darrow, to Lewis Brown 10 March 1931; both in folder of correspondence and miscellaneous items, Lewis Brown's papers. This was the first issue of the *Kellogg News.*

18. *Kellogg News* (3 March 1931); *Enquirer,* 24 November, 6, 7, 8, December 1930.

19. As quoted by Powell in *The Original Has This Signature,* 188. There is evidence that Hoover came to Battle Creek in 1932 and was shown around town by W. K. Letter, Hoover to W. K. Kellogg, from the Waldorf Astoria, N.Y., October 1936, letter in possession of Duff Stoltz, Battle Creek. See also *Enquirer,* 26 November 1930; letter, J. M. Carmody to Hugo Black, 9 December 1931, Hugo Black papers, Library of Congress, Washington, D.C.

Walsh later became one of the most powerful advocates of a national work-sharing policy. John M. Carmody, an editor of *Factory and Industrial Management* from 1927 to 1933, sent Hugo Black, then senator from Alabama, a batch of newspaper clippings and told him about the success of the six-hour day in Battle Creek. Black used this information to support the thirty-hour work-sharing bill he and Representative William Connery (D., Mass.) were sponsoring in the U.S. Congress.

20. *New York Times,* 15 April, 31 October 1931. The *Times* quoted officials' statement that 20 percent more workers had been hired, and that with "plant operations speeded up," Kellogg was "moving through . . . the greatest year in its history." Other accounts said 430 workers were added: Hoskins, "Is the Six-Hour Day Feasible?" See also *Moon-Journal,* 8 June 1937; Powell, *The Original Has This Signature,* 189. Unemployment still threatened jobs in Battle Creek, and Kellogg continued to look for innovative solutions. See *New York Times,* 25 September, 17 October 1931. Still, the six-hour day was far and away the most visible and successful of Kellogg's reemployment schemes.

21. *Business Week,* (22 April 1931): 16.

22. Hoskins, "Is the Six-Hour Day Feasible?" 16–18, 28.

23. Ibid.; See also letter, Lewis Brown to Chapin Hoskins, 9 June 1931, folder of correspondence and miscellaneous items, Lewis Brown's papers.

24. "Progressively shorter hours" was coined during the AFL's 1926 convention, when the unions voted to endorse the five-day week.

25. *Factory and Industrial Management* 81 (1931): 775, 776; See also letter, John M. Carmody, co-editor of *Factory and Industrial Management* to Lewis Brown, 2 October 1931, folder of correspondence and miscellaneous items, Lewis Brown's papers.

26. "Proof of the Pudding," 157–58.

27. For a comparison of Kellogg's views with those of recent socialist writers such as André Gorz, see Benjamin Kline Hunnicutt, "Kellogg's Six-Hour Day: A Capitalist Vision of Liberation through Managed Work Reduction," *Business History Review* 66 (1992): 475–522. For a full history of such economic views, see Benjamin Kline Hunnicutt, *Work Without End: Abandoning Shorter Hours for the Right to Work* (Philadelphia, 1988), 32–34; Benjamin Kline Hunnicutt, "The Economic Constraints of Leisure," in Mike Wade, ed., *The Constraints of Leisure* (Springfield, Ill., 1985), 242–86.

28. J. S. Mill, *Principles of Political Economy* (London, 1889, 1923), 749–51, quotations from 750–51.

29. The "backward-bending supply curve of labor," the oldest and most familiar of all economic models, went into circulation during the time of the Mercantilists. The model purported to show how workers offer their labor up for sale under a variety of wage conditions. The Mercantilists theorized that when wages were low, workers tended to supply more of their time and effort to work as wages increased. This is not surprising: as is true of everything else, the higher the price, the greater the supply for the market.

However, quite apart from demand, at some wage level the labor supply curve took a curious turn, after which higher wages encouraged less work, not more. The supply curve became negative or bent "back" (like a closing parenthesis). In keeping with the pessimistic Protestant/Calvinist view of the world, the Mercantilists attributed this phenomenon to human nature: human beings, lazy and corrupt by nature, would prefer leisure (or idleness) to wages and work once they secured a minimum level of existence. See Robert B. Ekelund and R. F. Herbert, *A History of Economic Theory and Method* (New York, 1975), 35–47, 111; J. K. Galbraith, *The Affluent Society* (New York, 1958), 121.

30. Mill, *Principles of Political Economy,* 750.

31. See Hunnicutt, *Work Without End,* 109–46.

32. Arthur Olaus Dahlberg's, *Jobs, Machines, and Capitalism* was published in 1932 and was widely heralded by businessmen, politicians, and academicians. Arthur Schlesinger observed that Dahlberg presented "the most effective statement" for continued work reduction during the Great Depression. See Schlesinger, *The Coming of the New Deal* (Boston, 1959), 91. Louis Rich observed that Dahlberg's ideas evolved directly from the works of Thorstein Veblen and his followers; See *New York Times,* 29 May 1932. Dahlberg, however, maintained that David Friday's *Profit, Wages, and Prices* and Stephen Leacock's *The Unsolved Riddle of Social Justice* had the most impact on him and had "started [him] upon a train of thought which eventuated in this book." *Jobs, Machines, and Capitalism* (New York, 1932), ix; also see the preface. The book received support in influential business circles and directly influenced Hugo Black, who used Dahlberg's arguments about technological unemployment and the need to spread work when

he introduced and defended thirty-hours legislation. Prominent scholars who lent their support included Edward Alsworth Ross, who wrote a foreword for the book, Kimball Young, and Edward A. Filene. Louis Rich praised the work as "one of the most thought provoking . . . within recent times." See *New York Times*, 29 May 1932. Dahlberg's themes were picked up by others, among them John H. Finley, associate editor of the *New York Times*, who argued that the new era of scientific achievement would lead to "spiritual accomplishments" and "the wisdom that comes with leisure", once machines produced more than the world "actually needs of the absolutely pivotal necessities of life." See *New York Times*, 25 March 1932.

33. Dahlberg felt that neither the multiplication of work nor the discovery of new markets would promote recovery. Rather, as Chase argued, these were forms of waste and inefficiency that needed to be controlled. Necessities produced before luxuries, productive work superseding the elaboration of unnecessary tasks—these were Dahlberg's guiding principles. Dahlberg, *Jobs, Machines, and Capitalism*, 103; see also 99–102.

34. Dahlberg attacked the alternative vision (the only theoretical competitor to progressively higher wages and continually shorter hours) that FDR was to make the ideological foundation of the "second" New Deal—the eternal creation of new work to replace work "lost" to capital and the machine. In Dahlberg's estimation, such a "radical" tack would require eternal and accelerating economic growth, perpetually expanding consumerism, a gigantic "waste" of natural resources and "human effort," and increasingly authoritarian governmental controls over the marketplace that would be even worse than socialism. Leisure, the final frontier of freedom for the masses, might lead to democratic culture, continuing education, widespread improvement in physical health, and spiritual growth. Dahlberg, *Jobs, Machines, and Capitalism*, 99, and chap. 3.

35. Instead of accepting shorter hours, business and industry had made the mistake of trying to create new markets, new jobs, and new goods and services in the age of abundance. Dahlberg, *Jobs, Machines, and Capitalism*, 233; see also 2, 122.

36. *Moon-Journal*, 24 November 1930.

37. In 1920 Brown left Emerson for "C. Charter Harrison, consulting management engineer and accountant of New York City." Over the next four year he "worked on the accounts of some of the leading businesses in the country, particularly the American Rolling Mill Company . . . [with personal] charge of revision of cost and general accounting methods." During his stay in New York he became a partner at Harrison Associates. In 1924, Brown left Harrison to take over management of Nichols and Shepard in Battle Creek, manufacturers and distributors of tractors, threshers, and combine harvesters, becoming president in 1928. Brown wrote that "under my management, the entire business was reorganized" in accord with the principles of scientific management.

38. Letter, W. K. Kellogg to Lewis Brown 26 July 1929, folder of correspondence and miscellaneous items, Lewis Brown's papers.

39. Brown's "Resumé," 1 May 1932, folder of correspondence and miscellaneous items, Lewis Brown's papers. During this time, Kellogg appointed Brown as one of the first directors of the Kellogg Foundation.

40. Lord Leverhulme, *The Six-Hour Day & Other Industrial Questions* (London, 1919). Lewis Brown's signed copy was dated "Sept. 1931" by Brown. The book is heavily marked, with notes penciled in the margins in Brown's hand. Brown's son, William Brown, loaned his father's copy of the book to the author.

41. Richard Cavendish, *"Lux Æterna," History Today* 38 (November 1988): 3. Leverhulme was also famous for his profit-sharing schemes and development of "continuous industry."

42. For additional accounts of voluntary work sharing, see David R. Roediger, "The Limits of Corporate Reform: Fordism, Taylorism, and the Working Week in the United States, 1914–1929," in Gary Cross, ed., *Worktime and Industrialization: An International History* (Philadelphia, 1988), 136; see also Best, *Study of a Change*; Hunnicutt, *Work Without End*, 148–53. In addition to Kellogg's and Goodyear, Sears Roebuck, General Motors at Tarrytown, Standard Oil of New Jersey, Hudson Motors, and several cotton manufacturers in New England instituted six-hours. The Baltimore and Ohio Railroad began a share-the-work program for shopmen in 1932, and on 8 October 1932 Remington Rand instituted a four-day week, a program that William Green endorsed.

By 1937, longshoremen on the Pacific Coast had won the thirty-hour week, and union agreements for a-six hour day or a thirty-five/thirty-six hour week were the rule in five major American industries: glass, coal mining, fur manufacture, and men and women's clothing. Approximately 66 percent of organized workers in newspaper publishing had negotiated agreements for less than forty hours; about half of them worked thirty-seven hours. The thirty-six-hour week was part of agreements covering two-thirds of motion picture operators and half the workers in the manufacture of hats. Two of the largest companies in the rubber industry and two large radio companies had the thirty-five- or thirty-six-hour week. About 5 percent of organized building construction workers had thirty-hour agreements; another 5 pecent worked thirty-five hours.

43. Scrapbook, Lewis Brown's papers; "Six-Hour Day Proves Success," *Kellogg News* (21 April 1931); see also ibid. (23 June 1931); Brown, "Operation of 6-Hour Day"; Lewis J. Brown, "What of the Six-Hour Day?" (pamphlet), 1931, folder of correspondence and miscellaneous items, Lewis Brown's papers. A copy of this pamphlet is available in the Presidential Papers, Herbert Hoover Presidential Library, West Branch, Iowa, (hereafter, cited as Hoover Papers). See also *Business Week* (22 April 1931): 16; *Enquirer*, 15 April 1931.

44. "The Kellogg Company's Experience with the Shorter Working Day (Four Shifts of Six Hours Each) at Battle Creek, Michigan" (1935), pamphlet published by the Kellogg Co.

45. Brown, "Operation of 6-Hour Day." See also Brown, "What of the Six-Hour Day?"

46. Brown, "Operation of 6-Hour Day"; see also *Enquirer*, 15, April 1931, where Brown noted that leisure provided: "Opportunities to cultivate farms or gardens . . . affording [workers] both wholesome exercise and a supply of fruits and flowers . . . Time to pursue educational courses, music, or other cultural studies. . . . increased incentives . . . less fatigue, resulting in more healthy, ambitious, alert, and aggressive working force . . . Opportunities for mothers who must support children to earn a living and yet have ample time at home to care for their families . . . I hesitate to stop here, for almost daily employees are finding additional advantages in the plan."

47. For a summary of the history of trading control off the job for control on it, compare David Roediger and Philip Foner, *Our Own Time: A History of American Labor and the Working Day* (New York, 1989), ix; and Gary Cross, *Quest for Time: Reduction of Work in Britain and France 1840–1940* (Berkeley, 1990), 13. Cross concludes, "The upshot of this analysis is that with industrialization workers accepted a trade-off: abdication of control over the pace and use of worktime in exchange for expanded access to nonworktime and increased income. This trade-off may be associated with the emergence of 'corporatism,' 'consumer society,' or 'Fordism.'" Roediger and Foner argue that "shorter hours simplified control of leisure, of intellect and even political power. It is tempting to see such demands for control over increased leisure as concomitant with workers' acceptance of increasingly alienated labor—as a tradeoff of control off the job for control on it."

Whether Kellogg workers accepted Brown's plan is the burden of Chapter Three of this book. For now it is enough to show that Kellogg management was making the strongest possible case for the tradeoff.

48. *Kellogg News* (7 April 1931); letter, Lewis Brown to James Couzens, 30 July 1931, folder of correspondence and miscellaneous items, Lewis Brown's papers. Brown also wrote, "It seems probable that American business will shortly face the need of providing for a shorter working day, and a wage providing for a decent American standard of living, if we are to keep our people busy and stabilize our prosperity." *Kellogg News* (21 April 1931).

49. Lewis Brown explained his departure from Kellogg's in this fashion: "October 1, 1931 I resigned my position [as president and general manager] on account of troubles in the Kellogg family and Mr. W. K. Kellogg re-established himself as president." "Resumé" 1 May 1932, folder of correspondence and miscellaneous items, Lewis Brown's papers.

After leaving Kellogg's, Brown continued to champion the six-hour day and repeat the arguments he used while he was in Battle Creek. See "Urges 6-Hour Work Day Here," *Rockford* [Ill.] *Morning Star,* 26 April 1932, folder of correspondence and miscellaneous items; see also Letter, A. G. Block, secretary of Barnes Drill Company, Rockford, to Lewis Brown, 28 April 1932, folder of correspondence and miscellaneous items, Lewis Brown's papers. "Cereals: Six-Hour Day Helps Kellogg's Co. Do More Work," *Newsweek.*

50. *Enquirer,* 4 December 1930.

51. *New York Times,* 2 August 1932; see also *New York Times,* 3 March 1931. Even before the widespread interest in the "New Leisure" surfaced in 1933–34, the "unemployment or leisure" theme was sounded by prominent people: see Henry Ford, *Moving Forward* (New York, 1930), 16–88, especially chap. 5, entitled "Unemployment or Leisure"; Ford and Crowther, "Unemployment or Leisure," 19; Ida Craven, "Leisure," *Encyclopedia of Social Sciences* (1932), 402–6; *New York Times,* 30 July, 2 October 1931, 2 August 1932.

52. *Kellogg News,* (12 May 1931), folder of correspondence and miscellaneous items, Lewis Brown's papers.

53. Letter, H. B. Hayden to Lewis Brown, 11 May 1932; letter, Lewis Brown to H. B. Hayden, 15 May 1932; letter, Leifur Magnussen, director of the International Labor Organization, to Lewis Brown, 19 May 1931; letter, Lewis Brown to Leifus Magnusson, 21 May 1931, folder of correspondence and miscellaneous items, Lewis Brown's papers.

54. *New York Times,* 2 August 1932; letter, Walter S. Gifford, director of the President's Organization on Unemployment Relief, to President Hoover, Box 319, 1A (3 August 1932), Hoover Papers; "Report of the President's Organization on Unemployment Relief," Box 339, Hoover Papers; letter, E. Dana Durand to W. C. Garner, 23 March 1931, Hoover Papers; letter, Wesley Mitchell to William C. Garner, 12 March 1931, Hoover Papers; "Statement on Spreading Work by the President's Organization on Unemployment Relief," 1 August 1932, Hoover Papers; letter, from A. W. Shaw, Shaw and Co., Chicago, to Lewis Brown 9 October 1931 (concerning Hoover's Committee on Recent Economic Changes), folder of correspondence and miscellaneous items, Lewis Brown's papers.

55. *New York Times,* 9, 10 December 1932, 15 January 1933; "Job Sharing: 5 Million Helped by Work-Spreading, Teagle Committee Estimates," *Business Week* (1 February 1933): 8; "Spread-Work Plans Gain Ground on the Employment Front," *Business Week* (3 August 1932): 7.

56. *New York Times,* 16, 21, 26 May, 30 June, 30 July, 22 September, 5 October 1932; W. Graf, *Platforms of the Two Great Political Parties: 1932 to 1944* (Washington, D.C., compiled 1944), 336, 354; R. F. Himmelberg, *The Great Depression and American Capitalism* (Boston, 1968), 41; L. C. Walker, "The Share-the-Work Movement," *Annals of the American Academy* 165 (January 1933): 13.

Letter, E. W. McCullough, manager, Department of Manufacture, U.S. Chamber of Commerce, to Lewis Brown, no date, folder of correspondence and miscellaneous items, Lewis Brown's papers.

57. S. Miller, Jr., "Labor and the Challenge of the New Leisure," *Harvard Business Review* 11 (1933): 462–67; *New York Times,* 7 October, 4 December 1932, 26 January 1933; "Labor's Ultimatum to Industry: Thirty-Hour Week," *Literary Digest* 114 (10 December 1932): 3–4; "Labor Will Fight," *Business Week* (14 December 1932): 32; "The Labor Army Takes the Field: A Shorter Work Week to Make Jobs," *Literary Digest* 115 (15 April 1933): 6.

58. H. P. Dutton, "Kellogg's 14-Month Experience with a 6-Hour Day," typescript, bound notebook, Lewis Brown's papers. In addition to being co-editor of *Factory and Industrial Management,* Dutton was professor of industrial management at Northwestern University at the time. The published version of the typescript is found in *Factory and Industrial Management,* April 1932.

59. "Kellogg Boosts Wages to New High," *Moon-Journal,* 7 November 1935. The passage quoted was highlighted in a clipping that Brown saved, bound notebook, Lewis Brown's papers.

In October 1935, Kellogg's announced another raise, increasing the minimum wage to $4.50 a day and the average hourly pay 5 cents. Average wages had already been raised 3 cents per hour in April 1934 and the bonus percentage increased. See "Kellogg Raises Wages," *Literary Digest* 120 (November 1935): 40, for the same quotation.

An internal memo from Walter C. Hasselhorn to E. H. McKay contains these company figures; average employment at Kellogg's was, 1,449 in 1930, increasing to 1,612 in 1933, an 11.2 percent increase. By 1938 the numbers had risen to 2,000, a 38.0 percent increase. Perhaps some of the increase is attributable to increased factory capacity, but in the 1933 memo management attributed the increase in payroll to the four shifts. See memo, Hasselhorn to McKay, 7 September 1933, Local No. 3 Archives.

60. *Los Angeles Examiner,* 30 March 1935, clipping, folder of correspondence and miscellaneous items, Lewis Brown's papers.

61. "Moral: Fatter Wages: Kellogg Goes Back to 1930 Pay Scales, Retains 6-Hour Day; Other Industries Advised to Study Plan," *Business Week* (16 November 1939): 9; "The Kellogg Company's Experience with the Shorter Working Day (Four Shifts of Six Hours Each) at Battle Creek, Michigan," pamphlet published by the Kellogg Company in 1935.

62. "Kellogg Boosts Wages to New High," *Moon-Journal,* 7 November 1935, clipping, bound notebook, Lewis Brown's papers.

63. *Kellogg News* (16 June 1931), folder of correspondence and miscellaneous items, Lewis Brown's papers.

64. "Kellogg's Security Plan," *Factory and Industrial Management*" 91 (December 1933): 81—85.

65. Lewis Brown, notes for "Dedication of new Kaffee Hag Coffee plant and our Employees' Recreational Hall" (no date), bound notebook, Lewis Brown's papers.

66. *Kellogg News*, (24 March 1931). Reports about the Kellogg Band, baseball, basketball, softball, volleyball, tennis, golf, and horseshoes teams were regular features of the *Kellogg News* in the 1930s, often appearing on the front page. Sports and activities were the paper's main fare—more articles appear on these than on any other topics. The first issue reported that Kellogg's fielded seven teams in city recreation leagues. The paper consistently advised workers to "turn out regularly at every game to cheer them on."

67. *Kellogg News* (7 April 1931).

68. *Kellogg News* (3 March 1931).

69. Author's survey, no. 431; see also "A Summary of the Kellogg Company's Experience with the Shorter Working Day" (Pamphlet), 1935; "Proof of the Pudding," 11, 112 157–58; Powell, *The Original Has This Signature*, 173, 189.

70. Quoted in Powell, *The Original Has This Signature*, 151, 203, 25, 203–5; "Proof of the Pudding," 157–58; see also Roy Eastman, "The W. K. Kellogg Story," *Advertising Age* 38 (6 March 1967): 102.

71. As quoted by Powell, *The Original Has This Signature*, 287, 289, 291. Also Jack Willoughby, "Legacy (Will Keith Kellogg)," *Forbes* 135 (25 March 1985): 88.

72. Powell, *The Original Has This Signature*, 18. James McQuiston observed that W. K. "started his foundation in 1930, the same year the six-hour day was started. . . . [he was] brought up in the Seventh-day discipline, like the Adventists. And he felt a responsibility to be a good steward of what the Lord gave him." Interview with James McQuiston, retired Kellogg manager, 11 August 1989. Like American Jews, the Adventists faced the problem of keeping their Sabbath on Saturday in a nation where Sunday religious observance was the rule. Blue laws complicated the work week for the Adventists, who like Jews were often forced to work on Saturday to make up for Sunday closings. Kellogg's concerns about the management of work hours may have this indirect link with the Adventists' struggles.

73. Powell, *The Original Has This Signature*, 19–21. See also Gerald Carson, *Cornflake Crusade* (New York, 1976), 11, 143–45; Ira Brown, "Watchers for the Second Coming: The Millenarian Tradition in America," *Journal of American History* 39 (1952): 342–46. According to Carson (103), Sister White continued to be active in the administration of the Sanitarium until the church broke its ties with John Harvey in 1907.

74. Although T. Coraghessan Boyle's *The Road to Wellville* (New York, 1993) and the movie by the same name are supposed to be about John Harvey Kellogg, they have little to do with the historical reality.

75. Tom Lutz, *American Nervousness, 1903: An Anecdotal History* (Ithaca, 1991), 221, 230, and passim; Powell, *The Original Has This Signature*, 54–55; Carson, *Cornflake Crusade*, 12, 76, 82; see also H. L. Mencken, *Happy Days* (New York, 1940).

76. *Printer's Ink* 111 (20 May 1929); *New York Times*, 17 May 1942; Powell, *The Original Has This Signature*, 56.

77. *Battle Creek Evening News*, 23 July 1915; *Enquirer*, 7 February 1938, 3 April 1950; Powell, *The Original Has This Signature*, 82.

78. Carson, *Cornflake Crusade*, 102; Powell, *The Original Has This Signature*, 59, 61.

79. Powell, *The Original Has This Signature*, 64, 65, 203, 204; *Enquirer*, 7 October 1951.

80. *Enquirer*, 7 October 1951; A. E. Wiggam, "The Most Remarkable Man I Have Ever Known," *American Magazine* 6 (December 1925): 14–15; see also *Good Health* 85 (September 1950): 205; Carson, *Cornflake Crusade*, 108, 122, 123.

81. *Enquirer*, 7 October 1951; Carson, *Cornflake Crusade*, 108, 198, 199, 207.

82. See the *Moon-Journal*, 6 January 1937, for an account of the Kellogg Foundation's granting $73,000 for a recreation center and Campfire Girls camp at Morris Lake. Also interview with Howard Roe, union official of the American Federation of Grain Millers (AFGM), 4 June 1990; Kellogg Foundation, *The First Eleven Years, 1930–1941* (Battle Creek, 1942); Kellogg Foundation, *The First Twenty-Five Years: The Story of a Foundation* (Battle Creek, 1955); Powell, *The Original Has This Signature*, 269–76, 310–25; Carson, *Cornflake Crusade*, 226–27.

83. Interview with Wayne Gleason, 5 May 1993; author's survey, no. 6; letter no. 51 from Wayne A. Gleason; letter no. 172 from Harold E. Davis; letter no. 185 from Brayden Plumb; letter no. 241.

84. Powell, *The Original Has This Signature*, 173.

85. Ibid. 211.

86. *Factory and Industrial Management* 81 (1931): 775, 776. The editors had spoken with W. K. just before they wrote, so an echo of his language may be heard. The editors continued, "[The six-hour day] recognized the changed balance between leisure to live and productivity to supply the means of living . . . and recognize[d] increased leisure with security as the most logical increase in the standard of living. [It was] the forerunner of a general movement aimed not only at meeting the widespread unemployment . . . but at providing a saner utilization of our resources of man power and machinery."

CHAPTER TWO

1. E. P. Thompson, "Time, Work-Discipline and Industrial Capitalism," *Past and Present* 38 (December 1967): 56–97, quotation on 85. In addition see Eric J. Hobsbawm, *Labouring Men: Studies in the History of Labor* (New York, 1964), especially chap. 17, "Custom, Wage and Workload," 344–71; Keith Thomas, "Work and Leisure in Pre-Industrial Societies," *Past and Present* 29 (1962): 50–62; Sidney Pollard, "Factory Discipline in the Industrial Revolution," *Economic History Review* 16 (1968): 254–71; Gareth Stedman Jones, "Working Class Culture: Working Class Politics in London 1870–1900," *Journal of Social History* 9 (1974): 460–508; Alasdair Clayre, *Work and Play: Ideas and Experience of Work and Leisure* (London, 1974); Herbert Gutman, *Work, Culture and Society in Industrializing America* (New York, 1976), 3–78; David Roediger and Philip Foner, *Our Own Time: A History of American Labor and the Working Day* (New York, 1989), 193; David Roediger, "The Movement for the Shorter Working Day in the United States before 1866" (Ph.D. dissertation, Northwestern University, 1980), 4–12.

2. E. P. Thompson, "Time, Work-Discipline and Industrial Capitalism," 84.

3. Ibid. 86.

4. John R. Commons et al., *History of Labor in the United States,* 4 vols. (New York; 1918–35), 1:170–72, 384–85, 479, 546; 2:89–90, 102–110, 475–79; 3:97–113; Harry A. Millis and Royal E. Montgomery, *The Economics of Labor,* 3 vols. (New York, 1938–45), vol. 1: *Labor's Progress and Some Basic Labor Problems,* 491–93; see also vol. 3: *Organized Labor,* 423; see Irving Bernstein, *The Lean Years: A History of the American Worker, 1920–1933* (Boston; 1960), 476 (quotation); Foster Rhea Dulles, *Labor in America* (New York, 1966), 106, 107; Marion C. Cahill, *Shorter Hours: A Study of the Movement since the Civil War* (New York, 1922), 14–19; Selig Perlman, *A History of Trade Unionism in the United States* (New York, 1921, 1950), 4, 45, 46; Sidney Fine, "The Eight-Hour Day Movement in the United States, 1888–1891," *Journal of American History,* 40 (1953): 441–61.

5. David Brody, "The Old Labor History and the New: In Search of an American Working Class," *Labor History* 20 (1979): 111–25.

6. Historians who have made contributions to a cultural history of work time include David Roediger and Philip Foner, authors of *Our Own Time,* and Gary Cross, *Quest for Time: Reduction of Work in Britain and France 1840–1940* (Berkeley, 1990). Other published works include the books and articles listed in n. 4 to the Introduction, and William McGaughey, Jr., *A Shorter Workweek in the 1980s* (White Bear Lake, Minn., 1981); Scott Christopher Martin's superb "Leisure in Southwestern Pennsylvania, 1800–1850" (Ph.D. dissertation, University of Pittsburgh, 1990), 7–10; Steven J. Ross, "Workers on the Edge: Work, Leisure, and Politics in Industrializing Cincinnati: 1830–1890"

(Ph.D. dissertation, Princeton University; 1980), iii–v, 317–404; John T. Cumbler, *Working-Class Community in Industrial America: Work, Leisure, and Struggle in Two Industrial Cities, 1880–1930* (Westport, Conn., 1979), 7–12, 28–38, 114–28; Roy Rosenzweig, *Eight Hours for What We Will: Workers and Leisure in an Industrial City, 1870–1920* (Cambridge, 1983), 222–28. See also David Montgomery, *Beyond Equality: Labor and the Radical Republicans, 1862–1872* (New York, 1967), 234–38; David Brody, *Steel Workers in America: The Nonunion Era* (New York, 1960), 171–73; Virginia Yans McLaughlin, "Patterns of Work and Family Organization: Buffalo's Italians," *Journal of Interdisciplinary History* 2 (1971): 299–314; Elizabeth Peck, "Family Time and Industrial Time," *Journal of Urban History* 1 (1975): 365–89; Alice Kessler-Harris, "Organizing the Unorganized: Three Jewish Women and Their Incomes," *Labor History* 17 (Winter 1976): 5–15; Benjamin K. Hunnicutt, The Jewish Sabbath Movement in the Early Twentieth Century," *American Jewish History* 69 (1979): 196–225.

7. Roediger and Foner, *Our Own Time,* 19. See also 1–25 and preface.

8. Ibid. vii.

9. Cross, *Quest for Time,* 4, 53, 54. See also vii–x, 1–20, 51–55.

10. Ibid. 20. For Cross's "leisure ethic," see 172, 179.

11. Ibid. 14.

12. Ibid. 34–42; Roediger and Foner, *Our Own Time,* 1–31; for revolutionary rhetoric as applied to shorter hours, see 34, 35, 42, 105.

13. Quoted in David Roediger, "Movement for the Shorter Working Day," 5.

14. Ibid. 46.

15. Cross, *Quest for Time,* 2.

16. Helen Sumner, "Causes of the Awakening," in Commons et al., *History of Labor* 1: 169–192. Sumner's chapter deals with the period before 1850. According to Commons and his associates, leisure was labor's earliest motive, the "cause of the awakening" of the American wage earner. In the 1820s and 1830s, the "most frequent cause of complaint among the workers was the lack of leisure." But after the 1918 publication of the first two volumes of their classic work, Commons and his associates rarely mentioned leisure again. Only Sumner's chapter emphasizes leisure as an important labor motive.

17. In *Our Own Time,* Roediger and Foner seek nothing less than "to reinterpret U.S. labor history" (xi), but they stop short of a full assault on the dominant economic interpretation, seeking rather to reconcile their social history with traditional economic analyses. Cross, in *Quest for Time,* is also interested in the "relinkage of political and social history"(4). Adding cultural and social motives to the economic drives that moved workers may be enough to advance the history of shorter hours, but the progressive shortening of the hours of labor raises questions about which set of motives, the economic or the social, was dominant. A

conflict between wages and hours is built into the workers' experience of the marketplace, and workers' views about what industrial progress is and where the modern world should be going are clearly conflicted as well.

Shorter hours raise an either/or historical question: more work for more of what industrial society creates, or more time outside the industrial workplace and marketplace for something else? Certainly the economic realm is tied to social and cultural forces. But the historical relationship, as the economists themselves insist, is either/or. It is therefore of critical importance to determine when, where, and whether economic or cultural forces were dominant.

It is my contention that cultural change rather than economic forces explains the death of the six-hour day in Battle Creek, but I do not deny the importance of economic experiences. As Sewell maintains, the historian's duty is to "capture [economic experiences] as experiences, as being construed by those who lived through them, as having *meanings* that need to be recovered." William Sewell, Jr., *Work and Revolution in France from the Old Regime to 1848* (Cambridge, 1980), 11.

18. Interview with anonymous Kellogg worker in her home in Battle Creek, 11 August 1989, (interview no. 12).

19. For example, David Roediger has made a strong case for the continuing importance of leisure. He argues persuasively that the leaders of both the ten- and the eight-hour movements in the nineteenth century were very much concerned with increased freedom from work, viewing it as something like a natural right won by the American Revolution, a form of emancipation comparable to the freeing of the slaves, and a religious (and specifically Methodist) achievement essential for the operation of "free moral agency." Roediger questions traditional interpretations that subordinate interest in free time to economic motives and he maintains that middle-class leaders, speaking for workers, consistently stressed the value of increased free time for cultural development, education, and moral and religious concerns. "Movement for the Shorter Working Day," 264–67.

20. Ross, "Workers on the Edge," iii–v, 317–404; James T. Adams, *Our Business Civilization* (New York, 1929), 17; see also 15–25, 191–96.

21. J. B. Gilbert, *Work without Salvation: American's Intellectuals and Industrial Alienation, 1880–1910* (Baltimore, 1977), vii–xv, 26, 29, 65–124; quotations from vii; Daniel Rodgers, *The Work Ethic in Industrial America* (Chicago, 1978), 28, 29, 65–124.

22. Rodgers, *Work Ethic in Industrial America*, 90, 107.

23. Ibid. 160.

24. Michael Seidman, *Work Against Work: Labor in Paris and Barcelona during the Popular Fronts* (Berkeley and Los Angeles, 1991), 169. Seidman presents a compelling "socially oriented, comparative" history of workers in Barcelona and Paris during the Popular Front era. A generation of historians have overlooked the

obvious fact that workers seldom shared the work myths of intellectuals and politicians. Uncritically accepting modern work as one of history's final goals and meanings, historians have been led, perhaps dominated, in this area by Marxist and labor historians who harbor the True Faith in a utopia of the workplace, modernization theorists who expect workers to adapt to modern work and find perfect freedom in doing what they have to do, and others who claim that in a work culture "workers find meaning" mainly in work and that labor is "literally meaningful." Labor historians have largely overlooked workers' continuing resistance to work and "the consequent coercion needed to overcome it" (ibid.). They ignore E. P. Thompson's identification of worker resistance as the *sine qua non* of the original imposition of industrial work discipline.

Against the ubiquitous work mythology, Seidman sets the "lived experience," deeds, and words of workers in Barcelona and Paris during the 1930s, finding a confrontation in which politicians' and intellectuals' faith in work was challenged by workers' experiences and aspirations. The same "workplace utopianism" that befuddles historians today misled the leaders of the Popular Front in Paris and the anarchosyndicalists in Barcelona and resulted, at least in part, in their downfall.

See also William Chase and Lewis Siengelbaum, "Worktime and Industrialization in the U.S.S.R.," in Gary Cross, ed., *Worktime and Industrialization: An International History* (Philadelphia, 1988), 183–216.

25. Surely, as the labor economists claimed and most historians still insist, workers also used time outside work for consumption. Long before the labor economists, industrialists like Henry Ford realized that free time was an economic asset because of the buying and consuming going on. During the 1920s businessmen and industrialists coined a phrase that summed up their ebullient view of advertising's future and leisure's unlimited potential: the New Economic Gospel of Consumption. Commercialized leisure, thus conceived and controlled, undoubtedly supported industrial growth and work discipline.

But, until very recently at least, this was not the whole story. Before the Great Depression, the cultural uses of leisure were often in open competition with consumption of industrial products. Abundant, increasing leisure offered an alternative to work and consumption. Leisure had a "humanitarian side," as Ford warned, that was dangerous and needed to be controlled by proper marketing methods (and, if necessary, the state) to keep workers working "full-time" and consuming at a satisfactory level. If workers were content to visit around their neighborhoods, chat on the front porch, or read at home instead of buying more things, expanding leisure posed a direct threat to the sale of Ford automobiles.

The economist Staffan Linder noted the change during this century from "time-intensive" to "good-intensive" leisure—from experiences that required more time and little money (such as conversation, community and church activities) to those that required relatively more consumption in less time (such as professional sports, movies, motoring, and eating out). See Staffan Linder, *The Harried Leisure Class* (New York, 1970),135. Without extreme distortion, one might restate Linder's conclusion in historical terms as a change from culturally intensive leisure to consumption-intensive leisure—a change that leads to the advent of a "Cultureless Leisure Class." But even as expanding leisure was being commodified during the first decades of this century, workers were also, in a contrary motion, turning to their own subcultures, still contributing their labor to the industrial economy, at least in part, as a means to outside ends. The "struggle about time" continued even as advertising expanded and new, attractive goods and services competed with traditional leisure patterns.

For most observers in the early part of this century, Henry Ford included, it was hardly a foregone conclusion that commercial amusements and "luxuries" would swamp "culturally intensive" leisure, or that perpetual economic growth would automatically win over expanding leisure. Instead, expanding leisure was a threat precisely because it represented value systems and a way of life outside the marketplace, offering a viable alternative to industrial work and capitalism. As long as workers considered work merely a means to an end, as long as they had things they would rather do than consume and work, shorter hours might be industry's downfall. A worker revolution would not be necessary to dethrone capitalism; American workers could do it simply by choosing to sell less of their time.

26. David Montgomery, "Gutman's Nineteenth Century America," *Labor History* 19 (1978): 419.

27. Following the fashion of some unfashionable economists, one may further propose that workers' cultural concerns were expressed directly in the marketplace. To the extent that workers chose higher wages, they were probably more interested in "the group of things purchasable with money;" to the extent that they chose shorter hours, they were probably more concerned with all the "non-pecuniary, alternative uses of time" that ethnologists, cultural historians, and anthropologists are now taking seriously. Detailed histories of work time offer the opportunity to find out more fully what Gutman's "rejection of economic man" means, to analyze what the alternative, outside cultural reality looked like, and to determine how the evolving cultural reality related to the evolving cultural experience of economic reality. See F. H. Knight, *Risk, Uncertainty and Profit* (New York, 1921, 1964), 116–17. This sort of speculation has led economists to make what Robert Lane called "The Claim" in "Markets and the Satisfaction of Human Wants," *Journal of Economic Issues* 12 (1978) 803–12. These economists have contended that the free market automatically assigns "value" to most if not all kinds of human motivations and satisfactions. See, for example, Alfred Marshall's familiar quotation in *Principles of Economics* (8th ed.), 17, 193, and Jack Barbash, *Job Satisfaction and*

Attitude Studies (Paris, 1976), 19; James Heckman, "Shadow Prices, Market Wages and Labor Supply," *Econometrica* 42 (1974): 679–94.

28. The text of the 1926 resolution is revealing:

Whereas under present methods of modern machine industry the workers are continually subject to the strain of mechanized processes which sap their vitality; and Whereas if compelled to work for long hours under modern processes of production, the vitality, health, and very life of workers is [*sic*] put in serious jeopardy. . . .

Resolved, that this convention place itself on record as favoring a progressive shortening of the hours of labor and the days per week and that the Executive Council be requested to inaugurate a campaign of education and organization to that end.

See Chester M. Wright, "Epoch-Making Decisions in the Great American Federation Labor Convention at Detroit," *American Labor World* (1926): 22–24; American Federation of Labor, *Report of the Proceedings of the 46th Annual Convention of the American Federation of Labor* (Washington, D.C., 1926), especially the Report of the Committee on the Shorter Workday, 195–207; for a reprint of the resolution see *Monthly Labor Review* 23 (1926): 1167.

29. Amalgamated Clothing Workers of America, *Advance* 1 (6 April 1917): 7; see also ibid. 2 (11 October 1918): 4; 2 (31 May 1918): 4; 2 (9 August 1918): 6; 2 (16 August 1918): 4; 3 (24 January 1919): 4–6; 3 (7 February 1919): 4; 12 (11 March 1927): 10; 17 (2 January 1931): 2; see especially 21 (19 April, 1935): 10, in which Joseph Schlossberg observed that, during the 1920s, "working people demanded leisure for participation in the enjoyments of life." During the Depression, however, "a new point" was realized: a recognition that "we work too many hours and we produce too much." See also International Ladies Garment Workers' *Journal* 1 (15 February 1919): 6; 1 (11 October 1919): 5; 9 (3 February 1928): 1, 3, 8; 9 (1 May 1930): 4–5.

30. Juliet Stuart Poyntz, "The Conquest of Leisure," *Justice* 1 (15 February 1919): 6; Hunnicutt, "Jewish Sabbath Movement"; Irving Howe, *World of Our Fathers* (New York, 1976), 430–538 and passim; Marcus E. Ravage, *An American in the Making* (1917; New York, 1971), 146–58, 173, 174; Irving Howe and Kenneth Libo, *How We Lived: A Documentary History of Immigrant Jews in America 1880–1930* (New York, 1979), 162, 164, 165, 201–204, 279, 280–92, 295; Elizabeth Hasanovitz, *One of Them: Chapter from a Passionate Autobiography* (New York, 1918), 146, 158–63, 177, 303–5; Joan Morrison and Charlotte Zabusky, *American Mosaic: The Immigrant Experience in the World of Those Who Lived It* (New York, 1980), 14.

31. See Editorial, *American Federationist* 34 (1927): 1300; see also "Labor Now Out for the Five-Day Week," *Literary Digest* 91 (16 October 1926): 9–11;

Monthly Labor Review 23 (1926): 1153–69; *Magazine of Business* 56 (August, 1929): 136–37; *New York Times,* 17 October 1926; the *American Federationist* issue for January 1926 included several articles on the importance of recreation and leisure. See also Editorial, "Recreation Declaration, The Atlantic City Convention—The Leisure Problem," *American Federationist* 33 (1926): 94; William Green, "5 Day Week in the Building Trades," *American Federationist* 35 (1928): 915; the April 1927 issue of the *American Federationist* was devoted to worker education; Matthew Woll, "Leisure and Labor," *Playground* 19 (1925): 322; "Recreation and the Labor Movement," *Playground* 18 (1924): 649; Leifus Magnusson, "Labor and the Leisure Movement," *Playground* 21 (1927): 656; "Utilization of Workers' Leisure Time—Report of the Director of the International Labor Office," *Monthly Labor Review* 31 (1930): 593. For labor's interest in leisure before 1926, see Eugene Lies, "Organized Labor and Recreation," *American Federationist* 20 (1923): 648.

32. William Green, "Leisure for Labor: A New Force Alters Our Social Structure," *Magazine of Business* 56 (August 1929): 136–37; see also William Green, "Workers' Education," *American Federationist* 34 (1927): 401 for "the cultural use of leisure." For labor's view in general see J. H. Maurer, "Leisure and Labor," *Playground* 20 (1927): 649–55; S. A. Shaw, "Now That Jerry Has Time to Live," *Survey* 52 (1924): 568–70; "Leisure Time of Workers," *Playground* 18 (1924): 342–47; George Eastman, "Letter to the Recreation Congress at Atlantic City," *Playground* 16 (1922): 409; "Resolution on Community Service Adopted at the American Federation of Labor Convention at Portland," *Playground* 18 (1924): 649; "State Education for Adult Workers in Massachusetts," *Monthly Review of Labor Statistics* 17 (1928): 975; Ralph Aiken, "A Laborer's Leisure," *North American Review* 232 (1931): 268; William Green, "The Five-Day Week: Inevitable."

33. William Green, "The Five-Day Week," *American Federationist* 33 (1926): 1025. In this article unemployment is mentioned, but the transition to leisure is under way; see also William Green, "The Five-Day Week," *North American Review* (1926): 567–74; *New York Times,* 9 December 1926; William Green, "Less Working Hours Is Logical," *American Labor World* (November 1926): 20; "The Proposed Five-Day Week," *Industry* 108 (23 October 1926): 1; "The Five Day Week, Facts for Workers," *Labor Bureau Economic News Letter* (November 1926): 12.

34. William Green, "Editorial," *American Federationist* 35 (1928): 785.

35. Matthew Woll, "Labor and the New Leisure," *Recreation* 27 (1933): 428; Woll, "Leisure and Labor," 322–23; AFL, *Proceedings of the 46th Convention,* 195–207.

36. Lewis J. Brown, "Operation of 6-Hour Day," reprinted in *Printer's Ink* 156 (27 August 1931): 33, and *Factory and Industrial Management* 82 (1931): 514.

37. See Benjamin Kline Hunnicutt, *Work Without End: Abandoning Shorter Hours for the Right to Work* (Philadelphia, 1988), chap. 3, "Leisure for Labor," and chap. 5, "Shorter Hours in the Early Depression."

CHAPTER THREE

1. Best's questionnaire, no. 314, National Archives, U.S. Department of Labor, Women's Bureau, Raw Data, Box 153, Records of Ethel Best's 1932 Kellogg Survey, Washington, D.C. (hereafter cited as Best's questionnaire).

2. Interview with Grace Lindsey at a Battle Creek restaurant, 5 a.m., 12 August 1989. Ping-pong became popular in the United States around 1927. The equipment was cheap and the space needed to play fairly small. Several amateur sports flourished at the time, competing for a while with the rival that finally submerged them—the nonparticipatory watching of professional sports, what Jay Nash in the 1930s called spectatoritis.

3. Interview with Leroy Despins, retired worker from the 1930s, 3 August 1994.

4. Letter no. 468 from worker who began at Kellogg's in February 1937.

5. Interview with Leroy Despins.

6. For William Green, president of the AFL, the Kellogg model was "shorter hours with the same weekly wages, higher hourly wages, and expanded payrolls." Throughout the thirties, labor repeated Brown's and Kellogg's claims about the importance of managing the diminishing, national demand for labor at the level of the individual firm and accepted Kellogg's vision of industrial progress as steadily increasing free time, reiterating the AFL's 1926 call for "progressively shortening the hours of labor." See for example, *New York Times*, 7 October, 4 December 1932, 26 January 1933; "Labor's Ultimatum to Industry: Thirty-Hour Week," *Literary Digest* 114 (10 December 1932): 3–4; "Labor Will Fight," *Business Week* (14 December 1932): 32; "The Labor Army Takes the Field: A Shorter Work Week to Make Jobs," *Literary Digest* 115 (15 April 1933): 6; letter, Hugo Black to P. A. Redmond, 23 December 1932, Hugo Black Papers, Library of Congress, Washington, D.C.

7. *Enquirer*, 1 December 1930. Subsequently, the *Enquirer* ran an Associated Press interview (dateline Washington, D.C., 12 December 1930) with Dr. William John Cooper, "commissioner of education," who predicted that by the year 2030 public schools would be more concerned with "how to live" than "how to make a living." Cooper based his prediction on a century of industrial progress that had steadily reduced work, and confidently asserted what other notables such as George Bernard Shaw and Julian Huxley were predicting: that automated machinery would "remove burdensome toil from the backs of man." Consequently, schools of the future would have to teach students "how to care for their health, how to

spend their leisure time to advantage, how to discharge their civic duties, how to make worthy homes and be capable parents." The local press also made much of the workers' delight in the six-hour day, Battle Creek's position at the forefront of labor's century-long fight for shorter hours, and the potential of the new leisure to change the town for the better. See *Enquirer*, 4 December 1930, 24 November 1932. Just as the national media were fascinated by the possibility of mass free time and took the "new leisure" seriously, Battle Creek's press assumed that the coming age would see the "problem of leisure" as its central concern. Battle Creek had once again become a pioneer outpost, now on a new frontier of free time.

8. "Six Months of the Six-Hour Day," *Factory and Industrial Management* 81 (1931): 775–76; see also "The Proof of the Pudding: Kellogg's 15 Month Experience with the 6-Hour Day," ibid. 91 (1932): 157–58.

9. Henry Goddard Leach, "Editorial: Humanizing Machines—II; Kellogg's Six-Hour Day," *Forum* 96 (September 1936): 97–98; Chapin Hoskins, "Is the 6-Hour Day Feasible?" *Forbes* 24 (July 1931): 16–18, 28 (quotation); *Business Week* (22 April 1931): 16.

10. *Business Week* (22 April 1931): 16; "Six Months of the Six-Hour Day."

11. For survey evidence of workers' opinion during the 1920s, see Ithaca, New York, School of Industrial and Labor Relations Collections, Consumer's League of New York Papers, Box 5B, File Folder 19, and Box 6A. See especially "Report of the Executive Secretary Meeting of the Board of Directors, February 8, 1927"; Consumer League of New York, "The Forty Eight Hour Law: Do Working Women Want It?" (New York: Consumer's League of New York, 1926–27), 35 pp. (pamphlet held by Wisconsin Historical Society, Madison, Wisconsin); see also Amalgamated Clothing Workers, *Advance* 12 (11 March 1927): 10.

In 1927 the Women's Bureau investigated the hours of work of 230,000 women in 2,600 establishments in 18 states. "The noise and speed of machinery . . . the complexity or the monotony of the job . . . undue fatigue . . . participation in community life . . . citizenship . . . interest in the home . . . home responsibilities . . . and leisure—and all that is implied" by leisure were the important reasons for the women's preference for shorter hours. No mention was made in this investigation (or in the Women's Bureau's 1928 Report) of either lost weekly wages or unemployment. See U.S. Department of Labor, "Bulletin of the Women's Bureau," *Bulletin* no. 58 (1927); "Women's Bureau Report," *American Federationist* 35 (1928): 709; see also U.S. Department of Labor, "Women in Delaware Industries," *Bulletin* no. 58 (1928).

12. Ethel L. Best, *A Study of a Change from 8 to 6 Hours of Work* (Washington D.C., 1933). The company's name was even kept confidential when the results were published. See letter, Ethel Best to Walter Hasselhorn, efficiency engineer, 12 July 1932, National Archives, U.S. Department of Labor, Women Bureau, Raw Data, Box 153 (hereafter cited as Box 153).

13. Of the 249 women who had worked the old eight-hour shifts at Kellogg's and had lost some pay when six-hour shifts came in, over 77 percent "preferred" six-hours. Of the 109 workers who had been hired after six-hours was instituted, 106 "expressed a decided preference for it" or were "very enthusiastic." Best, *Study of a Change*.

14. It is clear from the Best questionnaires that the agents discussed preferences with workers in hypothetical terms—that is, "Would you rather have 'more free time and less money' or 'more money and less time'?" Traditionally, economists have used similar questionnaire methods to draw conclusions about wage/leisure "preferences." The overwhelming majority of Kellogg workers who spoke of having such a "preference" said that they "preferred" the "extra time" to the "extra money." Certainly, many said they regretted having lost wages, but they expressed their preference in terms of a tradeoff. A small group said they preferred the "extra money," and a few vacillated or said they wanted both.

Best found it "significant that nearly 20 percent of the women with broken marital ties, in contrast to only about 10 percent of the single and of the married women, did prefer to work longer hours," adding that "possibly the greater economic responsibility of the women supporting homes without the aid of their husbands may have made the difference in earnings more important for them." This was Best's only reference to the economic pressures caused by the pay cut. But Best's claim that "broken marital ties" were important in accounting for worker preference is not supported by the numbers. Recalculation of her data shows no significant correlation between worker preference for eight- or six-hours and marital status. A dichotomy between women who were married versus those who were separated, divorced, or widowed produces a marital-status variable that shows no significant correlation with preference for six-hours or eight-hours.

TABLE 1. Preferences (rows) by marital status

Marital Status	Preferred 8-Hours	Preferred 6-Hours	Totals
Divorced, Separated, Widowed	11 (2.5%)	34 (8.5%)	45 (11%)
Married	54 (13%)	320 (77%)	374 (89%)
Total	65 (15.5%)	354 (84.5%)	419 (100%)

Best also neglected to tabulate the data her team gathered about the employment status of husbands. Surprisingly, women whose husbands were unemployed or employed part-time were no more likely to prefer eight-hours than those whose husbands were working full-time. Moreover, the author observed no significant statistical correlation between preference for six-hours and marital status (dichotomized as single versus married). These conclusions are based on statistical analysis similar to that in Table 1.

15. First, the team examined Kellogg's payroll books and compared wages paid before the change to six-hours and after hourly wages had been increased a second time. Management claimed that the total 25 percent hourly raise offset the original reduction in the work week from 40 to 36 hours.

Afterward, the team visited the 196 workers whose pay records they had examined (as well as an additional 61) and asked them what their average earnings were under the eight-hour and the six-hour schedules. The periods Best's team chose as the basis of comparison were September 1930 and April 1932. But the history of Kellogg's wages is so complicated that these numbers are misleading. During the fall of 1930, Kellogg tried out a five-day week to avoid laying off workers, reducing the work week from 48 hours to 40. The six-hour day reduced the work week again, but only to 36 hours, because Kellogg went back to six-day weekly operations in December 1930. But Best's most important finding was that workers *said* they had lost money on the deal—precisely how much was actually lost to the five-day week and how much to the six-hour day is not as important.

16. Best also confirmed Kellogg's claims about its larger payroll, noting that the number of women workers in the plant increased from 298 to 415, or 39 percent, one month after six-hours began, and that the number had continued to grow. She also confirmed that the women had received "a total increase [of hourly wages] of 25 percent over the rates in effect before the change in hours," even though weekly wages had declined.

In addition to Best's official report, published by the Department of Labor, she and the agents she directed left complete handwritten records of all 434 of their interviews. A treasure trove, Box 153 of the Women's Bureau's raw data files contains some of the best remaining evidence of workers' attitudes about work reduction. Best's analysis of the data stands up well upon reexamination, although her report has some flaws. She made one glaring omission in her attempt to explain the workers' attitudes. She mentioned that management's major goal was "to give work to more people without . . . increasing the cost of operations, and to do this without throwing the cost of shorter hours entirely on the employees." She also recognized that it was significant that virtually all workers hired after the company went to six-hour shifts enthusiastically supported the short schedule. But she neglected to include unemployment-reduction explicitly as a reason that workers hired before December 1930 preferred shorter hours. Letter, Ethel Best to Eugene McKay, general manager of Kellogg's, 12 July 1932, Box 153.

Further statistical analysis of the survey team's raw data shows little significant correlation between the amount of wages lost or gained by the six-hour day and preference for six- or eight-hour shifts; the correlation was significant at the .05 level but the correlation was only .190, "explaining" only 3 percent of the variation in the women's preference for six-hours in regression analysis. Recalculation by means of the chi-square produced a even weaker probability that there is a measurable relation between hours preference and earnings. A 2 (hours preference) by 9 (wage) table of frequencies shows that 83 percent of women who lost 26–30 percent of their paycheck preferred six-hours, as did 77 percent who lost 21–25 percent, 85 percent who lost 16–20 percent, 91 percent who lost 11–15 percent, 100 percent who lost 6–10 percent, and 84 percent who lost 0–5 percent. All whose earnings had improved preferred the short schedule.

The author observed no significant statistical correlation between preference for six-hours and marital status (dichotomized as single versus married); number of children; employment status of husband (employed, unemployed, or partially employed); respondent's age; or place of birth (dichotomized as U.S. versus foreign-born). The author also takes issue with Best's conclusion that a disproportionate number of workers who preferred eight-hours were on the evening and night shifts. More of these workers may have been dissatisfied because of the loss of the night bonus, but it is not clear that significantly more of them disliked the shorter schedule. In regression analysis, the author found only a .042 coefficient of correlation between preference for six-hours and the shift on which the respondent worked.

Those who preferred eight-hours and those who preferred six-hours were remarkably similar statistically. Women with seniority (based on the date the worker started at Kellogg's) were as likely to prefer six-hours as younger workers, even though women hired after 1930 were more liable "to be enthusiastic" or to "much prefer" six-hours. The one great difference was what the two groups said about the "extra hours." Those who "preferred" six-hours tended to say that the extra hours were a benefit, while those who "preferred" eight-hours tended not to, thus confirming Best's major conclusion that "the workers seem to feel that . . . they were being given time off for their reduced pay." Records of Best's 1932 Kellogg survey, Women's Bureau, National Archives.

17. Question 10a and 10c of Best's questionnaire.

18. See Best's questionnaire, nos. 221, 222, and 239 for "would hate to go back to the old shift"; no. 280: Nola Handy would "hate to have to work 8 hours"; no. 309: Iva Wood would "would dislike to work eight hours again"; nos. 353, 391: "it would be hard to work 8 hrs"; no. 285.

19. The best statement of the thesis is Arlie Russell Hochschild, *The Second Shift: Working Parents and the Revolution at Home* (New York, 1989); see also

Suzanne Desaulniers and Nancy Théberge, "Gender Differences in the Likelihood That Work Reduction Will Lead to an Increase in Leisure," *Loisir et Société* 15, no. 1 (1992): 135–52.

20. See, for example, Best's questionnaire, no. 86, Helen Broker; no. 195: Lucille Hicks spoke of "housework, washing, ironing, gardening"; no. 237: Alice Vande Siessen, fifty-eight years old, married, husband unemployed, use of extra time "sewing, housework and meals;" no. 154: Nola Denkoff, "fancy sewings, reading"; no. 324: May Partridge, thirty-one, two children, "has garden to show for extra time"; no. 341, Mary Repak said "Garden and needlework, showed agent a great deal of needlework and crocheting which she has done over the last two years . . . could not take care of a garden before . . . too tired."

It is tempting to use words like "hobbies," "crafts," or "leisure activities" in writing about such pursuits. Even though the Kellogg women use these words occasionally, they have become so encrusted with extraneous meaning (mostly associations with the trivial, the unrewarding, and the unimportant) that they would be misleading. An excellent case in point is the word "craft." Well into the twentieth century, "craft" had strong, positive connotations having to do with work, as in "craftsman." The word was being grafted to free activities during the 1920s and 1930s; in Battle Creek, "home-crafts" were being tried in the extra time. If work was losing its craft dimension, then perhaps individual skill and expertise could be kept alive outside the context of modern jobs, in leisure. Gradually, that usage was trivialized; "arts and crafts" became "pastimes," and "craft" and "hobby" shops sprang up in the city.

21. Best, *Study of a Change,* 9.

22. Best's questionnaire, no. 136.

23. Best's questionnaire, no. 158: Hilda Gibbs "puts up more fruit than otherwise"; no. 173: Ethel Wilson was "canning and preserving when interviewed"; no. 12: Ethel Einberry, "at present canning"; no. 60: Mary Kenyon, forty-five, canning during interview; no. 71: Vera Berys, twenty-two, married with two children, "time to put up preserves etc. that she could not do before"; no. 81: Mildred Hulbal canning during the interview; no. 325: Juanita Payne, twenty-five, was "canning strawberries when [the interviewer] was there," and said "she has time to accomplish more at home on the present schedule." Interviews with and letters from surviving workers provide additional historical insight into this remarkable activity.

24. Interviews with Paula Swan, president of AFGM, Local no. 3, 3, 11 September 1987, 18 October 1991.

25. Suzanne Gordon, *Prisoners of Men's Dreams: Striking Out for a New Feminine Future* (Boston, 1991), describes women's traditional concern for caregiving as part of a "transformative vision" that was once part of American feminism but has been neglected as women become "prisoners of men's dreams," such as competitive success at work. See her "Introduction."

26. Several women mentioned traditional skills that they were able to recover in the extra time. The craft the women mentioned most frequently was sewing, or "making clothes," followed closely in frequency by "gardening" (their gardens were predominantly flower gardens). But both Helen Hartwig and Grace Schragg spoke of building a house with their "partially employed" husbands in the two extra hours a day. Laurel Mott and Ada Story returned to farming on a small scale, primarily as an avocation but also in hopes of some extra income. Several of the Kellogg workers the author interviewed mentioned that farmers in the Battle Creek region liked the six-hour shift because it gave them time to farm. However, Best reported no full-time, serious farmers in her survey. The two part-time farmers her agents interviewed were similar to those the author found: gentlewomen (or -men) farmers who took up or returned to farming on a small scale, primarily for enjoyment and secondarily for some extra income. Most said they were happy to get the money out of farming that they put in. Again, the dominant "motive" was not necessity or function; their job at Kellogg's was the principal source of income, and the farming operation seldom paid for itself: several had to borrow from the company credit union to finance their "farming." See Best's questionnaire, no. 133: Laurel Mott and her husband "moved to the country after the 6 hour shift was put in . . . like to farm on a small scale. . . . start[ing] a strawberry and raspberry bed in the extra time." No. 143: Ada Story, forty-six, married living with daughter and son-in-law. She and the son-in-law worked the same Kellogg shift, driving back and forth together. They have some "land in the country" and a big garden. With six-hours shifts, both went to their garden "nearly every day, could not have done this on longer day."

27. Certainly, such crafts and skills had once been more governed by the press of circumstance, and many projects still had vestigial utilitarian functions: for example, several spoke of the money they saved by canning. But for most of the sixty-nine, the activities had been transformed, at least in part, because they chose to do them.

28. For culture as an "interlude" between or outside utility and status, see the discussion of Turner's liminal and Huizinga's play in the Introduction. For Gentile's Neo-Idealist ideas about cultural space, see Adriano Tilgher, *Homo Faber*, trans. Dorothy Canfield Fisher (New York, 1932), 164–66.

29. Quoted in Tilgher, *Homo Faber*, 165.

30. Scholars have recently noted that working women's views of work are still at variance with what work has come to mean for many in the modern women's movement. Rhetoric about the "the challenge of work" or a "liberating job," coming from a patrician such as James T. Adams in the 1920s or from feminists today, falls on disbelieving ears among the majority of women. Women's continuing discontent with work is described by Terry Wetherby, ed., *Conversations:*

Working Women Talk about Doing a "Man's Job" (Millbrae, Calif., 1977); Robert Coles and Jane Hallowell Coles, *Women of Crisis II : Lives of Work and Dreams* (New York, 1980); and Louise K Howe, *Pink Collar Workers: Inside the World of Women's Work* (New York, 1977).

The majority of the Kellogg women identified the extra time as free, even though a few used words such as "need" or "have to" when they spoke about home duties. Most of the 434 women talked in general terms about choice, ability, and ownership of their time outside their job at the plant. They also characterized the specific activities they were choosing as free. In stylized form, their syntax was, "I am able to" (indicating choice) "crochet" (the specific activity). Thus they identified both the act of choosing and the activity itself as free relative to other, less free and more work-like activities, such as doing dishes.

31. Joseph Pieper, *Leisure the Basis of Culture* (New York, 1952), 30 and passim.

32. *Enquirer*, 1 December 1930.

33. For examples of the undecided, see Best's questionnaire, no. 68: Lucille McRae, "nothing special to do with her extra time, but visits with friends, wanders around town"; no. 320: Annabella Pollock, "I don't know—I fool around, go downtown, help my mother"; nos. 366 and 367: "nothing special."

34. Some used the extra time for volunteer work and church. Edith Bodhe (Best's questionnaire, no. 139), a Catholic, could "attend church on all holy days"; no. 201: Crystal Howard, "gives more time for outside activities [she] spends all her extra time in church activities and volunteer activities . . . visiting the sick, etc." One of the women said she "has charge of a camp fire group."

35. Tilgher, *Homo Faber*, 168.

36. Interview with Grace Lindsey.

37. Author's Survey, no. 231 (unsigned).

38. See Michael Seidman, *Work Against Work: Labor in Paris and Barcelona during the Popular Fronts,* (Berkeley and Los Angeles, 1991).

39. See Best's questionnaire nos. 85, 102, 321, and 333, (corresponding to the quotations in the text).

40. Best's questionnaire, no. 125. But Grace Otto was unmoved by her husband's complaints, speaking eloquently about having "the best part of the day at home" and observing that she was glad that the center of her life was not going to be boxing Kellogg's cereal.

Edith Bodhe, fifty, single, was keeping house with an unmarried sister and brother when she told Best's interviewers that she "prefers 6 to 8 hours because she does not get so tired. . . . 8 hours would seem too hard." But Bodhe was "interrupted constantly" by her sister, who "said she preferred 8 hours for her sister because she [Edith] earned more and it keeps [Edith] out of the house for longer periods."

41. Letter, James McQuiston to Mary Anderson, director of the Women's Bureau, 20 January 1933, and attached report entitled "The Kellogg Six-Hour Plan," Box 153.

42. The author selected Kellogg workers from a list of retired workers provided by the Kellogg Retirees Association. Five hundered questionnaires were mailed to a randomly selected group of association members, 241 usable questionnaires (hereafter cited as "author's survey") and letters were returned. The survey was definitely biased in that the large majority of the workers contacted who had worked in the 1930s were young then and had just started work at Kellogg's. They would have been less secure in their jobs and more likely to be among the first workers laid off. Hence, they would have had a strong interest in work sharing. Older workers with seniority who would have benefited more from overtime work in the 1930s and would have lost more by the institution of six-hours had, for the most part, died (even though, without exception, the few workers questioned who had seniority in the thirties said they supported six-hours). Moreover, not all former employees joined the Retirees Association, and there was no way to control for deaths in general.

Phrases that Best found reappeared in the author's survey, including "free," "free to," "was able to," "my work," "my time," "gave me a chance to," "work-hogs," "greedy," "money hungry." Like Best's study, these personal interviews and narrative letters reveal rhetorical kinds of "central tendencies" that statisticians often overlook when they deal only with numbers.

43. Letter, Dab Farrell to author, 25 January 1989.

44. For "greedy," "work-hogs," and "enough," see especially letters to the author, nos. 44, 120, 185, 215, 237, and 356. The "work-hog" gave way to the "rabbit" as the outcast, or "deviant," among workers during the 1950s. A "rabbit" was a younger worker who worked fast for the various production bonuses, reducing the chance for older workers to get overtime.

45. Author's survey, nos. 37, 138, 142, 218, 298, and 431; anonymous interview no. 42, 11 August 1989.

46. Author's survey, nos. 469, 447, 427, 287, 284, and 401 (corresponding to quotations in the text).

47. Author's survey, nos. 197, 753, 178, 763, 593, and 219 (corresponding to quotations in the text). Also interview with Wayne Gleason, retired Kellogg worker, by Wendy Jenkins, 1 November 1991; interview with an AFGM executive vice president, 4 June 1990, 9 October 1990.

48. Letter, Ralph Parrish to author, no month, 1989; interview with Grace Lindsey.

49. Author's survey, no. 256. Also interviews no. 25, 33, 38, and 39; author's surveys, nos. 1, 5, 22, 45, 50, 57, 70, 86, 95, 96, 121, 128, 145, 148, 152, 155, 160, 165, 166, 168, 169, 192, 201, 226, 227, 229, 261, and 394.

50. Interview with Richard Cleveland, retired Kellogg worker, 3 August 1994; interview with anonymous retired male Kellogg worker, 11 August 1994.

51. Best's questionnaire, no. 208; interview with Leroy Despins.

52. Author's questionnaire, no. 298.

53. According to contemporary journalists' accounts, few workers were able to find second jobs. In the author's survey, fewer than 10 percent remember that they were able to find work outside Kellogg's during the depression, and then most worked only on an irregular basis.

54. Staffan Linder, *The Harried Leisure Class* (NewYork, 1970), 77–78, 214–24.

CHAPTER FOUR

1. Efforts to organize the grain milling industry began in the late 1930s and accelerated in the early 1930s, when the various unions in the industry established formal ties. The most important coalition was the Tri-State Council of Grain Processors, composed of local unions in Illinois, Iowa, and Missouri. In 1936, encouraged by political developments in Washington, the AFL assumed leadership of the organizational process and called a meeting of existing unions in Keokuk, Iowa, in April. In July, an AFL affiliate union, the National Council of Grain Processors (NCGP), formed in Toledo, Ohio, bringing together most of the unions in the industry. Continuing in a leadership role, AFL president Green appointed William Schoenberg as head of the new council and shortly thereafter replaced him with Meyer Lewis, who remained as president until 1940. Both Schoenberg and Lewis were appointed expressly for their organizational abilities, which they had demonstrated in the Midwest. See "Early Beginnings" and "A Brief History of the Grain Millers," typescripts, the archives of Local No. 3 of the American Federation of Grain Millers, Battle Creek, Michigan. Unsigned copy, letter, Secretary-Treasurer's office of the AFL to J. Lyle Sage, "organizer" in Battle Creek, 4 January 1937; unsigned copy, letter, Secretary-Treasurer's office of the AFL to J. Lyle Sage, "organizer" in Battle Creek, 6 January 1937; unsigned copy, letter, Secretary-Treasurer's office of the AFL to Edward Levitt, temporary secretary, "Federal Labor Union," No. 20,388, Battle Creek, dated 4 January 1937, all in Local No. 3 Archives.

2. The union records indicate that once unionization was inevitable, W. K. Kellogg was "in sympathy" with Local No. 20,388. "Early Beginnings"; *New York Times*, 29 May 1957. Also author's survey, no. 63, no date, from "A. M.," a Kellogg worker; *Moon-Journal*, 8 June 1937.

3. David Brody, *Workers in Industrial America* (Madison, 1975), 63–78, 134, chap. 6; Irving Bernstein, *The Lean Years: A History of the American Worker, 1920–1933* (Boston, 1960), 184–88.

4. More women agreed than disagreed with Lewis Brown. For agreement with the relay race idea, see Best's questionnaire, nos. 2, 25, 30, 52, 68, 88, 102, 108, 146, 197, 228, 302, 332, 345, 368, 396, C.E.W. I, C.E.W. T. (Several of Best's questionnaires were distinctive, identified by the initials "C.E.W." The author used alphabetic characters to reference these.) But an important minority said they were opposed to Brown's concessions and the production bonus. Sixteen objected to the line speed: Best concluded that fatigue was the second most common reason workers gave for preferring eight-hours. See nos. 8, 87, 105, 119, 213, 215, 354, 386, C.E.W. F, C.E.W. G, and C.E.W. M. Five objected to the loss of overtime payments, not agreeing with Brown about the bonus (e.g., nos. 180 and 193). Five objected to the loss of night differentials.

5. See *Moon-Journal,* 8, 10, 13 June 1937; *Enquirer,* 15 June 1937; Minute Book; Minutes from 15 November 1937 to 31 December 1938, Local No. 3 Archives (hereafter cited as Minute Book, 1937–38).

6. *Enquirer,* 9, 10, 13, 14, 15 June 1937; *Moon-Journal,* 10, 13, 14 June 1937. On 12 June 1937 the *Enquirer,* reported that Green had been "keeping in touch with the local negotiations through two long distance telephone calls." After 10 June negotiators turned to the "standard" six-hour day, which the union saw as a fall-back position. The *Moon-Journal* reported that there were indications 12 June that the union might waive the original demand for a union shop in return for higher wages and shorter hours. The basis of actual negotiations after 13 June was the list of proposals agreed to by a vote of the union membership the day before, a list topped by "standard six-hours."

7. *New York Times,* 29 May 1957, obituaries. See "Early Beginnings." According to one retired worker (author's survey, no. 162), "In 30s . . . when unions came in, Kellogg Company wanted 8 hours—at one time Kellogg had 4000 workers now [1990] about 2,000."

8. The *Enquirer,* 16, 17 June 1937, and the *Moon-Journal,* 15, 18 June 1937, reported that the union rejected the company's first proposal to allow these workers to remain on eight-hours because union members feared that having eight-hours in any of the plant's departments would undercut the majority's wishes. Personnel managers remember that the union's fears were realistic—that sentiment favoring longer hours remained active in the plant and tended to "pool" in the remaining eight-hour departments, keeping the issue alive.

9. *Enquirer,* 16, 17 June 1937.

10. *Enquirer,* 17 June 1937.

11. Ethel L. Best, *A Study of a Change from 8 to 6 Hours of Work* (Washington, D.C., 1933); *Enquirer,* 18 June 1937; *Moon-Journal,* 15, 18 June 1937. Contract between Kellogg's and Local No. 20,388, 23 June 1937, Local No. 3 Archives. Hereafter cited as Kellogg contract, 1937.

12. *Enquirer,* 18 June 1937.

13. "A Summary of the Kellogg Company's Experience with the Shorter Working Day" (pamphlet), Battle Creek, 1935; held by the Kellogg Company, Battle Creek, Michigan; photocopy in author's possession.

14. Kellogg Contract, 1937; *Moon-Journal,* 18 June 1937.

15. Quotation from "Minutes of a Meeting Called on 14 February 1938, Minutes Added 3 May 1938"; see also "Minutes of a Special Meeting of the Executive Board," 7 June 1938; letter, Meyer Lewis to Local No. 20,388, 8 July 1938, read at a special meeting of the local 11 July, copy in Minute Book, 1937–38. See also "Agreement between Kellogg and Local 20,388," including amendments effective 1 March 1943, Article VI, Section 1, paragraph *a*; all in Local No. 3 Archives.

16. Quotation from "Minutes of a Special Meeting Called 7 June 1938"; see also "Regular Monday Afternoon Meeting 18," April 1938; "Special Meeting Monday Afternoon," 25 April 1938; "Special Meeting Monday Night," 18 April 1938, all in Minute Book, 1937–38.

17. "Minutes Added 3 May 1938," in Minute Book, 1937–38.

18. Letter, Meyer Lewis to Local No. 20,388, 8 July 1938, read at a special meeting of the local on 11 July, in Minute Book, 1937–38.

19. Ibid.; see also Agreement between Kellogg and Local 20,388, including amendments effective 1 March 1943, Article VI, Section 1, paragraph *a* (hereafter 1941 Agreement with 1943 amendments) and "Minutes of a Special Meeting of the Executive Board," 7 June 1938, and "Minutes added May 3 1938," both in Minute Book, 1937–1938.

20. *Enquirer,* 20 June 1941. See also *Enquirer* 21, 22 June 1941; also, series of telegrams exchanged by E. H. Lovill of Local No. 20,388 and William Green and Sam Ming, January 1941; letter, Green to Ming, 16 July 1941, all in Local No. 3 Archives.

21. See 1941 Agreement with 1943 amendments; see also *Enquirer,* 20 June 1941.

22. *Enquirer* 19, 20 June 1941; *Moon-Journal,* 20, 21 June 1941.

23. See 1941 Agreement with 1943 amendments, Article VII, paragraph *g.* For the elimination of the bonus in the Mechanical Department, see memorandum, 17 July 1946, "To the Body of Local No. 20,388" in Local #3 Archives.

24. See 1941 Agreement with 1943 amendments.

25. *Enquirer,* 20 June 1941.

26. *Kellogg News,* (January–February 1943); 1941 Agreement with 1943 amendments, "Temporary Amendments to Contract," p. 29, in Local No. 3 Archives.

27. See 1941 Agreement with 1943 amendments; memorandum, 7 May 1944, Local No. 3 Archives.

28. Author's survey, nos. 18, 45, and 176.

1. Memorandum, 8 February 1946; letter, Ed Pilsworth to William Green, 2 March 1946, file folder dated 1946–47, Local No. 3 Archives.

2. Memorandum, 8 February 1946, file folder dated 1946–47, Local No. 3 Archives.

3. Ibid.; letter, Ed Pilsworth to William Green, 2 March 1946; letter, William Green to Ed Pilsworth, 12 March 1946, all in file folder dated 1946–47, Local No. 3 Archives.

4. Memorandum, 8 February 1946.

5. Letter, William Green to Ed Pilsworth, 12 March 1946.

6. Unsigned memorandum "To Local 20,388" from the local office, 11 September 1946; letter, J. N. Cummings to William Green, 17 April 1946, both in file folder dated 1946–47, Local No. 3 Archives. These numbers seem fairly constant. Best found that about the same percentage of women "preferred" six-hours in 1932. About two-thirds of the men in the five "eight-hour" departments voted for six-hours in 1937. Since the workers most in favor of working longer had gravitated to these five departments by 1937, the 71 percent total male vote for six-hours in 1946 may not represent an increase of male support at all.

7. Letter, J. N. Cummings to William Green, 17 April 1946, file folder dated 1946–47, Local No. 3 Archives. A male worker wrote to the author, narrating these events: "I worked at Kellogg's from 1934 to 1970. . . . During World War II the plant converted to 8 hour shifts because of lack of civilian employees. The company agreed [with the union] to return to the 6 hour shift after World War II ended. [But] after the war ended, the company wanted the employees to go to 8-hour shifts. This was voted plant wide several times because of the number of women involved. The company developed a plan to let each dept. vote individually by men and women separately." Author's survey, no. 456.

8. Unsigned memorandum "To Local 20,388" from the local office, 11 September 1946, Local No. 3 Archives; author's survey, nos. 176, 456.

9. "Memorandum of Minutes of 1st Meeting Regarding Contract Amendments Thursday, 12 June 1947"; "Minutes of Contract Negotiations Committee Meeting Thursday, 10 July 1947", in "Negotiations Minutes 1947–1948," notebook in Local No. 3 3 Archives. Also "Letter to Local 20,338" from the company, signed by Power Custer and R. S. Poole, with attached memo, "Proposed Amendments," 29 May 1947. Custer and Poole wrote, "We wish to propose consideration of a standard 8 hour day. . . . [C]onsideration must be given for the desires and benefits of certain groups of people [eight-hour supporters] who may be in the minority as far as the total membership is concerned."

10. "Minutes of Contract Negotiations Committee Meeting Tuesday, 8 July 1947"; "Minutes of Contract Negotiations Meeting Wednesday, 2 July 1947";

"Minutes of Contract Negotiations Meeting 16 July 1947," all in "Negotiations Minutes 1947–1948," Local No. 3 Archives.

11. "Minutes of Contract Negotiations Meeting Wednesday, 2 July 1947"; "Minutes of Contract Negotiations Committee Meeting Tuesday, 8 July 1947"; "Minutes of Contract Negotiations Meeting Tuesday, 16 July 1947"; "Minutes of Contract Negotiations Meeting Tuesday, 17 July 1947", all in "Negotiations Minutes 1947–1948," Local No. 3 Archives.

12. "Notes of Meeting on Contract Negotiations, 18 June 1947," in "Negotiations Minutes 1947–1948," Local No. 3 Archives.

13. "Minutes of Contract Negotiations Meeting 16 July 1947," in "Negotiations Minutes 1947–1948"; 1943 Amended Contract between Kellogg's and Local No. 20,388, August 1943; 1947 amendments to the 1941 contract between Kellogg's and Local No. 20,388, 24 July 1947; 1948 Amended Contract between Kellogg's and Local No. 20,388, 1 August 1948, all in Local No. 3 Archives. Author's survey, no. 150. The Miscellaneous Packing and Shipping Department apparently changed from an eight-hour schedule back to six-hours after the war even though it had been included as one of the eight-hour departments under the 1943 contract. It returned to eight-hours in 1947. Yards and grounds workers, watchmen, window washers, and painters also had an eight-hour day before the war and voted to retain it. Several departments not included as eight-hour departments in the 1941 contract did not return to six-hours after the war and so were allowed to vote on 25 July 1947. These included the cafeteria, the stores and salvage department, grain samplers, the wax paper department, garage, and truck drivers.

14. A year before, during the membership-wide ballot, only 29 percent of the men had voted for eight-hours; after the first department-by-department vote, nearly 35 percent of all male workers and a majority of senior male workers were on the eight-hour shift.

15. Author's survey, no. 150: "workers who opposed eight-hours" were "those without the seniority." No. 241: the reasons for the end of six-hours "were the union's demands for higher pay and fringe benefits and the company desire to automate and cut its workforce to affect these demands."

16. "Memorandum of Minutes of 1st Meeting Regarding Contract Amendments Thursday, 12 June 1947"; "Minutes of Contract Negotiations Committee Meeting Thursday, 10 July 1947"; both in "Negotiations Minutes 1947–1948," Local No. 3 Archives.

17. "Minutes of Contract Negotiations Committee Meeting Tuesday, 8 July 1947"; "Minutes of Contract Negotiations Meeting Wednesday July 2nd"; "Minutes of Contract Negotiations Meeting 16 July 1947"; all in "Negotiations Minutes 1947–1948," Local No. 3 Archives

18. "Minutes of Contract Negotiations Meeting Tuesday, 17 July 1947," in "Negotiations Minutes 1947–1948," Local No. 3 Archives; author's survey, no. 271.

19. The 1948 amended contract between Kellogg's and Local #20,388, 1 August 1948; memo R. S. Poole to "Kellogg Men and Women," 21 February 1947; both in "Negotiations Minutes 1947–1948," Local No. 3 Archives.

20. Memo, local No. 20,388 to "Members of Kellogg Local Union 20,388," 21 February 1947, in "Negotiations Minutes 1947–1948," Local No. 3 Archives. The emphasis is in the original documents.

21. "Notes of Meeting on Contract Negotiations, 18 June 1947," in "Negotiations Minutes 1947–1948," Local No. 3 Archives.

22. "Minutes of Contract Negotiations Meeting Wednesday, July 2nd"; "Minutes of Negotiating Committee 15 October 1948"; memo, R. S. Poole to "Kellogg Men and Women," 21 February 1947," in "Negotiations Minutes 1947– 1948," Local No. 3 Archives.

23. "Minutes of Contract Negotiations Meeting 19 July 1947," in "Negotiations Minutes 1947–1948," Local No. 3 Archives.

24. "Minutes of 1st Meeting Regarding Contract Amendments, 12 June 1947," in Negotiations Minutes 1947–1948," Local No. 3 Archives.

25. Ibid.

26. Memo, union to "Members of Kellogg Local Union No. 20,388," 21 February 1947, in "Negotiations Minutes 1947–1948," Local No. 3 Archives.

27. "Minutes of 1st Meeting Regarding Contract Amendments, 12 June 1947"; "Minutes of Contract Negotiations Committee Meeting, 8 July 1947"; "Method of Computing Kellogg Production Index," 18 July 1947; see also "Method of Computing Kellogg Production Index," 18 August 1947, all in "Negotiations Minutes 1947–1948," Local No. 3 Archives.

28. "Minutes of Contract Negotiations Meeting, 19 July 1947," in "Negotiations Minutes 1947–1948," Local No. 3 Archives. See also "Art of Wages," 10 July 1947, ibid.

29. "Minutes of Contract Negotiations Meeting," 19 July 1947, in "Negotiations Minutes 1947–1948," Local No. 3 Archives.

30. "Minutes of Contract Negotiations Committee Meeting, 10 July 1947"; "Minutes of Contract Negotiations Meeting, 14 July 1947"; "Production Incentive Plan," 29 August 1947; "Suggestions of the Committee for Productivity Improvement," all in "Negotiations Minutes 1947–1948," Local No. 3 Archives.

31. "Memorandum of Meeting with Negotiating Committee, 9 September 1947"; "Suggestions Committee for Productivity Improvement"; all in "Negotiations Minutes 1947–1948," Local No. 3 Archives.

32. "Minutes of Meeting with Union Negotiating Committee, 3 December 1948"; letter, AFGM Local No. 3 to P. D. Custer, 9 December 1948; both in "Negotiations Minutes 1947–1948," Local No. 3 Archives.

33. *Enquirer,* 21 May 1951; *Wall Street Journal,* 7 June, 15 July 1957; interview with Robert Willis, general president of the AFGM, 28 June 1990; interview

with an executive vice president of AFGM, 9 October 1990; interview with Jack Curtis, vice president and personnel manager at Kellogg's during the 1950s, 22 August 1990.

CHAPTER SIX

1. The epigraph is from "Time, Work-Discipline and Industrial Capitalism," *Past and Present* 38 (December 1967): 90–91; see also Gary Cross, *Quest for Time: Reduction of Work in Britain and France 1840–1940* (Berkeley, 1990), 13; Jeyland T. Mortimer, *Changing Attitudes toward Work* (Minneapolis, 1979), 3, 14, 15; interview with Howard Roe, executive vice president, AFGM, 9 October 1990; interview with Robert Willis, general president, AFGM, 28 June 1990; interview with Jack Curtis, vice president and personnel manager at Kellogg's during the 1950s, 22 August 1990. See also *Enquirer*, 21 May 1951.

2. Edwin A. Locke, "Job Attitudes in Historical Perspective," in Daniel Wren and John Pearce, eds., *Papers Dedicated to the Development of Modern Management* (n.p. [Academy of Management], 1986), 6–7.

3. Mortimer, *Changing Attitudes;* Sanford M. Jacoby, *Employing Bureaucracy: Managers, Unions, and the Transformation of Work, 1900–1945* (New York, 1985). See also Daniel Yankelovich, "Work, Values, and the New Breed," and Clark Kerr, "Introduction," both in Clark Kerr and Jerome M. Rosow, eds., *Work in America: The Decade Ahead* (New York, 1979); Edwin A. Locke, "The Nature and Causes of Job Satisfaction," in Marvin Dunnette, ed., *Handbook of Industrial and Organizational Psychology* (Chicago, 1976), 1297–1350; A. D. Chandler, *The Visible Hand: The Managerial Revolution in American Business* (Cambridge, Mass., 1977); D. A. Wren, *The Evolution of Management Thought* (New York, 1987).

4. Douglas McGregor, *The Human Side of Enterprise* (New York, 1960), 33, 34. See also Mortimer, *Changing Attitudes,* 16. The idea that instead of being a negative part of living, to be entered on the debit side of the workers' ledger, work could be transformed into a "normal good" has a twentieth-century origin. For the economist of the nineteenth and early twentieth centuries, and indeed for many modern theorists such as John Owen, the idea that work may become a normal good is an economic contradiction. "Perfect work," defined in these terms, is a contradiction because the more work becomes a "normal good," the lower its price will fall in a free labor market. Mortimer claims that most workers now accept the idea that work is a "central focus of life," even though "the existing body of research . . . suggests declines in satisfaction in virtually all segments of the working population" (16)." The myth of perfect work, of work as the center of life and a "normal good," is alive and well, but the reality is increasingly distant. The best research shows a widening gap between what people expect from their work and the actual work experience.

5. See also Frederick Herzberg, *Work and the Nature of Man*, (New York, 1962) 38.

6. As Frank Knight put it, "In so far as men act rationally . . . they will at a higher [income] rate divide their time between wage-earning and non-industrial uses in such a way as to earn *more money*, indeed, but to work *fewer hours.* Just where the balance will be struck depends upon the shape of the curve of comparison between money (representing the group of things purchasable with money) and leisure (representing all non-pecuniary, alternative uses of time)." F. H. Knight, *Risk, Uncertainty and Profits* (New York, 1921, 1964), 117; see also 31.

7. After forty years, writers are still struggling to overcome the dichotomy, and disabuse humankind of the notion that work and life are opposed in the industrial world. See, for example, Martin Morf, *The Work/Life Dichotomy: Prospects for Reintegrating People and Jobs* (New York 1989). See also Benjamin Hunnicutt, "The Economic Constraints of Leisure," in Michael G. Wade, ed., *Constraints on Leisure* (Springfield, Ill., 1985), and Jack Barbash, *Job Satisfaction and Attitude Studies* (Paris, 1976), 19, 257–65.

8. McGregor, *Human Side of Enterprise*, 42, 53.

9. Also see *Work and the Nature of Man*, chap. 5.

10. Abram T. Collier, "Faith in a Creative Society," *Harvard Business Review* 35 (May–June 1957): 35–41. Also Gordon George, "The Theology of Work," *America* 93 (2 April 1955): 4; Gunnar Hultman, "The Workplace—Do You Respect It?" *The Rotarian* 94 (May 1959): 54; Lansing Shield, "What's Wrong with Work?" *Readers' Digest* 60 (February 1952): 100–102. Shield offers this advice: "It is up to today's trustees of the American system to provide leadership that will win the workers of America to the philosophy of work, for by work alone may man exercise all his abilities and powers. Work is the purifier of man; work is life itself." Identification of work and hard work with the American character is also common in the decade. See Samuel Hopkins Adams, "It's an American Idea; Let's Not Give It Up," *Good Housekeeping* (March 1949): 33, 233.

11. Collier, "Faith in a Creative Society," 39–40.

12. Benjamin Hunnicutt, *Work Without End: Abandoning Shorter Hours for the Right to Work* (Philadelphia, 1988).

13. John Neuner and Benjamin Haynes, *Office Management: Principles and Practices* (Cincinnati, 1953).

14. "Leadership in the Kellogg Manner" (pamphlet), published by the Kellogg company (Battle Creek, 1957), hereafter "LKM"; "Code For Good Leadership," (pamphlet), published by the Kellogg Company (Battle Creek, 1958), hereafter "CGL"; both in the Willard Library, Battle Creek, Michigan.

15. "LKM," 4a,10aa. The page numbers are this author's convention, representing multiple sections with identical numbering in the same pamphlet. Section 1 is represented by numerals alone, section 2 by "a," section 3 by "aa," etc.

16. Custer's introduction to "LKM."

17. Jacoby, *Employing Bureaucracy*. Jacoby argues that industrial labor was "transformed" through a "historical process . . . of bureaucratization" and the rise of personnel management as a profession. "Good jobs" were the result: jobs with "stability, internal promotion, and impersonal, rule bound procedures" (2). But Kellogg's personnel managers were not content with mere changes in work's form. Putting more faith in the intangibles, attitudes and morale, they tried to redeem work at the plant by convincing workers that work done with the proper devotion was better than leisure—a "good job" was largely a product of attitude, and the right attitude toward work was a precondition to the enjoyment of life.

CHAPTER SEVEN

1. Eugene Genovese and Elizabeth Fox-Genovese explain that it was hardly possible for an "autonomous" working-class subculture to "resist successfully and totally the values and aspiration of the bourgeoisie" and that a "reciprocal influence with their oppressors" must be taken into account to appreciate workers' "tragic complicity in their own oppression." "The Political Crisis of Social History: A Marxian Perspective," *Journal of Social History* 10 (1976): 205–20.

2. See, for example, "Amendments to the Contract," 22 May 1957, Local No. 3 Archives; telephone interview with Robert Willis, general president of the AFGM, 28 June 1990. Willis suggested that "once the [W. K.] Kellogg era was over, then Kellogg, like everybody else, wanted to cut jobs—[this was] the biggest change in management philosophy [in Kellogg's history], no question about it."

3. Author's survey, no. 468.

4. Letter, Ralph Parrish to the author, no date, 1989, filed as author's survey, no. 351.

5. Author's survey, nos. 762 and 666, corresponding to the quotations in the paragraph; "Amendments to the Contract," 22 May 1957, Local No. 3 Archives.

6. Interview with Charles Blanchard, retired Kellogg worker, 10 August 1989; author's survey, no. 233.

7. John Lawrence, "Shorter Work Week: Many Rubber Workers Who Have It Spurn Leisure, Take Two Jobs," *Wall Street Journal,* 13 September 1957, front page.

8. One male noted that "primarily 8 hour shifts were considered male jobs & 6 hour shifts were considered female jobs. . . . [A]fter the women's movement, women tried and were successful in getting into some of the male dominated jobs." Author's survey, no. 23.

9. The *Enquirer,* 2 May 1951, reported that "Kellogg management says its policy is to have the finest conditions of pay, benefits, and general working conditions that prevail in the cereal industry."

10. Interview with Robert Willis, general president of the AFGM, 28 June 1990. Willis' conversation exemplified the new rhetoric of need. Basically he agreed with the company's position that job eliminations at Kellogg's were inevitable if the remaining workers were to be protected. Interview with Art White, retired Kellogg worker, 12 August 1989. Other interviews (nos. 2, 4, 6, 32, 46, 78, and 104) reflected the same language.

11. In sequence author's surveys, nos. 336, 666, 303, and 468.

12. Author's survey, nos. 320, 550.

13. Author survey, nos. 320, 303, 19, 455, and 22.

14. Interview with James McQuiston, 11 August 1989; see also *Enquirer,* 30 March 1973.

15. Author's survey, nos. 182, 227.

16. Author's survey, no. 46.

17. Interview with Alex Senyszyn, retired Kellogg worker, 12 August 1989.

18. Interview with an anonymous retired male worker, 11 August 1989.

19. *Saturday Evening Post* 230 (11 January 1958).

20. Author' survey, no. 136. Emphasis in the original. No. 471 admitted that he worked six hours, but only because "I was a college student."

21. Interview with James McQuiston, 11 August 1989.

22. Author's survey, nos. 131 and 136.

23. Author's survey, nos. 359, 460, 39, 67, 112, and 116.

24. Interview with James McQuiston, 11 August 1989. See also author's survey, no. 776.

25. Author' survey, no. 122.

26. Author's survey, no. 116; interview with James McQuiston, 11 August 1989.

27. Nelson Lichtenstein, "From Corporatism to Collective Bargaining: Organized Labor and the Eclipse of Social Democracy in the Postwar Era," in Steven Fraser and Gary Gerstle, eds., *The Rise and Fall of the New Deal Order, 1930–1980* (Princeton, 1989), 122–52; Nelson Lichtenstein, "Walter Reuther and the Rise of Labor-Liberalism," in Melvyn Dubofsky and Warren Van Tine, eds., *Labor Leaders in America* (Urbana, 1986).
Lichtenstein neglects what may have been the most important modern interclass accommodation: the shared belief in the centrality of work. As André Gorz points out, the transformation of work from a worker means to a capitalist end-in-itself was accomplished during the twentieth century. And one of the results of work's becoming the central cultural myth, shared by worker, manager, and capitalist alike, has been "the farewell to the working class." Gorz's thesis is nowhere better illustrated than at the Kellogg plant. André Gorz, *Critique of Economic Reason,* trans. by G. Handyside and C. Turner of *Metamorphoses du Travail* (London, 1988), passim.

28. David Roediger and Philip Foner, *Our Own Time: A History of American Labor and the Working Day* (New York, 1989), 267–68; Ronald Edsforth, "Goods over Leisure: Walter Reuther and the Origins of Consumer-Oriented Labor Liberalism," paper, quoted by permission, copy in author's possession; also Robert Asher and Ronald Edsforth, eds., *Autowork* (Albany, 1995), 168–69.

29. Benjamin Hunnicutt, *Work Without End: Abandoning Shorter Hours for the Right to Work* (Philadelphia, 1988), chap. 5.

30. Ibid. 159–65.

31. Edsforth, "Goods over Leisure," 168–75.

32. *IUD Bulletin,* May 1957.

33. As quoted by Asher and Edsforth, *Autowork,* 170.

34. *Business Week,* 17 April 1954.

35. *U.S. News and World Report* 41 (21 September 1956): 108.

36. *Nation's Business* 36 (February 1958).

37. Author's survey, nos. 84 and 105.

38. *IUD Bulletin,* September 1956.

39. For a summary of these developments see Asher and Edsforth, *Autowork,* chap. 6.

40. *Business Week,* 29 September 1956.

41. *IUD Bulletin,* October 1956.

42. *Fortune* 53 (May 1956); *U.S. News and World Report* 40 (20 April 1956): 139; *New Republic* 134 (13 February 1956): 10–11; *Business Week* (21 April 1956); *Wall Street Journal,* 13 September 1957.

43. Edsforth, "Goods over Leisure," 168–75.

44. André Gorz claims (as do Eugene McCarthy and Bill McGaughey) that the ending of labor's support for shorter hours has resulted, internationally, in the segmentation of workers and a widening division between a few workers who have good, secure, well-paying jobs and increasing numbers who are marginalized, left far behind in wages and out in the cold in terms of their culture's central myth of satisfying work. Gorz, *Critique of Economic Reason;* and Eugene McCarthy and William McGaughey, *Nonfinancial Economics: The Case for Shorter Hours of Work* (New York, 1989).

45. Author's survey, no. 166 was typical of the men's response to the prospect of leisure: "[Six-hours meant] "too much wasted time—less money—not as productive."

CHAPTER EIGHT

1. Author's survey, no. 456. Senior workers negotiated a revision of the 1941 contract, providing for the lay-off of employees with less than five years' service "before reducing the hours of work for the balance of the employees in that

division to less than 5 days," thus reversing work sharing at Kellogg's. See "Agreement," section 708, 1 August 1948. Similarly, Section 901, paragraph *d* reads: "Senior qualified people will be given priority for all extra days." see "Amendments to the Contract," 22 May 1957, Local No. 3 Archives. In time, such agreements automatically provided what each party wanted; the company got fewer workers, and the eight-hour workers gained additional overtime as the workforce was pruned during yearly slack periods.

2. Interview with Robert Willis, general president of the AFGM, 28 June 1990. Willis said that the voting procedure was "very controversial. . . . The person [who would] take up a petition to eliminate six-hours, other people would threaten, tearing them [the petitions] up."

3. Author's survey, no. 226; see also no. 231.

4. The union also "recognized" the problem of running a plant that had overlapping shift starting times, with workers coming and going all the time, and it applied subtle pressure on the six-hour workers while giving the appearance of neutrality in the voting process.

5. The change from majority to minority status is highly symbolic. For the historian, it represents the shifting of "deviance" on the work/leisure issue.

6. For workers transferring, see author's survey, nos. 108, 167.

7. Their identity as a group was formed primarily at the plant and in work-related organizations such as the 25 Year Club and the Retirees' Club. Most important to their group identity were their union affiliation and the union's department-by-department organization. Moreover, they had common concerns at work: their six-hour fight, their opposition to company initiatives, and the eight-hour petitions that were being circulated drew them together as a coherent minority force in the plant and at union meetings.

8. One worker wrote (author's survey, no. 108: "Hourly people who wanted to work 6 or 8 hrs would bid into the depts. which were on 6 or 8 hrs." See nos. 150 and 31 for the quotations in the text. Even though well-defined, the men's group was mixed, comprising employees who held a second job outside Kellogg's or who tried to farm, and a few authentic heretics who openly took issue with the "glory of work," thumbed their noses at long hours and overtime, and persisted in their own peculiar lifestyles and sets of values built on leisure—family life, hobbies, assorted avocations, hunting, fishing, loafing. Together with the women, these men continued to champion the rights of laid-off workers and criticize their fellow workers for being "work-hogs." See author's survey, nos. 51, 120, 219, and 226; interviews, nos. 32 and 49.

9. Examples include author's survey, no. 28, from a six-hour woman: "The company could put 'physical problem' workers from 8 hrs to lighter work in 6 hr. This was also a predominantly women's shift for lighter work and more family time."

10. This group was largely unorganized. Nevertheless, they tended to lead others by their vocal defense of the six-hour shift in union meetings, on the shop floor, and in the community. Toward the end, they became organized enough to hold meetings outside the aegis of the union—"six-hour's funeral" was attended by twenty or so of these "leaders" who had managed to keep labor's traditional shorter-hours vision alive. They were visible enough that company managers like McQuiston recognized them and spoke of them as a group. Moreover, the men identified themselves specifically as "six-hour men."

11. A few women talked about expanded choice in terms of the extra shift. One (author's survey, no. 399) wrote: "With 4 shifts it was easier for people to work the shift that they preferred." Another (no. 44) wrote, "I thought it great. There were 4 choices of time to work."

12. Author's surveys, nos. 512, 21; interview with anonymous retired female worker, 14 October 1991.

13. Interview with Joy Blanchard, retired Kellogg worker, 10 August 1989.

14. Author's survey no. 342; interview with Grace Lindsey, retired Kellogg worker, 12 August 1989.

15. Author's survey, nos. 127, 222, and 12; interview with Cecelia Bissell, retired Kellogg worker, by Rebecca Woodward, 21 November 1991; interview with anonymous retired male worker, 13 August 1989.

16. For workers who still talked in terms of "extra money" or of making a choice between money and leisure, see author's survey, nos. 51, 93, and 95; interview with Wayne Gleason, 5 May 1993; interview with Wayne Gleason, by Windy Jenkins, 1 November 1991; interview with Golda Sharpsteen, retired Kellogg worker, by Rebecca Woodward, 25 October 1991.

17. Author's survey, nos. 13, 17, and 310; interview with anonymous retired female worker, 14 October 1991.

18. Interview with Wayne Gleason, 5 May 1993.

19. Author's survey, no. 51.

20. Anonymous interview, no. 42, in Battle Creek, 11 August 1989.

21. For example, Joy Blanchard said, "See, . . . when I went to work and our two jobs were *enough*, you know, so we really didn't have to" work longer.

22. For six-hour mavericks who responded to the author's survey and who took responsibility for local unemployment by supporting work sharing, see interviews, nos. 3 and 29; author's survey, nos. 18, 29, 55, 84, 92, 127, 166, and 348. Moreover, most workers associate the return of eight-hours with a reduction in Kellogg's workforce. See, for example, author's survey, nos. 162 and 186.

23. For women who responded to the author's survey and used words like "greed," "work-hog," "enough," see author's survey, nos. 1, 2, 3, 11, 15, 44, 89, 120, 185, 215, and 237.

24. Author's survey, nos. 185 and 89; anonymous interview, no. 42, August 1989; interview with Helen Colles, retired Kellogg worker, by Melissa Brandt, 1 December 1991; interview with anonymous retired female worker, 10 October 1990.

25. Author's survey, nos. 44, 55, and 92, corresponding to the quotations in the paragraph.

26. Author's survey, nos. 44, 186, and 162 and anonymous interview, no. 42, in Battle Creek, 11 August 1989, corresponding to the quotations in the paragraph.

27. Interview with Cecelia Bissell, retired Kellogg worker, by Rebecca Woodward, 21 November 1991.

28. Interview with Art White, retired Kellogg worker, 12 August 1989.

29. Author's survey, nos. 185, 348, and 241, corresponding to the quotations in the paragraph. For others who commented negatively on the coalition, see author's survey, no. 176; "The union membership only wanted more money"; no. 222: "Kellogg's had tried several times to get a vote to go 8 hours plant wide for all. It would cut down on personnel and the benefits they had to pay out."

30. Interview with Cecelia Bissell, retired Kellogg worker, by Rebecca Woodward, 21 November 1991.

31. Author's survey, nos. 439, 56, 221; interview with James McQuiston, retired Kellogg manager, 11 August 1989.

32. Interview with Joy Blanchard, retired Kellogg worker, 24 July 1993.

33. Author's survey, no. 148.

34. Interview with Velma Plumb, retired Kellogg worker, by Robin Butler, 13 December 1991.

35. Interview with anonymous retired female worker, 14 October 1991.

36. Interview with anonymous retired male worker, 25 July 1993.

37. Workers express concern about local unemployment and support for work sharing in author's survey, nos. 13, 18, 44, 51, 55, 72, 84, 89, 92, 148, 166, 178, 320, 348, 455, and 460.

38. Author's survey, nos. 145, 231, 141, 77, and 32, corresponding to the quotations in the paragraph; interview with Cecelia Bissell, retired Kellogg worker, by Rebecca Woodward, 21 November 1991; author's survey, no. 57: six hours provided "more time to our self, and [we] weren't tired all the time and got along with the co. and people, and was able to be more productive."

39. Author's survey, nos. 78 and 31; interviews, nos. 104 and 42; and survey, no. 44, corresponding to the quotations in the paragraph. Art White remembered that "Kellogg supplied you with six brand-new uniforms a year, they laundered all your garments, tied them with a string, put them in your locker. And, my god, I don't get treated so good at home." Interview with Art White, retired Kellogg worker, 12 August 1989.

40. Author's survey, no. 219. Cecelia Bissell remembered that "it was the in-

surance and benefits that prompted them to keep pushing and pushing [against the six-hour shift] and finally [the union] didn't give [the company] any alternative. It was just automatically eight hours." Interview with Cecelia Bissell, retired Kellogg worker, by Rebecca Woodward, 21 November 1991.

41. Author's survey, nos. 12 and 108; interviews, nos. 42 and 51; interview with anonymous retired female worker, 24 July 1993.

42. Author's survey, no. 229; interviews, nos. 3 and 24; interview with anonymous retired female worker, 5 May 1993.

43. Interviews, nos. 3 and 4; interview with anonymous retired female worker, 9 October 1990.

44. Interview with Joy Blanchard, retired Kellogg worker, 10 August 1989. Other positive descriptions of the extra time as leisure appear in author's survey, nos. 50, 158, 189, 229, and 431.

45. Interview with Cecelia Bissell, retired Kellogg worker, by Rebecca Woodward, 21 November 1991.

46. For six-hour mavericks who responded to the survey and used the old language of freedom/control, see author's survey, nos. 28, 39, 57, 74, and 210; see also interviews, nos. 3, 4, 8, and 9. For the use of "leisure" and related language, see author's survey, nos. 50, 158, 186, and 229. For the continued use of "outside" activities, interests, etc., see interviews, nos. 3 and 36. For association of six-hours with "better" or "perfect" work, see interviews, nos. 3 and 4.

Like the women Best interviewed in 1932, most six-hour workers considered the extra free time to be a job benefit (see author's survey, no. 182), and continued to express considerable interest in transforming skilled work at home into freely chosen activities (see interviews, no. 112).

47. Interview with Kellogg couple in Battle Creek, 11 August 1989, (no. 42).

48. Author's survey, nos. 78, 31, 104, 210, 158, 200, 63, 182, 50, 74, and 39, corresponding to the quotations in the paragraph.

49. Author's survey, no. 48; interview with anonymous retired female worker, 5 May 1993.

50. Interview, no. 81; interview with anonymous retired female worker, 14 October 1991.

51. Interviews, no. 63.

52. Art and Donnelly White, retired Kellogg workers, 12 August 1989.

53. Interview with anonymous retired female worker, 9 October 1990 .

54. See Chapter Three.

55. Author's survey, no. 371.

56. Amy Saltzman, *Downshifting: Reinventing Success on the Slower Track* (New York, 1991).

57. Interviews, nos. 61, 63, 66, 74, 75, 81, 82; interview with anonymous retired male worker, 14 October 1991.

58. Interviews, nos. 74 and 75.

59. Interviews, nos. 61, 81, and 82; interview with anonymous retired male worker, 14 October 1991.

60. Interview with anonymous retired male worker, 14 October 1991.

61. Interviews, no. 3.

62. Interviews, no. 33. W. K. Kellogg often talked about maintaining the family farm as a hedge against the collapse of modern society—something to fall back on when the bubble burst. None of the workers the author contacted shared this sentiment. Instead, from the author's peculiar perspective, what they said resonated much more with a classical ideal. A. Bartlett Giamatti called Michael O'Loughlin's book, *The Garlands of Repose* (Chicago, 1978), the best book ever written about leisure. O'Loughlin describes the tradition of "Civic Leisure" in ancient Rome, represented in the writings and life of Virgil. After fulfilling his civic duty to Rome, Virgil retired to his farm and took up the activities of his youth. Whereas Virgil had "worked" at farming in his younger years to make a living, he did many of the same things in his retirement, "setting vines in rows" and "grafting pears." By so doing, according to O'Loughlin, he transformed work and the commonplace into freedom—the highest achievement of the Roman state. It was not world conquest or lavish consumption that were the apex of Roman culture; it was this "Civic Leisure."

Just so did the Battle Creek workers transform the ordinary, raising gardening and household skills to the realm of freedom, giving the products of "autotelic" activities away—or at least so it seemed to this writer, visiting there in the early 1990s.

63. Interviews, no. 42.

64. Interview with anonymous retired male worker, 10 October 1990.

65. Interviews, no. 5; interview with Charles Blanchard, retired Kellogg worker, 10 August 1989; interview with Mert Barber, past president of the Kellogg's Sportsmen's Club, 4 August 1994.

66. Interview with Joy Blanchard, retired Kellogg worker, 10 August 1989. In a 1993 interview Joy and her husband, Charles, both spoke with the author:

JOY: "[Six-hours] worked out good for us because he took care of the kids as much as I did, and so he knew what it was like to take care of these little preschoolers. We sure did [share household duties].
CHARLES: Fifty-fifty you might say.
JOY: We were way ahead of our time. Chuck took care of the kids. And he helped with the housework. And a lot of our friends were very astonished that he knew how to take care of the kids as well as I did.
CHARLES: Actually, it worked real well. I mean six-hours, and we'd switch off and on.

JOY: Yes we did [get to know our children very well]. . . . We were room parents, instead of me being a room mother, and he was there. And all the kids thought it was fantastic to have a father in school. And he was really active in the PTA all the time.

AUTHOR: Do you think that has changed, in terms of parents spending time with children?

JOY: Oh yes. Oh yes.

CHARLES: That's one of the main problems nowadays, I think.

JOY: That's why schools are having so many problems, I think, because parents are not getting involved, with the school, with their kids, and really knowing what's going on. All they do is sit at home and gripe.

Interview with Joy and Charles Blanchard, retired Kellogg workers, 24 July 1993, transcript and video available at KCTS, Seattle, Wash.

During the author's first interview with the Blanchards, Joy recalled: "I know our doctor said—this was when the kids were having regular checkups—and he said, 'Well, I don't approve of mothers working,' of course this was back thirty-five years ago, but he said, 'Really, Chuck has a rare opportunity for a father.' You know, every morning he got Steve and Rick up and gave them breakfast and was responsible for them all morning. He was working six to midnight, he was a room parent, you know. There always used to be room mothers, and he was a room parent, in that he would go down and supervise the parties and what-not at school, so he was very involved. . . . [Six-hours] really worked out well, and as I say, he knew what it was . . . to change diapers and give baths, and have the kids get into trouble in the neighborhood. One day they took off and he couldn't find them. They were down at Colburn school, playing on the playground."

67. Author's survey, nos. 56, 76, 109, and 271.

68. Interview with anonymous retired female worker, 9 October 1990.

69. Interviews, no. 100.

70. Interviews, nos. 42, 56.

71. Interviews, nos. 75.

72. See the exchange between Art and Donnelly White above.

73. Author's survey, nos. 43, 47, 87, 91, and 101; interviews, nos. 1, 5, 9, 12, 32, 33, 41, and 59.

74. Interview with anonymous retired female worker, 9 October 1990.

75. Eugen Fink, *Oase des Glucks Gedanken zu einer Ontologie des Spiels* (Freiburg, 1957), trans. Sister M. Delphine as "The Ontology of Play" in Ellen Gerber, ed., *Sport and the Body* (Philadelphia, 1979), 76; originally published in *Philosophy Today* 4 (Summer 1960): 95–110.

76. Interviews, nos. 64 and 78.

77. Interviews, nos. 14, 27, and 78.

78. Interview with anonymous retired female worker, 5 May 1993.

79. Interviews, nos. 8, 12, and 76.

80. Cornel West, *Keeping Faith* (New York, 1993), xi: "Prophetic criticism rests on what I understand to be the best of Euro-American modernity—the existential imperative to . . . [bestow] dignity, grandeur and tragedy on the ordinary lives of everyday people; and an experimental form of life that highlights curiosity, wonder, contingency, adventure, danger and, most importantly, improvisation. These elements constitute a democratic mode of being in the world inseparable from a democratic way of life and ways of struggle. Prophetic criticism is first and foremost an intellectual inquiry constitutive of existential democracy."

81. The author's intention is simply to differentiate language patterns, contrasting the words of managers and industrial psychologists (and, indeed, most other psychologists, biologists, anthropologists, etc., who presuppose universal need in their language and research) with the language of the workers. It is the historian's role to differentiate the truth claims contained in various language systems and refrain as much as possible from proclaiming which of the claims is the "real truth." Surely the profession of historians has learned this much from Foucault. Still, the truth system established on the "language of need" has typically tried to contain language like that used by the Kellogg workers in this century, and to tell "the real truth" about any "language of freedom" from the perspective of the "language of need." The modern presuppositions about "need" in the psychological and biological realms mirror the presuppositions about cause in the physical; both deny, by definition, the truth of language that makes claims about a free realm beyond need and cause. This is precisely why play and leisure have eluded science's theories as much as they have the marketplace's "matrix of logic." Nevertheless the mavericks' language may be compared favorably with the language of exceptional scholars such as Cornel West when he speaks of "existential" and "radical democracy."

82. Quoted by Adriano Tilgher, *Homo Faber,* trans. Dorothy Canfield Fisher (New York, 1932), 164–66.

CHAPTER NINE

1. *Wall Street Journal,* 13 September 1957, reported that 25 percent of the workers were on the six-hour shift.

2. *Fortune* 106 (29 November 1982).

3. *Enquirer,* 27 May, 3, 4 November 1982, 10 December 1979; *Kalamazoo Gazette,* 3 November 1982; *Detroit News,* 3 November 1982; letter, Christopher McNaughton, senior vice president at Kellogg's, to Jim Allen and Joe Sessions of AFGM, 5 November 1982, in "1980s Notebook," Local No. 3 Archives; *Enquirer,* 23, 25 May, 15 June 1983; Richard Lovell, "To Merge or Not to Merge:

A Weighty Decision for the City of Battle Creek" (M.A. thesis, Western Michigan University, 1983), copy held by the Willard Library, Battle Creek.

4. *Enquirer*, 23, 25 May, 15 June 1983.

5. *Enquirer*, 15 June 1983.

6. Jacques Rancière *La Nuit des Prolétaires* (Paris, 1981), vii.

7. Memo, Joe Sessions, AFGM business agent, to Local No. 3; memo, Kellogg management to "All Members of Local 3," "Incentive Package Applicable in Event of Successful Vote for Eight Hours"; both in "1980s Notebook," Local No. 3 Archives. *Enquirer*, 16 December 1984.

8. Memo, Joe Sessions, AFGM business agent, to Local No. 3; Memo, Kellogg management to "All Members of Local 3," Incentive Package Applicable in Event of Successful Vote for Eight Hours"; both in "1980s Notebook"; "Inter-union Correspondence, AFGM," Joe Sessions, AFGM business agent to Local No. 3, headed "Six Hour Representatives," 26 October 1984; all in Local No. 3 Archives. *Enquirer*, 13, 16 December 1984. Early on, the executive board of Local No. 3 recommended that members vote against the change because the elimination would cost about 160 jobs at the Battle Creek plant; see *Enquirer*, 20 July 1984.

9. "Incentive Package Applicable in Event of Successful Vote for Eight Hours," "July 1991 Notebook," Local No. 3 Archives.

10. "Communication," Joe Sessions to "Officers and Representatives of Local No. 3," no date, Local No. 3 Archives.

11. Quoted ibid.

12. Quoted ibid.; "Incentive Package Applicable in Event of Successful Vote for Eight Hours," "July 1991 Notebook," Local No. 3 Archives.

13. *Enquirer*, 12, 13, 16 December 1984; "Inter-union Correspondence, AFGM," Joe Sessions, Business Agent for the AFGM, to Local No. 3, headed "Six Hour Representatives," 26 October 1984, Local No. 3 Archives.

14. Author's survey, nos. 200, 222, 221, 241, 138, and 210, corresponding to the quotations in the paragraph. Working "under" eight- or six-hours is still a common expression, retaining some of the flavor of the older, more general critique of industrial and modern work.

15. Interview with Ina Sides, 24 July 1993, transcript and video available at KCTS, Seattle Wash.

16. Author's survey, nos. 222, 80, and 39, corresponding to the quotations in the paragraph; interview with Joy Blanchard, retired Kellogg worker, 10 August 1989. See also author's survey, nos. 17 and 236.

17. *Enquirer*, 13, 16 December 1984; memo, Kellogg management to "All Members of Local 3," "Incentive Package Applicable in Event of Successful Vote for Eight Hours," "1980s Notebook," Local No. 3 Archives.

18. Memo, Kellogg management to "All Members of Local 3," "Incentive Package Applicable in Event of Successful Vote for Eight Hours," "1980s Notebook,"

Local No. 3 Archives. Workers describe the end of six-hours in author's survey, nos. 28, 39, 44, 138, 200, 221, 222, and 241; see also interviews, no. 3: "The company made the decision—it sure wasn't the workers," and no. 9.

19. *Enquirer,* 9 February 1985; author's survey, no. 44.

20. Interview with Ina Sides, 24 July 1993.

21. Ibid. Several spoke again of the importance of the extra time for the family, and said that they regretted that work now would interfere with their family life. Interviews nos. 14 and 42.

22. Interview with Ina Sides, 24 July 1993.

23. Author's survey, nos. 123 and 93, corresponding to the quotations in the paragraph; letter, Velma Plumb to the author, 2 July 1994; interview with Betty Smyth, retired Kellogg worker, by Rebecca Woodward, 21 November 1991. Cecelia Bissell said, "The last four months I worked, I was never so miserable in my life. . . . I'll tell you how it was. [Before the switch to eight-hours] I liked the work. I liked everything about it. . . . [E]verybody enjoyed their work. You couldn't get a person to quit. And some of them, at mandatory sixty-five . . . wanted to stay. . . . Because it was like a big family. . . . [E]verybody cared about everybody." Interview with Cecelia Bissell, retired Kellogg worker, by Rebecca Woodward, 21 November 1991.

24. Author's survey, no. 146; interview with Cecelia Bissell, retired Kellogg worker, by Rebecca Woodward, 21 November 1991.

25. Interview with Smilia Popovich, retired Kellogg worker, by Windy Jenkins, 12 October 1991.

26. See for example "Less Snap, A Little Crackle—Any Pop?" *Forbes* 122 (4 September 1978): 35–36; Jack Willoughby, "The Snap, Crackle, Pop Defense," *Forbes* 135 (25 March 1985): 82–83; "Kellogg Company Looks Beyond Breakfast: Admitting the Cereal Market Is Mature, It Seeks Growth in Yogurt and Healthy Snacks," *Business Week* (6 December 1982).

27. Herbert Gutman, *Work, Culture and Society in Industrializing America* (New York, 1976); Virginia Yans-McLaughlin, *Family and Community: Italian Immigrants in Buffalo, 1880–1930* (Ithaca, New York, 1977); Sarah Eisenstein, *Give Us Bread and Roses: Working Women in the United States, 1890 to the First World War* (London, 1983); Theresa M. McBride, *The Domestic Revolution: The Modernization of Household Service in England and France 1820–1920* (New York, 1976); Patricia Branca, *Women in Europe since 1750* (New York, 1978), chap. 2 and epilogue.

Index

Century of work reduction, 1, 7, 46–50

CGL, 122–32

Chamber of Commerce, in support of work sharing during the depression, 32

Chase, Stuart, 23, 164

Chase, William, 55

Child care, sharing of, 174–75

Cincinnati workers, 54

Class: culture of work as basis for modern interclass accommodation, 238n.27; importance of full-time work for stability of, 142–44; leisure as time for building class identity, 200n.14; and shorter hours of labor, 7, 197–98n.10

Clevenger, Lou, 189

Clothing workers, 57–58

Coalition, eight-hour/higher wages/fewer workers, between senior male workers and Kellogg management, 7–8, 133–51, 152, 240n.1; beginning of, 89–91; in conflict with six-hour mavericks, 154–55; as dominant by 1960, 154; and language of Human Relations, 133; mavericks' recognition of, 162; problems of, after 1947, 105–9; as related to national labor developments, 146–51; rise of, 98–105; strengthening of, 94–95; triumph of, 185–86

Coalition, national, labor unions and Democratic Party, 146–51, 238n.27. See also Class

Coalition, six-hour/shorter hours/more workers: from the beginning of Kellogg's six-hour experiment, 13, 31; remnants of, after 1950s, 153–81; weakening of, 86,

89, 91, 93, 98–109, 133. See also Six-hour mavericks

"Code for Good Leadership" (CGL), Kellogg management's, 122–32

Collective bargaining, 86

Collier, Abram T., 119–20

Committee on Recent Economic Changes, Hoover's, 120

Commons, John R., 56

Community: collapse of, 10–12, 171–73, 199–200n.12; established during leisure, 171–73; work as providing, 128

Consumerism, 23

Consumption. See Gospel of Consumption, New Economic

Container department, incident in, 91–93

Control: of time, 8; abandonment of, for "full-time" work and overtime, 134, 162; giving up of, for leisure, 31, 86, 208n.47; on the job versus during time off, 30; and return of eight-hours, 106–7, 109

Corn flakes, invention of, 41–42

Cosier, Bill, 61

Cost of living. See Wages

Couzens, Senator James, 31

Craft, 226n.26; from positive to trivial usage of the word, 225n.20

Cross, Gary, 49–51, 56–57

Cultural explanation of the end of shorter hours (versus economic explanation), 6, 46–48, 52–55, 80, 193, 196n.5, 196–97n.8, 214–17nn.17, 25, 27

Culture: as autotelic, 73, 176–80; creation of, outside utility, function, and social role, 178, 199–200n.12, 200n.14; creation of, outside work, 74, 177–78; as reabsorbed by

work, 114, 121, 132, 165–81; as
the transformation of the utilitarian
in the realm of freedom/leisure, 71,
244n.62. *See also* Turner, Victor
Cummings, J. N., 99–101
Custer, Power, 87, 102, 106, 108–9;
and Human Relations management,
122, 124–25, 127–28

Dahlberg, Arthur Olaus, 23–26. *See
also* "Liberation Capitalism"
Despins, Leroy H., 61–62, 82
Deviants: reversal of, 152, 228n.44,
240n.5; as supporters of six-hours
after mid-century, 151; as work-
hogs in 1930s, 78
Discourse, cultural, 199–200n.12; in
Battle Creek, 3–8; community of,
11; trivializing of, 142–45
Doak, William, 32
Downsizing, 190. *See also* Six-hour
day, Kellogg's; Unemployment;
Work sharing

Economic growth, perpetual: dangers
of, 22–23, 24; expanding leisure as
an alternative to, 23
Economic maturity, 120
Edgerton, John (president of the
American Association of Manufacturers), 18–19
Edsforth, Ronald, 146–48, 151
Education, continuing: and shorter
hours, 62; use of, as preparation
for leisure, 176–77, 220–21n.7
Eight-hour day: management's pressure on workers to return to, 99,
101–3; senior male workers' support of return to, 103–5; transition
from eight- to six-hours, 16; transition from six- to eight-hours, 94–95

Eisenhower, Dwight, 150
End of shorter hours, 4, 5; as cause of
fragmentation of workers and
maldistribution of work, 239n.44
Extra-money, 139, 141
Extra time outside work, 7, 60; importance of, for family, 69–72,
77, 167–81; importance of, for
preservation of local culture,
67–69, 216–17n.25; Kellogg
women's claims to, 71, 73, 168,
178; rejection of, 72, 141. *See also*
Leisure

Factory and Industrial Management,
17–18, 22; survey of Kellogg
workers' opinions of six-hours,
62
Fair day's work for fair day's pay,
107, 133
Faith. *See* Work, industrial
Family: importance of leisure for, 23,
67–72, 77; loss of time for,
167–72, 245n.66
Farms and farming, 43, 226n.26; im-
portance of six-hours for continua-
tion of, 44; transformation of, into
leisure, 172–73, 244n.62
Fatigue, 16, 20, 230n.4
Filene, Edward A., 18
Fink, Eugen, 9, 178
Fishing, 174
Fixed costs. *See* Fringe benefits
Flexibility, 91–94
Foner, Philip, 48–49, 146
Forbes, 19; report on Kellogg work-
ers' opinions of six-hours, 63
Ford, Henry, 13, 15, 16, 40
Forum and Century (survey of Kel-
logg workers' opinions of six-
hours), 63

Freedom ascending versus need ascending, 114, 180; illusion of, 114; as reabsorbed by work and the marketplace, 114; realm of, outside industry and marketplace, 72, 80, 173, 177–78; as threat to established class, gender, and social roles, 144. *See also* Culture; Language of freedom associated with six-hours

Free time, as inescapable choice between unemployment and shorter work hours, 23. *See also* Leisure

Friday, David, 23

Fringe benefits: as reason for reducing Kellogg's payroll, 166, 242–43n.40; tailored to fit six-hours, 36–37, 90; under eight-hours, 101, 165–66

Front porch, empty, 171. *See also* Public spaces, loss of

Full-time work. *See* Work, full-time

Gardens, 37–38, 62, 71, 80

Gender: importance of "full-time" work in stability of gender roles, 142–44; and shorter hours of labor, 7, 138

General Foods, 94

General Motors, 18

Gentile, Giovanni, 71, 73–74, 180

Gilbert, James, 55

Gleason, Wayne, 158

Goodyear Tire and Rubber Company, 18, 28, 137; end of six-hour day at, 150–51

Gordon, Suzanne, 225n.25

Gorz, André, 192–93, 238n.27

Gospel of Consumption, New Economic, 4, 23–24, 26, 59, 120; transcending of, by Human Relations management, 121

Granola, 41

Granose, 42

Green, William (president of the AFL), 19, 23, 92, 99–100; on importance of leisure, 58; on Kellogg's return to six-hours after the war, 101; in support of Kellogg's six-hour day, 32, 59

Grievance procedures, 86, 146

Gulledge, G., 101

Gull Lake, 37, 44

Gutman, Herbert, 5, 6, 48, 56

Haas, Harry (president of the American Bankers Association), 32

Haldane, Viscount, 28

Hamilton, R. J. (Battle Creek mayor in 1937), 88, 93

Hammon, C., 101, 106

Harrison, D. M., 123

Hawthorn experiment (at Western Electric), 111

Heighton, William, 193

Henderson, Carol, 189

Herzberg, Frederick, 116–18

History, production of local and family, 176

Hobbies, 73

Holiday pay, 89

Holser, Donna, 60

Home duties, 66; choice of, over Kellogg job and housework, 70, 171; as complex and gradated series, 66–72; sharing of, by Kellogg couples, 174

Homemade goods, 69, 169–70; as transformation of the utilitarian into the realm of freedom/leisure, 71, 199–200n.12

Home projects, 82

Lamont, Robert P. (Hoover's secretary of commerce), on Kellogg's six-hour day, 32
LaMothe, William E., 182
Language: and historical reversal of patterns in Battle Creek, 139–42 (*see also* Deviants); importance of, recognized by Human Relations management, 110–22; importance of, recognized by Kellogg management, 128
Language of freedom associated with six-hours: and control, 65, 79; preserved by mavericks, 157, 167–68, 171–81; replaced by language of necessity, 139–42, 152, 246n.81; use of, by Kellogg workers in the 1930s, 63–64, 66–67, 74, 79; and use of possessive pronouns, 67
Language of morals, work-based, 135–36, 142, 164, 184; versus traditional language of morals, 164–65
Language of necessity, 65, 74; adoption of, by Kellogg workers, 133–52, 158; developed to support return to eight-hours, 100–101; expansion of, by Kellogg management, 182, 184; Human Relations management and, 114–15; hyperbolic forms of, 140; as "need ascending," 142, 180; as replacing language freedom, 139–42, 246n.81; as replacing work sharing, 151; resisted by mavericks, 157–60, 164–65; use of, by Kellogg management, 122–32; use of, by national labor leaders, 149
Leacock, Stephen, 23
"Leadership in the Kellogg Manner" (LKM), 122–32

Leeds and Northrop, 18
Leisure, 7, 82; active versus passive, 166–67, 173; Age of, 23; as alternative to devitalized work, 58; Brown on, 16; commercialized, 170; commodification of, 217n.25; defended by mavericks, 166–67; education as preparation for, 176–77; as escape from social and gender roles, 71–75; fear of, 142–43; feminizing of, 7, 142–46, 152; Green's support of, 58; importance of, for community, 167–81; importance of, for creation and preservation of worker culture, 54, 169–81, 199–200n.12, 200n.14; importance of, for family, 68–69, 77, 79, 167–81 (*see also* Family); importance of, for tradition and local culture, 169–81; increase of, as vision of work perfection, 54, 157; Kellogg women's claims to, 71; as "mental income," 16; as motive to work, 30; as outside of conflict and control, 178–80; as threat to established social, class, and status structures, 130, 142–45, 199–200n.12; as threat to industrial capitalism, 56, 216n.25; as threat to work, 130; time-intensive, 83; time-intensive versus goods-intensive, 216n.25; for traditional crafts and skills, 70; trivializing of, 7, 70, 100–101, 144–46, 152, 167, 225n.20; use of, to prepare for a career, 74; W. K. Kellogg on, 16; women and, 66; workers', 82–84. *See also* Shorter hours of labor
Leisured proletariat, 58
Leisure era, dawn of, 58
Lescohier, Don D., 19

Leverhulme, Lord William Hesketh, 27; on six-hour day, 28–29. *See also* "Liberation Capitalism"

Levitt, E., 101

Lewis, John L., 149

Lewis, Meyer, 85, 87, 92–93

"Liberation Capitalism," 13–14; fading of, with FDR's discovery of work creation, 34, 88; origins of, 21–26; replacement of, by Human Relations management's work-for-itself, 111; W. K. Kellogg on, 44–45

Lichtenstein, Nelson, 146, 238n.27

Liminal, the, 81, 144, 199–200n.12. *See also* Freedom; Turner, Victor

Linder, Staffan, 83

Lindsey, Grace, 60–61, 74, 80, 157

Litchfield, Paul, 18

LKM, 122–32

Local #20,388 of the NCGP: beginning of, 85–88, 229n.1; and first negotiations, 87–89; after World War II, 99, 101

Locke, Edwin A., 111

Lonning, Joe, 182

Lovelace, Dale, 87

Lump of labor, discrediting of, 34

Marx, Karl, 20

Maslow, Abraham, 112–14

Mass culture, coming of, 11, 83, 169–81

Mavericks. *See* Six-hour mavericks

Mayo, Elton, 111, 113

Mayorga, Nancy Pope, 143

McGregor, Douglas, 111–15

McQuiston, James, 140, 145–46

Meaning, human. *See* Work, industrial

Meany, George, 49, 149

Mechanical department, Kellogg workers in, 88, 162

Men, opinions of, about six-hours at Kellogg's, 76–80, 95. *See also* Surveys

Metropolitan Life Insurance Company, 37

Mill, John Stuart, 22, 28

"Millerites," 39

Miscellaneous Packing and Shipping Department, 88, 233n.13

Montgomery, David, 56

Motivation. *See* Worker motivation

Music, 73

National Council of Grain Producers (NCGP), 2, 85, 92. *See also* American Federation of Grain Millers

National Industrial Recovery Act, 86

National Office Management Association, 122

Natural history, leisure and, 175–76

NCGP. *See* National Council of Grain Producers

Necessity, economic: as all absorbing, 72, 113–14, 152; capitalism's ability to produce, 24; contested, 160; declining, 139; finite versus ascending and eternal, 112–13, 180; hierarchy of, 113–14; importance of, for eight-hour coalition, 133; versus luxuries, 23; obsolete, 112; perpetual, 115, 140; relative versus absolute, 139–42; use of, by Kellogg management, 122–32; use of, by Kellogg workers, 133–52. *See also* Language of necessity

Need. *See* Necessity

Neurasthenia, 40. *See also* Overwork

New Hampshire Plan, 15, 33, 89, 202n.7

Scientific management, 110
Seidman, Michael, 55
Senyszyn, Alex, 141
Sessions, Joseph, 187
Seventh-day Adventists, 39, 211n.72
Sewell, William H., 6
Shaw, George Bernard, 1
Shorter hours of labor: acceptance of cost of, by Kellogg workers, 98; as alternative to industrial order, 217n.25; as alternative to perpetual economic growth, 29; and beginning of shorter hours movement, 46; century of, 7; changes in organized labor's position and, 94; changing interpretations of, 48–52; as defeated by the politics of work creation, 34; disjunction between higher wages and, 53, 93–94, 99, 149, 217n.27; feminizing and trivializing of, 103–4, 142–46; in France and Great Britain, 49–50; historiographical analysis and revisions of, 46–57, 196–97n.4, 213–17nn.1-27; importance of, for worker culture, 26, 54, 217n.25; Kellogg management's rejection of, 130; Labor movement's abandonment of, 148–50; need for legislation for, 24; rejection of, by Human Relations, 112; remembered by Kellogg workers as continuous process, 78; resistance to, 24; six-hour mavericks persistence toward goal of, 159, 180–81; theories about cause of, 20, 110; as threat to centrality of work, 130; as threat to industrial capitalism, 56; uses of, by Kellogg women, 73. *See also* Six-hour day, Kellogg's
Sides, Ina, 3, 187–89, 191
Siegelbaum, Lewis, 55

Silver, Rabbi Abba, 23
Six-hour day, Kellogg's: as bargaining chip between labor and management, 133; beginning of, 13–15; benefits of, 16–17, 28–30; as continuation of "century of shorter hours," 57, 60, 78–79; death of, 158, 182–94; disagreements about, within families, 76; evaluation of, in 1935, 35–36; feminizing and trivializing of, 103–4, 144–46; and first day of operations, 1; funeral for, 188–90; as gender discrimination, 138; importance of, during organization of Local #20,388, 87–89; improvement of production rates under, 20; increase in Kellogg management's pressure on, 185–86; and issue of hourly pay versus weekly pay, 14, 99, 103; Kellogg workers' memory of end of, 187–88; made "permanent," 30; mavericks' defense of, 164–66, 168–81; mavericks holding out for, 153–81; men's retreat from, 144; men's views on, 75–84; national reaction to, 17, 21; organized labor and, 57–59; "preference" for, in 1930s, 63–64, 77–78, 224n.16; reasons for end of, 165; restoration of, after the war, 98, 101–3; shift schedules under, 16; size of payroll under, 15, 230n.7 (*see also* Payroll); as solution to unemployment, 18, 76, 78; suspension of, during World War II, 97, 232n.7; union demand for plant-wide, 87; use of, in advertising, 35–36; wages under, 64, 77–78, 98; women's views on, 60–75; work conditions at Kellogg's after death of, 190–91

Six-hour mavericks, 105; as concentrated minority, 154; in conflict with management and senior males, 154–55; as critical of men corrupting leisure, 170; defending extra time, 155, 168; defending leisure, 166–81; holding out for six-hours, 153–81; holding out for traditional view of progress as increased time off, 157; and language of freedom, 157–59, 167–68, 180; and moral language of individual responsibility for unemployment and work sharing, 164–65; and rejection of Human Relations language, 155; and resistance of language of necessity, 157–59, 164; and resistance of work-based language of morals, 164; as threat to union, 154; and traditional skepticism about work, 155–56; valuing time outside work and housework, 168; women as majority of, 154; and work sharing, 160–61
Skating, roller, 61
Skinner, B. F., 112
Sloan, Alfred P. Jr., 18
Smyth, Betty J., 190
Socialism, 14
Softball, 37
Southworth, Constance, 120
Speedup (of work), 76, 105, 230n.4. *See also* Relay-race, Lewis Brown's metaphor of
Spiritual needs. *See* Work, industrial
Sport: importance of, 73, 174; trivializing of local and amateur, 61
Sportsman club, 80, 174
Stan's Place, 188
"Stationary State," the economic, 22
Status. *See* Work, industrial

Strikes: discussed in 1947, 99–100; 1957, 109; 1941, 93–95
Surveys: author's 1988–95, 7, 75–77, 83, 228n.42; of workers' views on shorter hours, 221n.11. *See also* Best, Ethel; *Factory and Industrial Management*
Swan, Paula, 69

"Take This Job and Shove It," 55
Tank Farm, 154
Taylor, Frederick, 110
Teagle Commission for work sharing, 33
Tennis, 176
Theory X, Theory Y. *See* Worker motivation
Thirty-hour week, legislation for, 33, 59
Thompson, E. P., 6, 46, 109; and Irving Bernstein, 53, 56
Time-intensive versus goods-intensive leisure, 216n.25
Time: control of, 8; outside housework, 178–80; outside industry and the marketplace, 7, 72, 115, 168; unstructured, 8; wilderness of, 12, 60. *See also* Extra time outside work; Leisure
Time-hungry workers, 80
Tobias, Toby, 106
Tugwell, Rexford, 24
Turner, Victor, 9–10, 81, 115, 199–200n.12

Unemployment: as cause of shorter hours, 53; choice between unemployment and leisure, 23; fear of return of, after World War II, 98, 101; of Kellogg workers, 223nn.14, 16; mavericks and, 160–61; prob-

Work, industrial (*cont.*)
of, 110, 124–26, 130; impossibility
of joyous, 30; as its own reward,
111; maldistribution of, 163,
239n.44; as means to an end, 31,
57; metamorphosis of, 192–93,
238n.27; perfection as the continuous reduction of, 30, 157; perpetual, 115; preservation of, 8, 24; as
providing community, 112, 124,
128; as providing human meaning,
112–13, 116, 123–25; as providing
psychological needs, 112; as providing for spiritual needs, 114, 118–20;
for psychological growth, 118, 124;
resistance to, 55; rise of the world of
total, 72; salvation of, from erosion
of shorter hours, 34; transformation
of, 47. *See also* Work-for-itself
Work, perfect. *See* Work-for-itself
Work and the Nature of Man
(Herzberg), 116
Work as a moral solvent, 164
Work creation: beginning of politics
of, during New Deal, 4, 31–35; and
Human Relations' harnessing of
eternal need to modern work, 116;
as infinite, 113–14, 124; and Kellogg management, 124, 184–85; labor's support for, 101; organized
labor's embrace of, 147–51; versus
politics of work sharing, 34
Work discipline, industrial: changing,
31, 109; coming of, 46; from extrinsic to intrinsic basis, 115–16,
124–32; resistance to, 55–56;
strengthening of traditional, with
modern psychological principles,
130
Worker cultures: absorbed by work,
121, 132; importance of shorter

hours for preservation of, 47,
53–54, 198–99n.11, 217n.25; and
local concerns about unemployment, 53; loss of, with coming of
industrial work discipline, 36; preserved by six-hours, 169–81
Worker motivation: changing views of
Kellogg management on, 122–32; as
extrinsic to the job (wages and
hours—Theory X), 110; as intrinsic
to the job (attitudes—Theory Y),
111–15, 127; Kellogg workers on,
133–39; new importance of intrinsic, 112–15; problem of, 110; weakening of extrinsic, 111–12
Work ethic, 55–56
Work fetish, 164
Work-for-itself, 111–21, 238n.27; acceptance of, by some Kellogg workers, 134–52; Kellogg management's
use of, 127; McGregor's Theory Y
and, 112–15; management's theory
of, 115; mavericks' criticism of,
157. *See also* Herzberg, Frederick;
Worker motivation
Work-hogs, 62, 78, 105, 135, 161,
164, 228n.44
Work myths: and Human Relations,
111; John Harvey Kellogg's, 40–41,
216n.24; and Kellogg workers,
136–39; perfect job as, 75, 111,
235n.4. *See also* Work-for-itself
Work sharing: abandonment of, by
business for FDR's work creation
policies, 33–35; abandonment of, by
organized labor for work creation,
151; as cause of century of shorter
hours, 54; FDR's opposition to and
discrediting of, 34; during Great Depression, 4, 207n.42; Industrial
Conference Board's national survey

of, in 1932, 32; under Kellogg's six-hour day, 36; Kellogg workers and, 158–62; national drive for, 33; politics of, during the 1930s, 31–35; as presidential campaign issue in 1932, 33; as solution to work's maldistribution, 163; weakening of, at Kellogg's, 95, 102–3

Work skills, preservation of, during leisure, 69. *See also* Craft
World War II, return of eight-hours during, 97
Worship of toil, 24

Yiddish culture, the flowering of, and shorter hours, 58